Studies in Jewish Civilization, Volume 13: Spiritual Dimensions of Judaism

Proceedings
of the Thirteenth Annual Symposium
of the Klutznick Chair in Jewish Civilization-
Harris Center for Judaic Studies
September 17-18, 2000

D1522591

Studies in Jewish Civilization,
Volume 13:
Spiritual Dimensions of Judaism

Editors

Leonard J. Greenspoon
Ronald A. Simkins

The Klutznick Chair in Jewish Civilization
The Harris Center for Judaic Studies
The Center for the Study of
Religion and Society

CREIGHTON
UNIVERSITY
PRESS

Distributed by the University of Nebraska Press

Library of Congress Cataloguing in Publication Data

Studies in Jewish Civilization, Volume 13: Spiritual Dimensions of Judaism/
Leonard J. Greenspoon and Ronald A. Simkins, editors.
p. c.m—(Studies in Jewish civilization, ISSN 1070-8510; 13)
"Proceedings of the thirteenth annual Symposium of the Klutznick Chair in Jewish Civilization-Harris Center for Judaic Studies, September 17-18, 2000"
Half t.p.
ISBN 1-881871-42-8 (paper)
1. Spirituality, Jewish—Theology, history, criticism, interpretation, etc. Congresses. I. Greenspoon, Leonard J. (Leonard Jay), Simkins, Ronald A. II. Klutznick Chair in Jewish Civilization-Harris Center for Judaic Studies (13th : 2000: Creighton University)
III. Series

EDITORIAL
Creighton University Press
2500 California Plaza
Omaha, NE 68178

MARKETING & DISTRIBUTION
University of Nebraska Press
233 North 8th Street
Lincoln, NE 68588-0255

Printed in the United States of America

Dedicated to Norman and Bernice Harris

Table of Contents

Acknowlegments

Those who attended previous Symposia and readers of earlier volumes in this Series will immediately recognize elements of change, alongside elements of continuity, in this collection. In keeping with previous years, the Symposium for the year 2000 was devoted to a topic, Spiritual Dimensions of Judaism, which struck us as being significant, although in no way specifically related to the subject matter of earlier Symposia. This is how it has been from the beginning—each year we explore another area in the vast domain known as Jewish Civilization.

This year's Symposium, the thirteenth in the series, is distinguished as the first to be called the Klutznick-Harris Symposium. In addition to being named for the Klutznick family, who endowed the Chair in Jewish Civilization at Creighton University, it is now also named for our new co-sponsors, the Norman and Bernice Harris Center for Judaic Studies at the University of Nebraska-Lincoln. We are most grateful to the Center's director, Dr. Jean Axelrad Cahan, and to Mr. and Mrs. Harris, for combining our expertise and resources in this way. We look forward to many, many years of enhanced and enriched Symposia and publications.

We further extend our gratitude to numerous individuals and organizations, without whom our Symposium literally could not exist. Sunday is our day at the Jewish Community Center, where for the first time this year we worked with Carolyn Novicoff and Kathy Hirshman, whose efforts on our behalf were invaluable. Doreen Wagenaar, administrative assistant for the Harris Center, provided gracious and vital support during the Symposium; her coordination of publicity and support in the Lincoln area was especially important. Thanks also to Susan and David Davies, owners of Soul Desires Books in Omaha, who provided book displays and sales at the Jewish Community Center and Creighton University.

Ronald A. Simkins is co-editor of this volume and director of the Center for the Study of Religion and Society at Creighton University. His continued partnership, insights, and friendship are deeply valued. It is hard to find words, precisely because she is so good with them, to thank Adrian Koesters, who co-coordinated the symposium and served as editorial specialist in the production of this volume. We are most grateful for her contribution.

We also gratefully acknowledge the support, in most cases support that has continued over the years, of those upon whose generosity we depend. We will never take it, or you, for granted:

Jewish Educational and Library Services of the Omaha
 Jewish Federation (JELS)
The Creighton College of Arts and Sciences
Dorothy and Henry Riekes
The Ike and Roz Friedman Foundation
The Eve and Louis Wintroub Endowment
The Henry Monsky Lodge of B'nai B'rith
The Creighton University Committee on Lectures, Films, and Concerts
The Jewish Chautauqua Society

Volumes in the Studies in Jewish Civilization series are usually published once a year. This volume is being published within the same calendar year as *Studies in Jewish Civilization 14: Women and Judaism*, so that symposia presentations may reach a wider audience more quickly. We thank Creighton University Press and its editor, Brent Spencer, and the University of Nebraska Press and its editor-in-chief, Gary Dunham, for giving us the go-ahead for this accelerated schedule and the means to make it happen.

We dedicate this volume, the thirteenth in our series but the first with our new name and sponsorship, to Bernice and Norman Harris. Your exemplary generosity and leadership are an inspiration.

Editor's Introduction

In reviewing the articles as I prepared to write this introduction, I was struck by how well their authors—although addressing different aspects of the topic from divers viewpoints—complement each other. Collectively yet independently, they forcefully make a number of points: the quest for spirituality (however defined) is an authentically Jewish one; the requisite materials for this quest are predominantly textual (even when the arts are involved); study necessarily precedes, but is not a full substitute for, action; spiritual concerns elevate our sense of being a part of, as opposed to apart from, a community; and finally, the quest for Jewish spirituality is an arduous one—but well worth the effort.

It is immediately apparent that these five points, taken as a whole, are not neutral; rather, they are polemical in nature and structure. Thus, for example, our authors are not sympathetic to those who argue for exclusively extra-Jewish avenues to spirituality, and they are decidedly unimpressed with any and all pop culture shortcuts to authentic Jewish spirituality. They also concur in their view that the attainment of spiritual insights has rarely been an end unto itself. Moreover, they are convinced that today, the beginning of the twenty-first century, is a propitious time to talk about, and act on, elements of spirituality within Judaism.

In the task of arranging chapters in our volumes, subject matter, approach, and author are all relevant. The first article, Hava Tirosh-Samuelson's programmatic essay, clearly provides a context for the articles that follow. It was well received by scholars and audience alike as the keynote address at the Symposium itself; it serves equally well as the introduction for this volume, containing as it does wide-ranging analyses of historical, methodological, and contemporary issues. To enhance its value, Tirosh-Samuelson has appended an annotated bibliography that is especially useful and accessible for non-specialists.

The five chapters that follow form an historical sequence. Yehuda Gellman juxtaposes the seemingly passive Abraham of Genesis 22 (the binding of Isaac) with the same patriarch four chapters earlier, who pointedly questions divine justice prior to the destruction of Sodom and Gomorrah. Gellman's contemporary understanding of the Aqedah, which emphasizes radical openness to change in the face of what is known and valued, relies on such disparate sources as Søren Kierkegaard and the Rebbe of Izbica.

Charles D. Isbell likewise delves into the Hebrew Bible, in his case the prophet Micah, for insights into the true meaning of spirituality. Called upon to deliver a memorial address for his grandfather, Isbell imaginatively recreates—for an audience consisting largely of lawyers and jurists—the courtroom scene of Micah, chapter six, in which the Lord is plaintiff; the people of Israel, defendant. Within the context of the not-surprising victory of the plaintiff, Isbell uncovers the surprisingly simple core values that should underpin all religious observance.

Steven Sacks moves the discussion forward to the rabbinic period, focusing on the three pillars—Torah, Temple service, and acts of lovingkindness—upon which the world was said to be founded. In particular, Sacks looks at the potential, and real, conflict that can exist between the imperative to study and the perceived need to carry out certain actions. The prioritization of such concerns remains relevant even today for individuals seeking to negotiate between (and among) spiritual principles and ethical (but secular) activities.

A perennial question: What matters more, what we do or why we do it? As expertly explicated by Zion Zohar, Rabbi Bahya ibn Pakuda, living in the Golden Age of Spain, formulated a response that broke with earlier Jewish thought and profoundly influenced later ethical thinking. In Bahya's judgment, actions are ethical only if they reflect the underlying intention or *kavannah* of the heart that is informed by the will of God. Bahya's wisdom, Zohar adds, can also be applied in the somewhat tarnished but still golden age of today.

There are few figures in Judaism better known (and, in some quarters, beloved) than the Baal Shem Tov (or Besht), the founder of Hasidism. But, as Morris Faierstein notes, scholars have been divided over how to assess the historical Besht in his roles as miracle worker and spiritual teacher. In interpreting the data, Faierstein calls attention to the many intentional parallels between the accounts of the Besht and the earlier hagiographical biographies of Rabbi Isaac Luria (also known as the Ari).

The remaining chapters in this collection do not in general follow an easily discernible pattern, yet they seem to flow effortlessly and naturally from one to the next in their present order. Ori Soltes' magisterial survey and analysis of contemporary art heads this section. Richly illustrated, Soltes' commentary on eleven Jewish artists—some well known, others less so—

emphasizes elements of continuity and novelty in works that stress the mystical and spiritual in Judaism. Often, he observes, these elements come to the fore in the interplay of words and images.

Words and images also come together in synagogue architecture, the topic of the next two papers. Thomas Kuhlman looks at a number of American synagogues to support his well-argued contention that a relationship between spirituality and architecture can and in fact does exist. He presents some familiar buildings, such as Newport's Touro Synagogue and Beth Elohim in Charleston. Given the Symposium's setting in Omaha, Kuhlman also provides examples from this city's rich past, present—and future.

At the close of his paper, Kuhlman refers to the work of Martin Shukert, a town planner and urban designer based in Omaha, who is also intimately involved in the planning and designing of local synagogues. We are pleased that Shukert accepted our invitation to articulate a first-hand account of what it is like to "design for God" in contemporary America.

Prayer and prayer books are activities and items we associate generally, although not exclusively, with synagogues. Omaha art historian Jenni Schlossman examines prayer books, especially recent editions prepared by the Reconstructionist movement, with an eye toward illuminating the power of art to further the process of reflection and meditation. In particular, she looks at the adaptations of traditional *shiviti* plaques (which embrace both words and images) contained in works fashioned by Betsy Platkin Teutsch and other artists.

Prayer books have traditionally been made up primarily of words; this is not likely to change. But the words themselves can be said to illustrate, among other things, spiritual dimensions of Judaism. As Charles Isbell eloquently points out in this second of his contributions, verbal illustrations of spirituality are often framed in the common, "earthy" language appropriate to the laborers and farmers who were the original authors or earliest audience for many of our most popular prayers. Their full significance eludes many in today's mostly urban congregations. Isbell's evocative reconstructions of the "earthy" contexts of such prayers, enlivened with personal recollections, go a long way toward bridging the chronological and sociological gaps that separate us from our forebears.

Rela Mintz Geffen begins her article, the last of this book's chapters, by chronicling the factors, both internal and external or contextual, that have expanded and enhanced rites of passage as vehicles or expressions of spirituality for contemporary American Jews. She then provides examples of new or embellished rites. These include ceremonies for newborn daughters, parallel to traditional rituals celebrating the birth of a son, and the proliferation of explanatory manuals for birth ceremonies, weddings, funerals, and other occasions.

We are aware that the articles in this volume do not cover all, or even most, of the dimensions of Judaism that may be characterized as spiritual. But such quantitative coverage was not our goal. Rather, we have sought to introduce our readers to certain qualities of the spiritual within Judaism, in the hope that these texts and illustrations will both acquaint them with important issues and concepts and spur them on to further study—and action—on their own. We hope and pray that we have in some small measure succeeded.

Leonard J. Greenspoon
Omaha, 2002
ljgrn@creighton.edu

Contributors

Morris L. Faierstein

Meyerhoff Center for Jewish Studies
University of Maryland
College Park, Maryland 20852
kotsker@yahoo.com

Rela Mintz Geffen

Office of the President
Baltimore Hebrew University
Baltimore, Maryland 21215
Rela1@aol.com

Jerome (Yehuda) Gellman

Department of Philosophy
Ben-Gurion University of the Negev
Beer-Sheva 84105 Israel
gellman@vms.huji.ac.il

Charles D. Isbell

Department of Philosophy and Religious Studies
Louisiana State University
Baton Rouge, Louisiana 70803
cisbell@cox.net

Thomas A. Kuhlman

Department of English
Creighton University
Omaha, Nebraska 68178
takuhl@creighton.edu

Steven D. Sacks

Divinity School
University of Chicago
Chicago, Illinois 60637
sdsacks@midway.uchicago.edu

Jenni L. Schlossman

4048 Kristy Circle
Omaha, Nebraska 68112
bezaliya@earthlink.net

Martin H. Shukert   RDG Crose Gardner Shukert
                                     900 Farnam Suite 100
                                     Omaha, Nebraska 68102
                                     mshukert@rdgusa.com

Ori Z. Soltes   1718 P Stree NW, Suite T-9
                                     Washington, DC 20036
                                     orisoltes@aol.com

Hava Tirosh-Samuelson   Department of History
                                     Arizona State University
                                     Tempe, Arizona 85287
                                     Hava.Samuelson@asu.edu

Zion Zohar   Sephardic Studies Program
                                     Florida International University
                                     Miami, Florida 3380
                                     zohar@worldnet.att.net

Studies in Jewish Civilization,
Volume 13:
Spiritual Dimensions of Judaism

Proceedings
of the Thirteenth Annual Symposium
of the Klutznick Chair in Jewish Civilization-
Harris Center for Judaic Studies
September 17-18, 2000

Jewish Spirituality: Past Models and Present Quest

Hava Tirosh-Samuelson

THE CONTEMPORARY THIRST FOR SPIRITUALITY

Spirituality is "in" today. In books, magazines, Internet sites, educational materials, academic conferences, and informal adult Jewish education, spirituality is the buzzword. The evidence is unambiguous: Jews are seeking spirituality, exploring it, talking about it, and pondering how to make it a part of their lives. How can we explain this phenomenon? Why was this not the case thirty or forty years ago? What prompted this resurging interest in the spiritual dimension of Judaism?

Let me venture a brief and admittedly incomplete answer to these questions. When Jews settled in America, their primary concern was physical survival as individuals. To survive as individuals entailed acculturation into the rich tapestry of American immigrant society. For this purpose, traditional Judaism had to be reformed, changed, and reinterpreted. In the second half of the nineteenth century, this transformation was carried out by Reform Judaism for the Jewish immigrants from Germany and other Central European countries; at the turn of the twentieth century, Conservative Judaism carried out the reinterpretation of traditional Judaism for the Jews of East European descent.

Both Reform and Conservative Judaism were committed to Americanize the Jewish immigrants, and in both cases Americanization came at the expense of the spiritual dimension of Judaism. Not only was the need to adapt to the new world overwhelmingly difficult, the process of adaptation and acculturation was carried out in terms of synagogue rituals or observance of obligatory commands rather than in terms of inner spiritual life. Moreover, for Reform Judaism the spiritual aspect of Judaism was exceptionally problematic because its seemingly superstitious practices negated the Enlightenment rationality to which Reform Judaism was committed. Modern, scientifically oriented Reform Jews considered the very rituals and beliefs of traditional Judaism, which constituted the core

1

of Jewish spirituality, as obstacles to Americanization and a downright intellectual embarrassment. Similarly, Conservative Judaism, which focused its energies on resolving the tension between halacha [Jewish law] and modernity and used the academic study of the history of Jewish law to legitimize proposed changes, was least interested in the preservation and cultivation of spiritual practices that the East European immigrants brought with them to the New World. It is no surprise that Jewish immigrants in the first and second generations had little interest in or knowledge of the spiritual treasures of Judaism.

If until the 1940s the major question was the survival and acculturation of individuals, the annihilation of one third of world Jewry in the Holocaust shifted the concern from the survival of individuals to the collective survival of the Jewish people. In the post-Holocaust years preoccupation with Jewish survival was inseparable from concern about the struggle of the nascent State of Israel in the perpetual war with its Arab neighbors. These physical needs have dominated the public Jewish agenda in America and made economic and political support for the State of Israel the axis of Jewish self-definition. This support for Israel, however, was perfectly compatible with the successful integration of Jews into American society. As Louis Brandeis and Horace Kalen showed, there was no necessary conflict between defining oneself as an American Jew and lending support for the State of Israel. Like other ethnic groups in America, the Jews now had a state to which they felt emotionally attached without forsaking their American identity. As Americanization and Zionism became two sides of the same coin, American Jews were defining themselves in secular categories (i.e., as an ethnic group or a culture), rather than in religious terms (i.e., as a community of faith bound by a certain religious lifestyle). Thus, even though organized Jewish life in America continued to take place in synagogues, the spiritual depths of Judaism have become increasingly irrelevant to American Jews.

For American Jewry, the post-World War II years were a success story, despite the need to come to terms with the horrors of the Holocaust. The Jewish community in America erected magnificent synagogues, created an impressive network of communal services, and established outstanding fundraising machinery primarily for the sake of lobbying on behalf of the State of Israel. Impressive as these are, these achievements have little to do with the interior life of the soul or with the spiritual dimension of human life. It is no coincidence that the baby boomers (and now their children) grew up in suburban synagogues in which there was neither exposure to nor discussion of the spiritual dimension of Judaism. In the midst of economic prosperity, social mobility, political influence, and cultural visibility, the second and third generations of American-born Jews were experiencing a certain void. Something was amiss in the midst of their success story.

This spiritual vacuum led many young Jews in the late 1960s and through the 1970s to enter various counter-culture movements, including civil right protests, the women's movement, anti-war protests, and even the recreational use of drugs. At the same time, disappointed with the suburban synagogue, young disillusioned Jews found their way to alternative religious practices, be they New Age cults, established Eastern traditions such as Buddhism, or Jewish Orthodoxy and Hasidism. The remarkable resurgence of the latter was in part due to the *ba'aley teshuvah* [the returnees], whose endorsement of traditional Jewish life was a critique of the suburban synagogue and its inability to address Jewish spiritual needs. Fund raising, social action, political lobbying, programs of brotherhoods and sisterhoods, and numerous philanthropic associations did not succeed in quenching the spiritual thirst of baby boomers and their children.

It is against this background that we can understand what is known as the Jewish Renewal Movement of the 1980s and 1990s. Due to the remarkable work of religious visionaries such as Rabbi Zalman Shachter-Shalomi and Shlomo Carlebach already in the 1970s, Jews were introduced to the spiritual dimension of Judaism through music, story telling, meditation, and counseling. When the interest in the spiritual dimension of Judaism was combined with the boom in the academic study of Judaism in numerous Jewish Studies program, the search for spirituality yielded more concrete results. The literary sources of the Jewish spiritual tradition now became available in new English translations along with contemporary commentaries, summaries, and popularizations. Through them, the spiritual dimension of Judaism has become available to American Jews, inspiring a reinterpretation of Judaism for the postmodern age. By the end of the 1990s, a new way of being Jewish had become well established in America. To be Jewish now means not merely donating a sum of money to the UJA (United Jewish Appeal), being active in the institutions of the local federation, or occasionally traveling to Israel, but also practicing meditation, contemplation, visualization of letters, and breathing techniques, or dabbling in astrology and aspiring to achieve out-of-body experiences. The Jewish Renewal Movement has shown that Jews could quench their spiritual thirst by turning to the rich legacy of the Jewish tradition itself.

The sad irony, however, was that as the Jewish baby boomers became aware of the spiritual dimension of Judaism, they were also woefully unable to appropriate it. The suburban synagogues did not provide the spiritual seekers with the linguistic skills necessary to access the literary sources of Judaism or with the conceptual framework necessary to fathom its symbolic depth. A genuine recovery of the Jewish spiritual tradition requires mastery of Hebrew, understanding of Judaism as a symbolic system, attentiveness to the theological claims of Judaism, and openness to the rhythm of Jewish ritual life. The serious seekers of Jewish spirituality would overcome the obstacles and acquire the necessary skills along with endorsement of Jewish religious life; but for many who crave instant spirituality, a superficial dabbling with Jewish spirituality has become common. That a few non-Jewish media stars also found their way to Kabbalah has further made the Jewish spiritual tradition very fashionable.

THE MEANING OF SPIRITUALITY

That Jews today are interested in spirituality is clear. But what exactly does "spirituality" mean? I contend that the term spirituality is used today rather loosely and vaguely to express a certain critique or dissatisfaction with established forms of a given religion. Thus, for Jewish seekers of spirituality the term connotes the antidote to whatever they find problematic in organized Jewish life. Jewish spirituality represents to some a rejection of the overemphasis on politics, fund raising, material success, and social mobility. To others, Jewish spirituality could mean a desire for intimacy and a rejection of the large, impersonal synagogue where members seldom get to know each other. The quest for spirituality signifies to still others a critique of the aesthetic limitations of Jewish communal life and a desire to enhance the artistic quality of Jewish life. "Spirituality" is thus used as a catchword for whatever one finds lacking in contemporary Judaism and is adduced as the reason for feeling alienated from Judaism. Such loose usage of the term spirituality is useful if we seek to understand how Jews view themselves, but it obscures the nature and content of Jewish spirituality.

A more accurate meaning of "spirituality" [in Hebrew *ruhaniyut*] has its roots in Greek philosophy. "Spirituality" is the opposite of "corporeality" or "materiality" [*gashmiyut* or *homriyut*]. This is an ontological distinction between two aspects or dimensions of reality. The material or corporeal aspect is that which has extension in space, changes over time, and consists of tangible, physical properties accessible to the senses. By contrast, the spiritual is that which does not exist in space and time and has no tangible properties. The spiritual, however, is no less real than the corporeal. In fact, in Platonic metaphysics, where this dichotomy originated, the spiritual is more real than the material because the latter is but an imitation of the former. Furthermore, Platonic ontology identifies the real with the good, making the spiritual superior to the material or corporeal.

These ontological distinctions have profound implications for the interpretation of human life. Humans are understood to be not just bodies that disintegrate at death, but compositions of a corporeal body and a non-corporeal soul. How one interprets the relationship between soul and body may vary, but all those who speak about spirituality in this second sense of the term presuppose, first, that humans are endowed with the ability to transcend their embodiment; second, that the end of human life lies not in the satisfaction of corporeal needs or the enjoyment of material goods, but in the cultivation of that which enables humans to experience the non-corporeal aspect of reality. To seek spirituality in the second sense of the term means to cultivate a life that is conducive to the well being of the soul, the non-corporeal aspect of the human, so as to attain the spiritual end of human life, however defined.

The most spiritual aspect of reality is God, and therefore the third meaning of spirituality pertains specifically to the desire to come close to God, even to unite with God. This is the mystical aspect of Jewish spirituality. Historically, how to achieve intimacy with God and what this intimacy consists of varied from one spiritual program to another, in accordance with the theoretical assumptions of the program. As we shall see, for the Jewish philosophers who privileged the intellect, closeness with God meant attaining intellectual perfection—prophecy being the highest expression of this perfection. The most elevated form of prophecy was understood to be the union of the human intellect with God's mind or with the ideas in God's mind. By virtue of this intellectual union, the prophet gained knowledge of the laws by which God governs the world, knowledge that constitutes the hidden meaning of God's revelation. For other Jewish spiritualists, especially the theosophical Kabbalists, intimacy with God meant penetrating the rhythm of God's inner life and even influencing that rhythm through the performance of divine commands with the proper intention. For still others, intimacy with God entailed an ecstatic experience in which the human soul, or a part of the soul, dissociated itself from the body and temporarily united with God. This union resulted in either an ability to apprehend the structure of the created universe or an ability to tap into the reservoirs of divine energy and employ them so as to change the created world.

Since God is non-corporeal, intimacy with God could be achieved only if humans reach a similar degree of non-corporeality. The spiritual programs in Judaism clearly privileged the non-corporeal aspects of humans, the soul or parts of the soul such as the intellect. While these spiritual programs accepted embodiment as a good, because God created the human body, they also considered the body as a potential obstacle to spiritual progress. Thus, some programs specified ascetic techniques to curb, neutralize, or suppress the body, while other programs prescribed ways to spiritualize or refine it. They therefore devised practices in which the physical aspects of the body produced energy that was directed toward a non-corporeal goal, intimacy with God.

It is important to note that regardless of how a given spiritual program understood intimacy of the soul with God, Jewish spirituality tends to focus on the individual rather than on the collective dimensions of Jewish life. Each and every Jew is enjoined to lead the kind of life that leads to the salvation of the individual soul. The aspect of a collective, political dimension of Judaism, especially the Jewish messianic vision of the remote future, is rather muted as Jewish spiritualists turned inward to cultivate the inner life of the soul. Spiritualists were not much interested in the political ingathering of all Jews into the Land of Israel in the messianic age, even though they affirmed the belief in the future coming of the messiah. Likewise, Jewish spiritualists were less concerned with the dramatic events of the end of time, which included the collective resurrection of the dead, although some of them did speculate on the ways in which an individual soul will be reunited with a particular body. The intimacy with God, which they attempted to attain, is an individual goal, though it has some collective ramification. If all Jews are engaged in it, reality will be transformed and with it the place of Israel in the world.

Finally, a fourth, more technical meaning of spirituality pertains to certain recommended procedures and practices that make it possible for humans to transcend their embodiment. Whether the goal of human life is defined as attainment of holiness, envisioning the invisible God, achieving intimacy or union with God, or immortality of the soul, such a spiritual program consists of practices that are said to produce the desired result. The spiritual path may include observance of divine commands, as much as it could encompass techniques to alter one's state of mind or produce ecstasy and out-of-body experiences. Spiritual techniques may or may not be related to specific normative practices. Most commonly, a spiritual program involves ascetic practices intended to control, subdue, or transform the cravings of the human body, depending on the perception of the body as either an obstacle to spirituality or a means to it.

When I speak about Jewish spirituality, I use the term in the second, third, and fourth senses defined above. Out of my comments about two medieval spiritual programs will emerge three main claims: first, rabbinic Judaism understood itself in spiritual terms, although the precise meaning of Jewish spirituality would change over time. Second, Judaism endorsed the ontological distinction between the spiritual and the corporeal, whose origin can be traced to Greek philosophy; the deepest aspect of self-understanding was based on philosophical assumptions that originated outside of Judaism. And third, Judaism articulated elaborate procedures to cultivate the inner life of the soul so as to attain the ultimate end of human life: the immortality of the soul. My data come primarily from two medieval programs of Jewish spirituality: rationalist philosophy and theosophical Kabbalah. Although these were not the only programs of Jewish spirituality, they were definitely the most important in the history of Judaism. I discuss philosophy and Kabbalah comparatively not only to impart a more accurate historical understanding of these intellectual strands within Judaism, but also to encourage us to realize that there is no necessary contradiction between spirituality and rationality.

A comparative discussion of rationalist philosophy and theosophical Kabbalah is appropriate because they had much in common. Both reached their zenith in thirteenth century Spain and presented themselves as the answer to the Jewish needs of their day. Both shared a set of metaphysical and cosmological assumptions borrowed from ancient Greek philosophy as interpreted in the Middle Ages. Both elaborated highly sophisticated speculative systems to explain the structure of reality and the place of humans in it. Both spiritual programs focused on the well-being of the individual soul and recommended specific actions that produced the proper relationship between the soul and the body, and both defined the ultimate end of human life as the immortality of the individual soul. Finally, both programs viewed themselves as the correct interpretation of rabbinic Judaism and presented themselves as the preferred way to attain the rabbinic ideal of holiness. To understand philosophy and Kabbalah as parallel spiritual programs, it is important to realize how they both emerged within the religious paradigms of rabbinic Judaism.

SPIRITUALITY OF RABBINIC JUDAISM

Rabbinic Judaism is the form of post-biblical Judaism that emerged after the destruction of the Second Temple in 70 CE. The centrality of halacha (Jewish Law) in rabbinic Judaism makes it difficult for people today to realize that rabbinic Judaism understood itself in spiritual terms. Moreover, it is difficult to think about post-biblical Judaism as a spiritual program because the Bible does not have any word that can be translated as "spiritual." Why? The answer is that the Bible lacks the ontological distinction between the spiritual and the corporeal. Regarding God, the Bible unabashedly speaks of YHWH in corporeal and anthropomorphic terms; regarding humans, the Bible speaks about the living human being as an organic unity [*nefesh hayah*]. The vitality of the human is determined by the quality of the interaction with God, an interaction that is framed in terms of purity and impurity, of the holy and the profane. Since the Bible understood God to be literally present in the midst of the Israelite camp, the main task of the Israelite nation was to ensure that God's presence was never contaminated. Contamination of the divine presence, however, is brought about not only through actions that violate the boundary between the sacred and the profane—the actions specified by the purity laws of the Bible—but also through intentional acts in relation to other human beings. In other words, in biblical religion there was no distinction between the interior and the exterior, between the corporeal and the spiritual, between ritual action and moral intention. All aspects of human life were understood in the context of the separation between the sacred and the profane, and their goal was to ensure that one could stand in holy relationship with God.

Israelite religion defines the goal of Jewish life in terms of holiness and commands Israel to be holy "for I the LORD your God am holy" (Lev 19:2). Already in the Bible, then, holiness is understood in terms of a relationship with God, a relationship that is based on the principle of imitation, or being like God. The dynamic relationship between God and Israel is framed in the Bible in terms of an everlasting covenant [*berit*] between God and Israel. This is a perpetual love affair that cannot be abrogated by either God or Israel, even though it can change dramatically in accordance with the actions of the partners to the covenant, God or Israel. The sign of God's everlasting commitment to Israel is the revelation of the Torah at Sinai. The Torah articulates the path that Israelites must follow if they are to flourish and prosper as human beings who can stand in relationship with God. Biblical religion, at least since the seventh century BCE, makes it clear that the attainment of holiness is possible only to those who live the life of Torah that God revealed to Israel and that such life involves a set of commandments that enable humans to be more like God.

During the Second Temple period, biblical religion underwent changes as the Bible reached its final edited version. Until 332 BCE, the majority of Jews lived in the Persian Empire, and some Babylonian and Persian beliefs, most notably the resurrection of the body, found their way into the Bible. But after the conquests of Alexander the Great, Jews lived in a hellenized environment, and their religious beliefs reflected the encounter with Greek philosophy and culture. The belief that the human is a composition of a corporeal body and an incorporeal soul entered Judaism from the surrounding Hellenistic culture, giving rise to a new understanding of the holy life and, in turn, of Jewish spirituality. The mark of the holy life during one's lifetime became the ability of the soul to experience life after death in "the world to come" [*haolam haba*].

In post-biblical rabbinic Judaism, entering the "world-to-come" is the goal of human life, but there is considerable vagueness about it nature. In some rabbinic texts "the world-to-come" is a spatial category that describes a certain location, though not necessarily a terrestrial location. It is a realm in which the dead exist in some fashion, although there is no agreement about the nature of their existence. In other texts, "the world-to-come" is a temporal category that pertains to the end of cosmic history, and again there is no agreement about the details of the end of time. And, finally, there are rabbinic texts where "the world-to-come" pertains to a certain mode of being, an ideal type of Jewish life that stands in opposition to the vagaries of life in this world [*haolam hazeh*]. Whether "the world-to-come" is understood temporally, spatially, or existentially, the rabbinic texts situate the depiction of "the world-to-come" in the context of the Jewish doctrine of retribution. Inclusion in the "the world-to-come" depends on the degree of righteousness achieved during one's lifetime. There is a causal relationship between the quality of one's life in this world, namely, the degree to which one's life was governed by Torah, and one's ability to enjoy the ideal future life, whether that occurs immediately after the death of the body or in the remote eschatological future.

In its entirety, then, rabbinic Judaism can be viewed as a comprehensive and detailed program to attain the spiritual goal of human life. In the most general terms, the rabbinic spiritual path consists of three major components, as summarized by Avot 1:2: Torah, *avodah*, and *gemilut hasadim*; that is, the study of God's Torah, the performance of rituals commanded by God, and interpersonal interaction through acts of lovingkindness. Through Torah study, worship, and acts of kindness, Jews could imitate God and bring the divine presence to dwell in their lives in this world. The claim of rabbinic Judaism is quite clear: the more Jews imitate God's ways and sanctify life through the practice of mitzvot, the more Jews can be assured of life in "the world to come," whether this life comes immediately after the death of the body or in the remote, post-historical future.

The life of Torah study, worship, and good deeds combined corporeal and non-corporeal aspects. Roughly speaking, these two aspects overlap the legal and non-legal dimensions of the Jewish tradition. The corporeal aspects of Jewish life, namely what Jews ought to do, are governed by halacha. But the rationale for observing God's commandments was elaborated through non-legal literature or Aggadah. Together, the legal and non-legal aspects of rabbinic Judaism produced an organic way of living that encompassed all aspects of human life, replacing the practice of Judaism in the Temple, which now lay in ruins.

The legal and non-legal aspects of rabbinic Judaism capture the interplay between the physical and spiritual aspects of human life. On the one hand, the holy life is to be carried out through actions of the body that sanctify all aspects of life: space, time, the body, human relations, and social institutions. But on the other hand, the process of sanctification must never be merely perfunctory or external. It must involve the proper intention [kavannah], so that the mitzvah can be carried out for the sake of God rather than for one's own sake. As the rabbinic scholars increasingly absorbed Greek modes of thought, they began to locate human intentionality in the soul. Under Greek influence, the rabbis understood the soul to be distinct from the body.

Rabbinic Judaism did not articulate a consistent psychological theory to explain the relationship between body and soul or the operation of the soul. Yet it is clear that the rabbis (especially in the Talmudic period) were aware of the complexity of interior life and cultivated certain practices to enhance it. For some, the cultivation of interior life meant the attainment of ecstatic, out-of-body experiences, in which the soul of the practitioner could ascend to the celestial world to "envision God in His beauty." These ecstatic journeys were induced by special procedures, and their major concern was how to protect themselves against the danger of the experience. The journey of the soul to the celestial realm was considered very dangerous because one could lose one's sanity or even die. To protect themselves against these dangers, the ecstatic visionaries had to arm themselves with verbal formulas that acted like protective shields, since they were comprised of divine energy stored in the very letters of the linguistic formulas.

These ecstatic and visionary experiences were not meant for the entire Jewish community. They were practiced by a small group of religious savants, whose social location and relationship to rabbinic Judaism is still not clear. Whether these ecstatic experiences were undergone by rabbis who were at the center of the rabbinic class or rather by Jews who were opposed to the rabbinic class, whose works were later appropriated by rabbis, remains an open question. What matters is that the content of the ecstatic experiences was considered secret, to be divulged only to the few, primarily through oral teaching. Eventually, toward the end of the Talmudic era, these traditions were written down and edited, most likely in Babylonia, and in this form the material arrived in Italy. With the settlement of Italian Jews in Germany, these esoteric teachings migrated northward to Germany, where they eventually gave rise to new kinds of speculations and ethical directives. I refer to the spiritual program of the German pietists in the thirteenth century, known in Hebrew as *Hasidey Ashkenaz*, whose literary legacy is *Sefer Hasidim* [The Book of the Pietists] attributed to R. Judah ha-Hasid (Judah the Pietist). Despite the influence of the Hekhalot and Merkabah literature on the pietists of Germany, for the most part ecstatic and visionary activity remained marginal in rabbinic Judaism.

The dominant mode for the expression of rabbinic spirituality was not the ecstatic experience but the imaginative and creative interpretation of Torah. In their homiletical literature—the midrashic collections and the Aggadot of the Talmud—the rabbis gave full freedom to their imagination, speculating about God, the covenant with Israel, human destiny, and the afterlife. These literary speculations, beautiful and inspiring as they were, did not constitute a full-fledged systematic spiritual program. That development took place only after philosophy was absorbed into Jewish consciousness in the tenth century, when most Jews resided in Muslim lands.

Jewish spirituality, then, is a product of the Middle Ages and the early modern period. In medieval Germany, France, Spain, Italy, North Africa, Egypt, Palestine, and Ottoman Turkey, medieval Jewish thinkers articulated complex spiritual regimens. All of them were predicated on certain theories concerning the structure of the universe, the place of humans in the universe, the relationship between body and the soul, the purpose of human life, and the meaning of divinely revealed Scriptures. On the basis of these theories, Jewish spiritual disciplines either added certain practices to an already existing ritual life or interpreted existing practices and beliefs in accordance with their distinctive outlook. Some of these practices were decidedly ascetic, including isolation, seclusion, frequent fasting, ritual immersion, night vigils, and even self-mutilation. Other practices were aimed at altering ordinary consciousness through controlled breathing, physical postures, induced weeping, visualization of Hebrew letters, or recitation of divine names. Most if not all of these practices were carried out within the parameters of Jewish Law, but they surely enlarged the scope of Jewish devotional life. In some cases, spiritual practices were indeed derived from or influenced by non-Jewish spiritual traditions, Muslim, Christian, or Hindu.

Cultivation of the inner life was not undertaken for its own sake or for the sake of feeling good. Rather it meant to accomplish one thing: enhance the quality of Israel's interaction with God. The difference between philosophy and Kabbalah is to be found in the way each of them understood the nature of God and the capacity of Israel to communicate with God. We now turn to discuss philosophy and Kabbalah with greater specificity.

MEDIEVAL PHILOSOPHY: SPIRITUALITY AS INTELLECTUAL PERFECTION

In a nutshell, the crux of philosophic spiritual programs was the claim that to attain perfection one must perfect the intellect, since it is the intellect that is the essence of humans. But underlying this intellectualist vision is a complex system of beliefs that I will attempt to summarize briefly.

The point of departure for medieval Jewish philosophic spirituality was the metaphysical distinction between matter and form. Form pertains to *what* a thing is, whereas matter pertains to *that* a thing is. Another way of understanding this distinction is to say that matter pertains to extension in space, whereas form pertains to thought; matter pertains to particulars, whereas form captures the universal; matter is perceivable through the senses, whereas form is knowable by the intellect. According to the medieval Jewish philosophers who followed Aristotle, in the world as we know it both matter and form are necessary and interdependent; a form cannot exist without matter and vice versa, matter cannot exist without form. However, there is a level of reality that is non-corporeal, in which exist disembodied forms. These are intellectual substances, of which God is supreme because God is least corporeal.

God

All medieval Jewish philosophers were religious believers; they all presupposed the existence of God, and they all believed that humans are capable of gaining some knowledge about God. Who is the God of the philosophers? The God of the philosopher is a non-corporeal entity. God is an intellect, or a mind, that is engaged in one activity only: thinking or contemplating. God's contemplation is non-corporeal because the content of God's thinking is God. God think about Himself and his thinking is causative. God's thinking give rise to a world other than God. As a result of God's thinking, the world came into being, though how exactly God caused the world to come into being was a matter of debate among medieval philosophers. What matters to my comments is this: for medieval Jewish philosophers, spirituality was associated with the mental activity of thinking. If God is primarily an intellect that thinks, to be most like God is to develop the capacity to think, a capacity that the medieval philosophers believed was created by God.

The Human

The biblical text already asserted that humans were created in the divine image. Maimonides and all those who followed him interpreted the "image of God" to mean the capacity to think and to distinguish between truth and falsehood. Our ability to know truth is thus the basis for our ability to imitate God and to come close to God, to the extent this is possible for humans who are embodied creatures. Precisely because humans are embodied, their knowledge is by nature finite, prone to mistakes, and hindered by all sorts of sensual obstacles. But, in principle, human access to God is possible because of the intellect and is carried out by means of cognitive activity. Our task, then, is to perfect the intellect so as to become more like God, to the extent that humans can be like God. The spirituality of the philosophers was thus intellectualist.

The human intellect, according to the rationalist philosophers, was one of the functions of the human soul. All medieval Jewish philosophers held that humans are comprised of a body and a soul, and they tended to follow Aristotle in considering the soul as the organizational principle of the body. The soul itself has several functions; some are more dependent on the body than others. The least physically dependent function of the soul is the intellect, and it makes humans distinct from all other animals. Yet even the intellect is not totally divorced from corporeality or physicality. The intellect derives knowledge from sensations. Through the senses the soul gathers raw data about the world that it processes and from which it extracts what can be known about the world. That knowledge, claimed the philosophers, is grasped by the intellect and determines the quality of the intellect and in turn the destiny of the individual knower. The more abstract, universal, and necessary knowledge one possesses, the more one has a chance to survive the death of the body.

Given the philosophic focus on the intellect, what about our emotions or other mental functions that do not involve the intellect? Do they function in any way in philosophic spirituality, or do they represent an obstacle to spirituality? At least for Maimonides and those who followed him in the thirteenth, fourteenth, and fifteenth centuries, the emotions and the imagination were considered obstacles for spiritual life because they were directly linked to the body. To have a spiritual life of philosophic contemplation, the emotions must be properly curbed, restrained, and even suppressed. They must be ruled by the intellect that directs all human activities and intention toward what is objectively good.

The spiritual life of the philosophers thus required a lot of self-control through habitual practice of good acts. What makes a given act good is that it is not too little, not too much, not too fast, not too slow; in short, that it is "just right." Through repeated action of such good acts, humans can acquire the virtues, the disposition to behave in the right way at the right time and for the right motive. We may easily recognize Aristotle in this view of the virtues. Indeed, the Jewish philosophers adopted the Aristotelian understanding of virtue and integrated it with the rabbinic understanding of holy life. Through the right action in the mean, we acquire the virtues that enable us to live the good life and experience well-being, or happiness, in this world.

Revelation

If we can know a lot about the world and if we can figure out how to live the good life, it may seem that, according to the Jewish philosophers, we do not need any special assistance from God. If so, did the Jewish philosopher find the revelation of God's will in the Torah redundant? Not at all! All medieval Jewish philosophers believed in divine revelation, as asserted by the rabbinic tradition. Not only did the Jewish philosophers never doubt the historicity of revelation, they also believed that what the Torah teaches is absolutely true. The Torah is absolutely true because its recipient, the prophet Moses, had attained the highest degree of intellectual perfection. Moses' perfection in his prophetic activity was due to the fact that he was least affected by his human body, especially his imagination, a mental faculty that can always divert the intellect away from the truth. In all other prophets, the imagination colored their ability to apprehend truth, but in the case of Moses his prophecy was pure, unadulterated, and unencumbered by the imagination or by bodily function. It is another way of saying that Moses was the most spiritual human being who ever lived or who will ever live. Hence the Torah of Moses is a spiritual entity, though its spirituality is hidden or covered through the veils of language.

The Torah of Moses teaches philosophic truths in a figurative speech that befits the fact that humans have a body and a soul. The truths of the Torah are twofold or have two different functions: some of the Torah's teachings are meant to perfect the body; namely, to ensure that those who live by the Torah will live the good life as individuals who must exist with others in societies. The Torah thus contains many instructions and laws that secure the best social order. In addition, the Torah contains truths that perfect the soul, or more precisely the intellect, and make humans like God. This body of knowledge that Moses made known to Israel has salvific power. Those who attain this knowledge can survive the death of the body and attain the immortality of the intellect.

The task of the philosopher is to lift the veils that cover the philosophic truths of the Torah through the act of interpretation. The fact that the truths of the Torah were seen to be veiled meant that the spirituality of the philosophers was both esoteric and elitist. Because the truth is non-corporeal, it is difficult to comprehend; hence the truth requires the mediation of figures of speech that enable the finite human mind to grasp it through simile. But most human beings are unable to grasp subtle and profound truths; hence they never capture the meaning beyond the figure of speech. Minimally, the philosopher must expose the philosophic meaning of the Torah to competent disciples, who can thereby gain access to the immortality of the soul. When such interpretation and teaching take place, it becomes evident that the laws of the Torah are compatible with the acquisition of virtues and that the content of the Torah's views is absolutely true.

Given this understanding of Torah, it is easy to see why medieval Jewish philosophers maintained that there was no conflict between being a religious person and being an intellectually rigorous scientist, much as there was no conflict between cultivating the virtues and following the commands of God. The spiritual life of the philosophers was lived through the acquisition of moral and intellectual virtues, culminating in the knowledge of God, to the extent that God can be known by humans. It is this desired knowledge that constitutes the ultimate end of human life according to medieval Jewish philosophers.

The Ultimate End of Human Life

The ultimate end of human life, according to the philosophers, is the knowledge of God. But of what exactly does that knowledge consist? Maimonides said that it consists of the knowledge of God's governance of the world. According to him, the essence of God remained unknowable even to the most perfect philosopher, Moses, but the way God relates to the world is accessible to humans. Other philosophers, like the fourteenth century philosopher Gersonides, were more optimistic about human knowledge and maintained that we have some knowledge of who God is, though this knowledge is indirect; namely, through analogies. Be that as it may, the philosophers held that it is the perfection of the intellect that ensures personal immortality. Knowledge of necessary, eternal truths, constitute what remains of us after the death of the body.

The ultimate end of human life is thus the bliss of uninterrupted intellectual activity, the most joyous activity of all, unencumbered by the physical limitations of the body. Philosophic spirituality, then, is contemplative and even mystical because it posits the union between the knower, the object of knowledge, and the activity of knowing. Given the supremacy of contemplation, it is obvious that for the philosophers the actual performance of commandments has only an instrumental value. It creates the social order and the life style that are conductive to the life of contemplation. This emphasis on contemplation also marginalizes concern for the remote future as depicted by traditional Jewish messianism or the collective resurrection of the dead in the eschaton.

In sum, the medieval Jewish philosophers articulated a spiritual path that was based on the acquisition of moral and intellectual virtues through habitual practice of the mean. This spiritual program did not negate the three components of Jewish spirituality—Torah study, worship, and acts of lovingkindness—but gave them a new interpretation. The study of Torah was given the highest value and was now carried out in light of philosophy, taught by non-Jews. The performance of commandments through prescribed rituals was given an instrumental value: the commandments created the best social order in which intellectual perfection can be attained. And acts of lovingkindness toward other humans were considered part of the imitation of God's action in the world, but their utility was also instrumental; they prepared one for the knowledge of God. For the philosophers, the interior life focused on the act of studying the hidden, philosophic meaning of the Torah and the attainment of intellectual perfection by which we become most like God: a mind engaged in eternal contemplation.

With a better understanding of rationalist spirituality, we can now turn to theosophical Kabbalah and clarify what it shares with philosophy and where it differs. By studying these two spiritual programs comparatively, we are able to gain a deeper understanding of the history of Jewish spirituality and the relevance of past models for the present quest.

KABBALAH: SPIRITUALITY AS PARTICIPATION IN GOD'S LIFE

The origins of Kabbalah can be traced to the rabbinic period, but as a self-conscious program for the interpretation of rabbinic Judaism Kabbalah emerged in southern France and the late twelfth century and flourished in Spain during the thirteenth and fourteenth centuries. Kabbalah experienced a second revival in the sixteenth century in the Land of Israel, and kabbalistic ideas would give rise to the acute messianism of the Sabbatian movement in the mid-seventeenth century and to the Jewish revival movement of Hasidism in the mid-eighteenth century. Like rationalist philosophy, kabbalistic spirituality was rooted in rabbinic Judaism, especially in the homiletical dimension of the rabbinic program, but whereas the philosophers intellectualized the rabbinic legacy, the Kabbalists relished the imaginative creativity of the rabbis and considerably embellished it. To some extent, it is correct to say that Kabbalah emerged as a polemical response to the dissemination of rationalistic philosophy; in fact, it was an attempt curb rationalist philosophy because it was believed to be a deviation from the rabbinic program. Yet, it is misleading to say that rationalist philosophy and Kabbalah are two diametrically opposed spiritual programs.

No less than philosophy, Kabbalah was an outgrowth of strands within rabbinic Judaism; no less than philosophy, Kabbalah was intended for the educated elite and not for the masses; no less than philosophy, Kabbalah presupposed the existence of a hidden meaning of divine revelation which only the Kabbalist can know. Moreover, I would claim that medieval Kabbalah could not have come into existence without the growth of philosophical thinking about Jews. Certain concepts, themes, and methods of Scriptural interpretation in Kabbalah were derived from previously developed philosophy, even though they were given a different twist. So what characterizes Kabbalah as a distinct spiritual path in Judaism?

God

Like the philosophers Kabbalists were aware of the Otherness of God. They too wished to protect the transcendence of God that they claimed it to be "without limit," or infinite. God as infinite [or *eyn sof*] is unknown and inaccessible. The essence of God remains inaccessible to human knowledge and is not the object of human worship. But the hiddenness of God does not exhaust divine reality. According to the Kabbalists, God has revealed his essence through ten dynamic powers, called *spherot*; these aspects are the attributes which makes it possible for humans to know quite a lot about God and to communicate with God.

The philosophers taught that communication with God is possible, but limited to what humans can know about God's governance of the created world. By limiting human knowledge to divine providence, the philosophers limited not only human knowledge of God but also divine personhood. Indeed, the philosophers were quite embarrassed about any attempt to speak about God in human terms and interpreted these terms away by employing allegorical methods. The Kabbalists, on the other hand, wished to protect a personalist conception of God, which they claimed was the authentic meaning of rabbinic Judaism, and they thought that God's personality, and indeed God's inner life, is made known to humans through the ten *spherot*. Thus kabbalistic theosophy was the attempt to fathom the mystery of God's personality and the dynamics of God's inner life.

For the Kabbalists, God was thus a of unity the ten *spherot* that interacted with each other incessantly. Does that mean that the Kabbalists did not believe in the unity of God? Not necessarily. The Kabbalists were as much monotheists as the philosophers were, but they believed that unity is expressed in multiplicity rather than in simplicity. Moreover, the unity of the divine world is to be found in the delicate balance and harmony between the ten *spherot*, powers that react, respond, and interact with each other and with the reality outside the *spherot*ic realm. The God of the Kabbalists is a living reality rather than a static idea. This living reality is the source of all that exists, and as such it experiences polarity and conflict. Ideally, divine reality should be balanced, but due to human sins, this polarity is out of balance and in need of repair.

The most daring notion of the kabbalistic conception of God is that the divine world is governed by the polarity of masculinity and femininity. The Kabbalists took very seriously the notion that we are created in the divine image. We are like God not because we have the capacity to think, but because divine reality itself is constellated as a human being. The *spherot*ic realm is thus arranged in the shape of a human person, and God's inner life possesses the same intellectual, emotional, and even sexual qualities known to us from human life.

The energy that pulsates through the Godhead is sexual in nature. The processes within the Godhead are governed by the rhythm of sexuality: penetration and withdrawal, union and separation, marriage and divorce. The constant flux of the *spherotic* realm reflects both the ever-changing nature of human psychic and bodily processes as well as changes in God's relationship with the created world. In particular, the supernal drama reflects both the intimacy and the vicissitudes of the eternal love between God and Israel.

More than any other aspect of God, the Kabbalists focused on the last or tenth Sefirah, the feminine aspect of God. Referred to primarily as Shekhinah—the Talmudic term for Divine presence—the Kabbalists imaged the divine female as Queen, Bride Sister, Daughter, Wife, Matron, Mother, Earth, Sea, Moon, Field, Orchard, and a host of related feminine symbols. The divine female represents the relational dimension of the Deity. The Shekhinah is the face that God shows to the created world, especially to Israel. As a liminal boundary between the Godhead and the reality outside it, she is both the entry gate into the Godhead and the channel through which divine efflux is transmitted to the created universe.

The Shekhinah's relationship with the masculine forces of the Godhead is unstable, affected by human deeds. Human sins empower the domain of evil (the reification of profane forces) and induce discord in the supernal world, represented by the sundering of the divine male and female. In contrast, righteous conduct—through the performance of the commandments—reunites the masculine and the feminine aspects of the Godhead, restoring the bisexual Godhead to its primordial harmony. In turn, the re-pairing of the Godhead results in the abundance of divine efflux to the created universe, the sign of redeemed reality. Thus, the Kabbalists articulated the intrinsic connection between knowledge of God, the ability to impact God, and the redemption of reality.

But how did the Kabbalists know that God is an androgynous being? Where did they find support for their claim that the mystery of divine life pertains to procreation and not only to creation? The answer is very similar, though not identical, to the one given by the philosophers when they attempted to reinterpret Judaism philosophically. We can have some knowledge about God first because we are "created in the divine image" and second because God has revealed himself to us. While structurally this is the same, philosophy and Kabbalah interpreted creation in the divine image and revelation quite differently.

The Human

Human beings, or, more precisely, Israel, are similar to God not just because they are endowed with the ability to know truth, but also because the human soul has an ontological affinity with God. More specifically, the human soul is a divine particle; it is a substance carved from the very essence of God. Echoing Platonic theories of the soul, the Kabbalists maintained the preexistence of the soul, which unites temporarily with the body for the duration of one's life. Being a divine substance, however, the soul aspires to return to its divine source when the body dies. However, the sins that humans commit during life are a hindrance to the return of the soul to its origin. Thus, the major purpose of kabbalistic spirituality is to protect the initial holiness of the soul from being contaminated by the body. This protection is possible through the performance of divine commandments with the proper intention. We shall return to this point below. For now suffice it to note that for the Kabbalists the tension between the soul and the body is more acute than for the philosophers.

Not surprisingly, kabbalistic spirituality had strong ascetic tendencies. It was not only concerned with the acquisition of virtues through the habitual practice of the mean, but also developed techniques for the suppression of passions and temptations. Some of these techniques varied in their severity over time. They were most severe after the expulsion of the Jews from Spain; their severity can be explained not only as an attempt to expiate sins, but also as an influence of Christian and Muslim spiritual practices. These ascetic practices included frequent fasting, ritual immersions, self-flagellation, long night vigils, induced weeping, and wearing of sackcloth. They were especially prominent in Safed after the expulsion from Spain, though their origins can be traced to German Hasidism of the thirteenth century. More commonly in kabbalistic spirituality, the body was not suppressed but rather spiritualized and purified through the very performance of mitzvot that all Jews are enjoined to perform. To understand how the rituals of the Jewish tradition can function in a purifying way, we need to understand the kabbalistic conception of Torah.

Revelation

For the Kabbalists, the Torah made known the processes that govern God's inner life. Since God's inner life is non-corporeal, the Torah had to be communicated through veils which befit human embodied nature, precisely as the philosophers suggested. However, the esoteric or hidden meaning of the Torah is not comprised of philosophic truths but the mystery of God's personality. The Torah, in other words, is minimally God's biography (for those who believe that Moses wrote the Torah) or, better still, God's autobiography. Reading Torah is the main path toward the retelling of God's hidden, personal story.

The Kabbalists assumed that the Torah is literally written in the language of God. It is the language in which God created the world and in which God revealed his innermost self. The meaning of Hebrew words, therefore, is not conventional or artificial but substantive: the Hebrew language of the Torah captures divine reality symbolically. The task of the Kabbalist is thus to decode the symbols of the Torah that are to be found in its narratives and laws. The narratives of the Torah are not simply stories about events in mundane life, but symbolic expressions of processes within the Godhead. If so, there is nothing trivial or insignificant in the Torah. Every word, every letter, the order of the words in the sentence, the place of the verse in the portion, and the relationship of one Torah portion to another reflect the rhythm of divine life.

For the Kabbalists, as well as the philosophers, Torah study is the most direct path to knowledge about God and knowledge of God. But they read Torah very differently. Whereas the philosophers find in the Torah directives for the most just society and the most correct opinions, the Kabbalist finds in it the mysteries of God's personality. Thus, when the Kabbalist reads the Torah, he does not remain apart from the act of reading, but becomes an active participant in the divine life. Kabbalistic Torah interpretation is thus both a sacramental activity (when the reader participates in the life of the divine) and a transformative experience (when both the reader's subjective reality and the objective reality to which it refers are transformed). The purpose of kabbalistic Torah study, moreover, is redemptive: it brings about the redemption of the Kabbalist, his community, the world, and even God.

Worship

If we understand the kabbalistic approach to the study of Torah, we can speak more generally about the kabbalistic conception of the mitzvot. Unlike the philosophers, who believed that the performance of divine commands has only an instrumental value, the Kabbalists held that the commandments have intrinsic value. Jews should perform the mitzvot "for human sake" "for the sake of God." What does that mean? The rituals of the Jewish tradition, say the Kabbalists, are transformative and redemptive. Through the performance of commandments, Jews can perfect themselves, society, the cosmos, and even God. God, too, is in need of redemption because divine reality is broken and in disarray due to human sins. Through the performance of divine commands, humans can repair divine reality and bring about the redemption for which the Jews have been waiting.

In this spiritual program the theurgical and the mystical aspects of rituals are closely intertwined. On the one hand, the Kabbalist performs the mitzvot in order to achieve a mystical union with God—that is, *devequt*. Through proper mental concentration, the Kabbalist spiritualizes himself so that his soul is liberated from the body to be united with the Shekhinah, or female aspect of God. As a result of that union, the Kabbalist creates yet another union—the unification of the Shekhinah with her husband, *Tife'eret*, which manifests the theurgical function of worship. The Kabbalists' mental energy is thus the key that unlocks the mysteries of the Shekhinah, enabling her to be receptive to the penetration of her husband, *Tife'eret*.

In kabbalistic spirituality, the human and the Torah are aligned symbolically and structurally. According to Kabbalah, a human being possesses 613 limbs, which parallel the 613 mitzvot and the 613 limbs of the primordial man, the constellation of the Godhead. Each mitzvah Jews perform on earth has a direct referent in the *spherotic* world. The performance of a mitzvah thus perfects the performer and the addressee of the mitzvah, God. In the genderized symbolism of Kabbalah we may phrase this principle as follows: through the performance of mitzvot the Kabbalist brings about the reunion or re-pairing of the masculine and feminine aspects of the Godhead. Torn apart from each other because of human sins and the aggressiveness of demonic forces, the divine male and female are now united by virtue of kabbalistic performance of the mitzvot. Thus the male Kabbalist acts as a female conduit to the heavenly erotic event.

As a holy ritual, the mitzvot must be performed in absolute purity. If we take Torah study as the paradigmatic mitzvah, it means that only Jews, or, more precisely, only Jewish males who live by the Jewish purity code, can penetrate the symbolic text and bring about the unification of the male and the female. Whether the Kabbalist must engage in actual sex with his lawful wife in order to accomplish the divine reunion or can merely fantasize about holy sex while engaging in Torah study with his male comrades is still an open question.

The theurgical import of ritual according to Kabbalah meant that Kabbalah invigorated halachic Judaism. Though Kabbalah emphasized the importance of the spiritual dimension of the mitzvot, the interiorization of religious life did not corrode the actual performance of the mitzvot. On the contrary, the symbolic meaning that Kabbalah imparts to each and every aspect of the mitzvah meant that actual performance has an intrinsic value. Each and every mitzvah, to the minutest detail, has a cosmic and metaphysical significance. Thus, the road to communion with God lies not in mere understanding of the rationale of the commandments or in the creation of a just social order, but in the combination of external performance and internal intention or *kavannah*.

Whereas the philosophic spiritual program focused on the attainment of intellectual perfection, the kabbalistic spiritual path focuses on the cultivation of concentrated intention. The Kabbalists highlighted the need to perform each and every mitzvah with the proper mental attitude. One has to be very mindful of the mitzvah and never do it out of rote or in order to fulfill one's duty. But this is not all. Mindfulness here means that one must accompany the external performance with an internal act of mental concentration. That act is the spiritual energy by which the performer is able to connect a bodily action to a specific locus in the divine world. Mental concentration creates the energy that elevates the mundane act to the supernal world. When the Kabbalist performs a given ritual with the proper *kavannah*, he not only spiritualizes himself, but also creates a new spiritual entity that transcends mundane reality and ascends upwards toward the *spherotic* world. Put differently, kabbalistic ritual is a creative act; if you wish, an artistic act. I would thus venture to say that the Kabbalists could be viewed as the artists of medieval Judaism. They perfected Jewish legal tradition and the mythic worldview to such a degree that they empowered the Jewish tradition and made it perfectly reasonable for Jews to retain their allegiance to the tradition.

Kabbalistic and philosophic spiritual programs differ from each other in regard to the performance of the mitzvot. For the philosophers, the practice of the precepts of Judaism was instrumental to the acquisition of moral and intellectual virtues. To the Kabbalists, the observance of the rituals of Judaism enabled the mystic to participate in the inner life of God. More specifically, it meant that the Kabbalist could fathom the rhythm of divine life and influence that rhythm by connecting his thought with the proper aspect of the divine realm. Ideally, the Kabbalist would be able to unite the masculine and feminine elements of the divine that were severed in the remote past through the first sin of Adam. The mitzvot are not just instruments for the contemplation of God, but acts possessed of intrinsic merit: they enable the Kabbalist to become a partner of God. The Kabbalist communicates with God both through the body and through the mind. While performing the commandment in the body, the Kabbalist accompanies performance with mental concentration that is directed toward a particular locus in the divine landscape.

APPLYING PAST MODELS TO THE PRESENT QUEST

With this exposition of rabbinic Judaism, philosophy, and Kabbalah we can now make some concluding remarks and reflect on the meaning of the past models to the quest for spirituality today. Our first conclusion is that spirituality is a feature of the rabbinic way of life, of the life of the dual Torah. It is impossible to be Jewishly spiritual outside the structure of the concepts, themes, and sensibility defined by rabbinic Judaism itself. How we interpret rabbinic Judaism is a matter of debate and disagreement, but I am convinced that for Jews, spirituality is feasible only within the conceptual framework of the life of Torah. Medieval philosophy and Kabbalah illustrate how it is possible to interpret the received tradition in very different ways to express diverse spiritual needs.

The data suggest a second conclusion: Jewish spirituality is unavoidably textual: it must be anchored in Scripture whose meaning is fathomed through the act of interpretation. No matter how a Jew interprets what the Torah means, there can be no spiritual program outside the process of Torah interpretation. For Jews today, this means that to devise meaningful Jewish programs of spirituality, Jews must be familiar with the Torah, read it in Hebrew, and understand its unique features. Fluency in Hebrew is particularly central to those who are attracted to Kabbalah, since Kabbalah regards the letters of the Hebrew alphabet as the most elementary building blocks of reality. To dabble in Kabbalah and seek to benefit from its spiritual powers without the knowledge of Hebrew is meaningless.

The centrality of the act of study in Jewish spirituality leads to a third conclusion. Spirituality in Judaism cannot be identified with emotionalism, let alone unfocused or fuzzy thinking. Rather, Jewish spirituality has a strong intellectual dimension in regard both to the theories presupposed by a given spiritual program and to the centrality of study in the spiritual life. Philosophers and Kabbalists alike were highly learned in the literary sources of Judaism, even though they were also informed about and open to non-Jewish spiritual and intellectual traditions. If Jews today seek to cultivate the spiritual life, they must make their priority the study of Torah, in the broadest sense of that term, at the expense of other pursuits. Such study, however, should not be divorced from contemporary science, both the natural and the social sciences, to the extent that these sciences are true.

The speculative character of Jewish spirituality, however, does not negate its concern with proper action. Our fourth conclusion pertains to the human need to act in a certain way in order to imitate God and thereby perfect the world. The two medieval spiritual programs presupposed that we live in an imperfect, that is, unredeemed world. Jewish spirituality is an ongoing process of perfecting the imperfect, of redeeming a reality that is unredeemed though not unredeemable. Such assumptions accentuate human responsibility toward the world and call upon us to be actively involved in the mending of the world through Torah study, rituals, and good deeds. Responsibility toward others requires that Jewish spirituality cannot be another form of contemporary self-indulgence or a way to escape from the ills of the world. Rather, Jewish spirituality entails making the material needs of other human beings our own spiritual concern and doing something about it.

That a spiritual program involves action in this world leads to our fifth conclusion: Jewish spirituality is both this-worldly and otherworldly. For everyone, the repair of the world begins in this life, though it is never completed in this life and is never accomplished by one person. The spiritual path points toward another reality, a more perfect reality in which God rules, but the ideal is never fully realized in this world. Jewish spirituality prescribes a certain path that can never by fully realized in one's own lifetime. Thus, it is in principle a mistake to attempt to force the realization of the ideal in order to bring about the messianic age because it will be premature and harmful. Put somewhat differently, Jewish spirituality is both theocentric and anthropocentric. It is theocentric because it considers God the goal of human life, but it is anthropocentric because it believes that humans have the capacity to become more than just disposable bodies that are destined to decay. Jewish spirituality makes the human a partner of God by calling on us to cultivate that which is divine in us.

My comments should make it clear that the spiritual thirst among Jews today can indeed be quenched by the rich spiritual sources of Jewish tradition, provided Jews avail themselves of it. The return to our spiritual resources will not only enrich the quality of our Jewish life; it will also address the shortcomings of human life in modern, post-industrial Western nations at the dawn of the twenty-first century. In an age governed by technology, Jewish spirituality is profoundly humanizing. It calls on us to cultivate that which is divine in us by devoting our life to contemplation as well as to action. In an age that is governed by a cacophony of deafening sounds and disrespect for language, Jewish spirituality bids us to listen to words very carefully as well as to cherish silence. In an age that vacillates between ruthless hedonism and scientific secularism, Jewish spirituality reminds us that we are both body and mind, and that bodily rituals and actions toward other persons complement contemplation of the mind and meditation of the heart. In an age that is ruled by digital images that rob our capacity to imagine creatively, Jewish spirituality invites us to develop our imagination without using ready-made images and to find inspiration in words rather than in pictures. In an age consumed by the pursuit of material success and comfort, Jewish spirituality suggests to us that life can be spiritually rich without material trappings. Whether we wish to abide by the insights of medieval Jewish spirituality is up to us.

SUGGESTIONS FOR FURTHER READING

Ariel, David S. *The Mystic Quest: An Introduction to Jewish Mysticism*. New York: Schocken Books, 1988.

An excellent introduction to the Jewish mystical tradition that makes modern scholarship on Kabbalah accessible to the general reader.

Cooper, David A. *A Handbook of Jewish Meditation Practices*. Woodstock: Jewish Lights, 2000.

A very useful introduction to the practices of Jewish mysticism by a spiritual teacher and expert in meditation for whom Kabbalah is not merely a subject of academic scholarship but a living reality.

Frank, Daniel H. and Oliver Leaman (eds.). *History of Jewish Philosophy*. London and New York: Routledge, 1997.

The best reference book about the Jewish philosophical tradition from antiquity to the present. Written by specialists in Jewish philosophy, it covers both individual thinkers and intellectual trends, all situated in their proper historical context. Each chapter includes a bibliography of the relevant primary sources and studies by modern scholars.

Giller, Pinchas. *Reading the Zohar: The Sacred Text of the Kabbalah*. Oxford and New York: Oxford University Press, 2001.

An accessible, well-written work based on detailed familiarity with the zoharic text and mastery of modern scholarship on Kabbalah. The study highlights the complexity of the zoharic text, its mystical doctrine, and its impact on Jewish culture.

Ginzburg Elliot, K. *The Sabbath in the Classical Kabbalah*. Albany: State University of New York Press, 1989.

A thematic analysis of Sabbath symbolism in classical Kabbalah with a focus on the *Zohar*. Jews who observe the Sabbath will find this book most useful for unpacking the motifs of the *kabbalat shabbat* ritual.

Green, Arthur. *Seek My Face, Speak My Name: A Contemporary Jewish Theology*. Northvale, N.J.: Jason Aronon, 1992.

Written by a leading academic scholar of Kabbalah and Hasidism, this book is an example of how the mystical tradition can shape contemporary Jewish theology.

Hallamish, Moshe. *An Introduction to the Kabbalah*. Translated by R. Bar-Ilan and O. Wiskind-Elper. Albany: State University of New York Press, 1999.

An excellent thematic treatment of kabbalistic doctrines that provides informatin about major Kabbalists and their texts, all in the proper historical context. Attention is paid to both Zoharic and Lurianic versions of Kabbalah.

Idel, Moshe. *Kabbalah: New Perspectives*. New Haven: Yale University Press, 1988.

A very innovative study by an Israeli scholar who has challenged the reigning theories of Gershom Scholem, the leading modern scholar of Kabbalah. Instead of understanding Kabbalah as a set of speculative doctrines, this book focuses on its experiential dimension and offers a typology to understand types of mystical experiences. It is based on prodigious scholarship of kabbalistic texts extant primarily in manuscripts.

_____. *Studies in Ecstatic Kabbalah*. Albany: State University of New York Press, 1988.

A collection of three studies about a major thirteenth century mystic, whose spiritual approach is a peculiar combination of Kabbalah and the philosophy of Maimonides.

_____. *Language, Torah and Hermeneutics in Abraham Abulafia*. Translated by M. Kallus. Albany: State University of New York Press, 1989.

Another collection of translated studies about Abraham Abulafia for the advanced reader who is intrigued by this important Jewish mystic. The studies are especially useful to those interested in the nature of mystical experiences and the connection between language and religious experience in Kabbalah.

Kaplan, Aryeh. *Jewish Meditation: A Practical Guide*. New York: Schocken Books, 1985.

A non-academic introduction to kabbalistic spirituality by an Orthodox rabbi who was a practitioner of Kabbalah. The book opens up the experiential dimension of Kabbalah as the spiritual aspect of halachic

Judaism.

Liebes, Yehuda. *Studies in the Zohar.* Translated by A. Schwartz, et al. Albany: State University of New York Press, 1993.

A collection of three studies by an Israeli scholar who is a creative and original interpreter of the *Zohar*.

Maimonides, Moses. *The Guide for the Perplexed.* Translated by S. Pines. Chicago: University of Chicago Press, 1963.

The most authoritative translation of the seminal text of Jewish philosophy. This edition includes an essay by Schlomo Pines on the literary sources of the *Guide* and an introduction by Leo Strauss, a major modern interpreter of Maimonides.

Safed Spirituality. Translated by F. Lawrence. Ramsey: Paulist Press, 1984.

A collection of primary sources by the mystics of Safed in the sixteenth century that present the spiritual world of this mystical community in its historical context.

Scholem, Gershom. *Major Trends in Jewish Mysticism.* New York: Schocken Books, 1946.

The most comprehensive overview of the Jewish mystical tradition by the leading scholar of the tradition. Although many of its claims have been challenged in recent years, this book remains the foundational text of modern scholarship on the Jewish philosophical tradition.

_____. *On the Kabbalah and Its Symbolism.* Translated by R. Manheim. New York: Schocken Books, 1965.

A collection of foundational essays about the nature of kabbalistic symbolism and about the relationship between symbolism and ritual in Kabbalah.

_____. *Origins of the* Kabbalah. Edited by R. J. Zwi Werblowsky. Translated from the German by A. Arkush. Philadelphia: The Jewish Publication Society, 1987.

This book is essential for the advanced student who is interested in the emergence of Kabbalah in the twelfth century. Despite its academic style, it is quite accessible. While much has been discovered since its first publication, the main claims remain in place.

Sirat, Colette. *A History of Jewish Philosophy in the Middle Ages.* Cambridge: Cambridge University Press, 1985.

Until recently, this book was the most useful overview of medieval Jewish philosophy. Its strength lies in summaries of existing scholarship and an extensive bibliography.

Tishby Isaiah. *The Wisdom of the Zohar.* Translated by D. Goldstein. 3

vols. London and Washington: The Littman Library of Jewish Civilization, 1989.

An anthology of translated zoharic passages arranged thematically. Each section has extensive introductory essays that situate the ideas of the *Zohar* in their relationship to rabbinic Judaism and to Jewish philosophy. If a reader can have only one text about the *Zohar*, this is it.

Twersky, Isadore, ed. *A Maimonides Reader.* New York: Behrman House, 1972.

A most useful anthology of excerpts from Maimonides' legal, philosophical, and epistolary writings.

Wolfson, Elliot R. *Through a Speculum that Shines: Vision and Imagination in Medieval Jewish Mysticism.* Princeton: Princeton University Press, 1994.

For the advanced reader, the strength of this volume lies in the close reading of texts, bridging the alleged differences between rationalist philosophy and Kabbalah, and tracing the evolution of literary motifs over time. Its originality lies in the argument that visualization of God is central to Jewish mysticism.

_____. *Circle in the Square: Studies in the Use of Gender in Kabbalistic Symbolism.* Albany: State University of New York Press, 1995.

A collection of previously published essays about the gender aspect of Kabbalah. For the advanced reader who has more than basic knowledge of Kabbalah, its main thesis is that Kabbalah remains profoundly male-centered, despite its focus on the feminine aspect of God. The implication of the book is that when properly understood, kabbalistic feminine imagery of the divine is not compatible with feminist sensibilities.

Zohar: The Book of Enlightenment. Translated by D. Matt. Ramsey: Paulist Press, 1983.

A small selection of texts from the zoharic corpus that successfully captures its poetic power.

The Meaning of the *Aqedah* [Binding of Isaac] for Jewish Spirituality

Jerome (Yehuda) Gellman

INTRODUCTION

The book of Genesis presents us with two contrasting pictures of Abraham. The first is Abraham of Genesis 18, where Abraham argues with God over the approaching destruction of Sodom. Abraham challenges God to spare the righteous, with the striking verse: "Far be it from you to destroy the righteous with the wicked…. Shall the judge of the entire world not do justice?" This Abraham stands before God with full confidence in his deepest moral convictions, invoking his moral sensibilities to rebuke the creator of heaven and earth. This Abraham asks God to respect his human autonomy and personal integrity. In this picture of Jewish spirituality, the person of faith stands upright before God.

The second Abraham is in Genesis 22, Abraham of the *Aqedah* [the binding of Isaac], who, in total submission to God's command and in full self-denial, goes forth to sacrifice his dearly loved son, Isaac. This Abraham, knowing no autonomous moral truths, sets out to kill an innocent child because God has told him to. This is the Abraham of surrender to God. In this picture of Jewish spirituality, the person of faith appears bowed before God.

Recent Jewish thinkers have framed the question: "Which Abraham should serve as the governing image for Jewish spirituality?" The late Israeli thinker, Yeshayahu Leibowitz, argued that the *Aqedah* represents the victory of a God-centered religion over an anthropocentric religion. The Abraham of Sodom thought of God as serving human social needs and therefore having to endorse a human ethical understanding. True Jewish spirituality, Leibowitz maintained, happens when a person serves God for no human ends whatever. This is what Abraham learned at the *Aqedah* when he had to sacrifice everything for God, including his own moral sense.

Rabbi David Hartman has rejected the *Aqedah* model in favor of a covenantal spirituality in which God honors and nurtures human integrity and autonomous judgments. Covenantal spirituality involves a reciprocal relationship between God and a person, in which both appear as partners. Therefore, Hartman advances the Abraham of Sodom as the model of Jewish spirituality. The *Aqedah* for Hartman should be thought of as an aberration, a quirk, of normative Jewish spiritual understanding.

I am interested in challenging the very terms in which the question is formulated. Based on this challenge, I will be proposing a new understanding of the contemporary significance of the *Aqedah*.

LEIBOWITZ ON THE *AQEDAH*

Leibowitz developed his understanding of the *Aqedah* through the pair of terms *lishmah* and *shelo-lishmah*. Both refer to the motivation of our actions. A motivation *shelo-lishmah* involves acting for human interest, either for the personal interest of the agent or for the good of others. The *lishmah* motivation means acting for the sake of God; i.e., because the act is mandated. Thus, for Leibowitz, *shelo-lishmah* is equivalent to acting for any reason other than the act having been mandated. *Lishmah* means to act from a sense of obligation, and nothing more. For Leibowitz, the obligatory nature of the act comes from its being mandated by halacha [Jewish law]. Although for Leibowitz the undertaking to abide by halacha is freely chosen by a person, the choice is to place oneself under the obligation of halacha for no motive other than keeping halacha itself.

Leibowitz enunciates his position most clearly in an essay entitled, "Abraham and Job."[1] In this essay, Leibowitz argues that the *Aqedah* experience is a corrective to Abraham's earlier understanding, as represented by Abraham's admonition to Abimelech in the episode of Abimelech and Sarah. In admonishing Abimelech for a lack of fear of God, Leibowitz asserts, Abraham reveals his conception of God as one who functions to preserve the moral-social order. "From Abraham's rebuke to Abimelech," writes Leibowitz, "it follows that fear of God has a human-social function."[2] In so understanding, Abraham fails to appreciate the fear of God as an end in itself, directed toward God and the commandments and not toward any human end. Abraham's relationship to God is one of *shelo-lishmah*. In a similar vein, Leibowitz advances his assessment of the Sodom episode, where Abraham argues with God on moral grounds, calling on God to do justice in "judging the world."[3] Here too Abraham relates to God as the insurer of a moral-social order.

The *Aqedah*, for Leibowitz, thus replaces Abraham's previous God-conception with a concept of serving God, *lishmah*, for the sake of doing the command of God alone. In the case of the *Aqedah*, "fear of God is expressed solely in Abraham's ability to nullify all human values."[4] The *Aqedah* experience serves to change Abraham's understanding. He now learns that "his faith is not defined by any human moral definitions." No longer is Abraham to think of humanity as in the center, with God as a "functionary" providing its needs, not even its moral and social stability. Instead, God is in the center. People do God's word because it is God's word. Morality mixes with religion, then, only to the extent that religion becomes idolatrous, placing human beings in the center instead of God. For Leibowitz, then, Abraham is not a paradigm of Jewish spirituality at Sodom; he is an underdeveloped religious personality.

HARTMAN ON THE *AQEDAH*

David Hartman has summarized Leibowitz's attitude to the *Aqedah* as follows:

> The paradigm of the religious life for Leibowitz, the archetype of the love of God, the model of genuine worship of God, is Abraham at the *Aqedah*, at the moment in which Abraham was prepared to sacrifice his son Isaac.[5]

The *Aqedah* is thus a corrective and nullification of Abraham's Sodom mentality. The *Aqedah* teaches all of us to overcome the anthropocentric approach to God.

Hartman's most developed views on the *Aqedah* appear in the essay "Judaism as an Interpretative Tradition," where he speaks of two "organizing images" of God and of "two classical models of religious consciousness" that begin with Abraham.[6] One is expressed in the conversation between Abraham and God concerning the destruction of Sodom. Abraham questions God's apparent willingness to destroy the innocent along with the guilty, "Shall not the Judge of all earth deal justly?" (Gen 18:25). Here Abraham appeals to God not based on a "prior revelation," but with reference to "some generally accepted moral code of discourse" that compelled him to challenge God.[7] This Abraham was impressed with the "inherent normative force and validity" of principles of morality. To Hartman, this Abraham had a "strong sense of moral autonomy." For this paradigm of Abraham:

moral autonomy is not an expression of hubris or of the need to assert human independence, but is compatible with and integral to a religious consciousness that believes that the God you worship would never violate your fundamental moral intuitions of justice and love.[8]

The second paradigm is Abraham at the *Aqedah*. Hartman poses the rhetorical question: "Does the divine command not violate Abraham's moral intuitions, his fatherly sensibilities and feelings, and even God's own promises?"[9] Abraham at the *Aqedah*, for Hartman, represents the paradigm of "total submission and unconditional surrender," including the surrender of his deepest moral sense. [10]

Hartman decisively favors the Sodom paradigm of Abraham, wherein "God's laws must reflect...my understanding of reality and morality. Not sacrificing what I believe to be fair and just is not a violation of my belief in God or in divine authority."[11] Thus, for Hartman, two competing paradigms represent two competing religious phenomenologies. One, the *Aqedah*, presents a phenomenology of religious submission, while the other, Abraham's defending Sodom, contains a phenomenology of human dignity.

Hartman and Leibowitz are deeply divided over the question of whether the Sodom story or the *Aqedah* story should serve as the leading paradigm of Jewish spirituality. Leibowitz defends the *Aqedah* paradigm in the name of the denunciation of all human interest when a person serves God. Hartman defends the Sodom paradigm in the name of our deepest moral sensibilities and in the name of the willingness to a live a religious life of "autonomy."

Despite the enormous division between Hartman and Leibowitz, they share to the end their way of posing the issue and their method of solving the problem. What they share is a conviction that one or the other, Sodom or the *Aqedah*, must be chosen as the leading paradigm for Jewish spirituality. They are each convinced that Jewish spirituality requires one paradigmatic story to guide its adherents. They differ over only what that paradigm should be.

I want to suggest a different approach to the issue of Sodom versus the *Aqedah*. In this approach, neither the *Aqedah* story nor the Sodom episode serves as a paradigm for Jewish spirituality. Instead, we are to see the two episodes as together pointing precisely to the lack of a single "paradigmatic" episode for Jewish spirituality. Seen in this way, the *Aqedah* and how it functioned for Abraham, no longer serves so much as a tale about "morality and religion," but as a metaphor for a more encompassing stance toward faith, within which the question of morality is but a specific instance.

To explain and draw out the implications of my proposal, I will turn to the thought of the Danish philosopher Søren Kierkegaard and to the theology of the Hassidic Rebbe, Rabbi Mordechai Joseph Leiner of Izbica. My contemporary interpretation draws on their common thought, despite the great differences in milieu in which they thought and lived.

KIERKEGAARD AND THE *AQEDAH*

In his work *Fear and Trembling,* Kierkegaard presents Abraham at the *Aqedah* as a knight of faith, when he heeded the word of God and went to sacrifice Isaac.[12] In his journals, Kierkegaard distinguished between the knight of resignation and the knight of faith. The knight of resignation is a lesser figure in Kierkegaard's eyes than the knight of faith. To bring out this distinction, we can present three different "Abrahams," depending on the way Abraham goes about the sacrifice of Isaac.

Abraham One: Abraham One is the person of confidence. This Abraham knows that the sacrifice will not be. He is certain he will return with Isaac. Abraham is confident of this because the sacrifice runs counter to the moral law. God would never command this. In addition, the commandment usurps God's promises for Isaac. Abraham One goes to the *Aqedah* with confidence and hope. He knows that the future will be with Isaac. While travelling to the place that God will show him, he might daydream here and there about what kind of wife he would be pleased for Isaac to marry, what kind of home Isaac would live in, and even what kind of individual Isaac might make of himself. This Abraham never goes beyond the finite. As Sylvia Crocker has put it, "The ordinary man of hope already knows what God expects of man, *any* man: the moral law specifies it."[13]

Abraham Two: Abraham Two is the knight of resignation. He makes the movement that Kierkegaard calls "infinite resignation": he renounces Isaac absolutely and forever, and he does so in submission and self-denial before the word of God. According to Kierkegaard, the knight of resignation fails the test of the *Aqedah* because he shares knowledge of the future with Abraham One. According to Crocker:

> The knight of infinite resignation listens as a person to God as a Person....But his listening is only intermittent. As soon as he apprehends what it is God asks of him, he closes his personality to God...he regards the structure of the future as a settled matter.[14]

The structure of the future is settled for Abraham Two no less than for Abraham One. This Abraham will also daydream on the way to the *Aqedah*. He will be absorbed in what the future will now be like without Isaac. Perhaps he and Sarah will move to a new, smaller tent. He will have to find someone to carry on his mission or instead think of a retirement home on the sea. He rehearses how he will tell Sarah about the demise of their son. Abraham Two passes well beyond the *Aqedah* before it ever takes place. He too does not pass the test.

Abraham Three: This Abraham is the knight of faith. He passes God's test. Kierkegaard depicts the knight of faith as having contradictory beliefs that only faith can comprehend. The knight of faith believes with all his soul that he will be losing Isaac forever, and he also believes with no less fervor that he will get Isaac back. He believes both, says Kierkegaard, "in virtue of the absurd." On the standard interpretation, Abraham's contradictory state is interpreted cognitively: Abraham is in a complex cognitive state that involves believing two contradictory propositions to be true. Following Crocker, I propose that Abraham's state is best understood as a state of openness and readiness regarding the future.[15] The knight of faith is equally prepared for either option. He is prepared not in the sense of merely being able to cope with whatever happens, but in the sense of being open to and embracing whatever God (i.e., the future) will bring. The person of faith is in an enduring state of full receptivity to God's word. The future is in God's hands, not his own. On the journey to the mountain, Abraham is ready for whatever will transpire. This Abraham journeys to the *Aqedah* with an open future.

This does mean that the person of faith has no plans and makes no effort to produce a future course of events. Existentially, to acknowledge that the world is in God's hands does not imply quietism about the future. To engage in the world, to plan and build for the future, belongs to our human condition. Quietism makes us less than human. What makes one a person of faith is the ability to acknowledge failure of plans and dreams, to imagine oneself as otherwise than defined by her or his projects.[16] Neither does acknowledging failure mean taking the failure as a "sign" from God that this is not to be, and thus desisting from one's project. On the contrary: to acknowledge the failure means to accept that failure alone, while being entirely open to the future. Accepting failure, then, is perfectly consistent with taking the broken pieces in hand and starting all over again with the same project.

Abraham at the *Aqedah* is infinitely resigned to the loss of Isaac and is infinitely prepared to live with Isaac. What does that mean? It means that the *Aqedah* is a metaphor for the readiness for any eventuality, including the eventuality that one might come to see one's most cherished convictions stand in need of replacement. It is to see that one day one may want to change one's convictions and be prepared to change them without seeing oneself extinguished thereby. To be ready in this way is to listen at every moment and not to be closed to the word.

The person of faith makes the "leap of faith." Popularly, the leap of faith involves a person's closing his eyes, as it were, and leaping grandly into the stance of faith. The "leap" is thought to be without grounding and without reason. It is a leap beyond evidence and beyond what can be known to be true. Often a leap of faith serves as a metaphor for an irrational decision in favor of religious faith, against all odds.

However, this popular formulation of the "leap of faith" is far from Kierkegaard's explanation.[17] M. Jamie Ferreira, in a closely argued paper, has shown that the leap of faith does not at all involve a willful, blind jump.[18] Rather, the leap of faith is a qualitative change in a person that happens when she or he becomes a person of faith. The change is qualitative in that it does not issue from an accumulation of gradual quantitative increments. It happens when a threshold is met and then everything leaps—all at once—into a different structure and meaning. The leap is comparable to a gestalt switch. When a gestalt change takes place, it is not gradual. The switch is quick and holistic. In just this sense, there is a leap of faith. The person of faith undergoes the leap, as it were, and undergoes it not gradually but immediately.

I would add to Ferreira's insightful analysis the following point from Kierkegaard's *Fear and Trembling*. Kierkegaard compares the knight of faith to a dancer who is able to "leap into a definite posture in such a way that there is not a second when he is grasping after the posture, but by the leap itself he stands fixed in that posture."[19] The knight of faith lands directly into the posture of the dance. He does not fall and then have to adjust to the choreography. The accomplished dancer descends intact into the movement of the dance: just so the knight of faith. The knight of faith lands upright and totally within the situation. The leap of faith, then, is not only a leap to faith, but also a leap by faith, in the sense of being fully prepared for what comes next, whatever it is. No matter what it is, the leaper falls into it ready and in step.

THE REBBE OF IZBICA

A similar approach to faith occurs, I believe, in the singular thought of the Hasidic Master, Rabbi Mordecai Joseph Leiner, the Rebbe of Izbica (1802-1854).[20] His notion of faith comes across through his consistent, idiosyncratic use of the verse, "When it was time to act for God, they violated your Torah" (Ps 119). In rabbinic writings, this verse was used to ground a principle by which the rabbis could promulgate a law that would violate a standing law for a purpose they deemed justified. The classic example of this was the decision to commit the oral law to writing despite a previous prohibition against doing so.[21] This was done so that the oral law would not be "forgotten." Thus, the principle served as a second-order normative principle governing the body politic and social exigencies. In the hands of the Izbicer, it becomes a principle guiding an individual in the privacy of his or her own soul. For it provides the justification for a person to listen to the voice of God at a particular time and place, even when doing so conflicts with the permanent network of obligations a person otherwise bears. Thus Rabbi Leiner transforms this principle far beyond its rabbinic intent as a juridical principle.

The Izbicer's concept of an individual's sinning at God's behest has its roots in the Talmudic notion of a "sinning for Heaven's sake."[22] The cases in the Talmud of "sacral sin" are limited to historical events where national leaders act for the sake of the common good. The Izbicer's category of sinning in response to God's call, however, applies as well to individuals who do not play historical roles and pertains to the relatively limited purview of the life of a private person.

The Izbicer returns again and again to the idea of being prepared to act in accordance with God's special, present will for you, even if this means transgressing the laws of the Torah. Here are a few examples. He writes of the person who looks for God to "illuminate him and reveal to him anew God's will." And this sometimes requires doing an act against halacha, for it is "time to act for God."[23] The Izbicer Rebbe also says there is a difference between a righteous person [a *tzadik*] and a person who is "straight of heart." The former guides his life "according to the principles of the Torah." "Straight of heart" refers to one whose heart is pulled after the will of God: "Even though on the outside it appears at times that he will digress from the path of the Torah, this too is the will of God."[24]

At the same time, the Izbicer cautions that we must use extreme care to determine that what might strike us as God's special will for us really is such and not a demonic desire or egocentric interest. Thus, the Izbicer writes of the need to scrutinize ourselves "seven times seventy" times before acting on what we take to be God's will if it contradicts the laws of the Torah. We must first make every effort to repress the desire to transgress the Torah from what appears to be God's own wish. If all efforts to repress come to naught and "that desire still remains, then [we] will know for sure that [the desire] is from God."

Surely, the issue of knowing that the voice one hears is God and not the devil is deeply troubling, and the Izbicer was well aware of the problem.[25] I do not wish to pursue that side of the topic, however. Rather, I want to ask, what are we to make of this man's obsession with transgressions that God desires?

The key lies in the Izbica Rebbe's commentary on Exod 20:20: "You shall not make with me, for yourselves, gods of silver and gold." The Rabbi comments that this comes to teach us not to serve God out of pure habit, such as what we learned from our teachers and parents.[26] What he means is that in Jewish spirituality, we are not to make our service to God something rigid, like an unmoving statue of silver or gold. Rather, we are to be open at every moment to the possibility that we might have to act differently from, even contrary to, what we have been taught in the past. I would add: and we must be prepared to depart from what we ourselves once thought was sacred truth.

I suggest, therefore, that what draws the Izbicer to his widened notion of sinning for God is not an obsession with sin, nor the expectation that a person will indeed be called by God to commit a sin. Rather, the Izbicer expresses the profound importance of a person's being able to imagine sinning for God, if that's what it should come to. There is all the difference in the world between a person who thinks he knows for sure and in advance what God wants, every minute and every place, and a person who is able to hear God's voice anew, if need be. The former holds a primary commitment to a system in which God disappears into a tiny dot. The latter holds a primary commitment to God and so will do whatever is God's will. The ability of a person to imagine sinning for God's sake is a test of whether the person's primary devotion is to a system or to God.

In pragmatic terms, the ideal Izbicerian believer lives with a primordial ability to revise or abandon his or her most cherished values and conceptions. The Rabbi of Izbica, like Kierkegaard, ascribes a contradictory belief to Abraham: Abraham believed he was going to sacrifice Isaac, yet "believed in the promises as before. They did not weaken for him. And this faith cannot be fathomed by the [ordinary] human mind."[27] Abraham

believes he will lose Isaac, and believes that he will not lose him. I propose
that the existential meaning of this contradiction for the Rebbe, as for
Kierkegaard according to Sylvia Crocker, is that Abraham was open, fully
and willingly, to two different futures. He was not locked into his past
understandings. He was a Kierkegaardian person of faith.

A NEW UNDERSTANDING OF THE *AQEDAH*

Building on Kierkegaard and the Rebbe of Izbica, I propose that the deepest
contemporary meaning of the *Aqedah* revolves around the question of
whether one is able to conceive of oneself as having been mistaken, of
having misunderstood, or of having failed to comprehend all aspects of
the context in which we live and act.

So understood, the issue surrounding the contrast between Abraham
at Sodom and at the *Aqedah* is not over which paradigm is to dominate.
On this approach, neither episode is paradigmatic. The *Aqedah* message
can be understood only in tandem with the Sodom story. At Sodom,
Abraham expresses his deeply entrenched conviction concerning the
impossibility of God's acting against (what Abraham perceives to be) the
present moral imperative. Abraham has an entrenched view about the true
moral principles and about how they apply to his present situation. There
may be some uncertainty here, yet it is only the uncertainty of how to
work out the details of his convictions. God then comes and challenges
Abraham to become the person of faith. With the *Aqedah* command, God
tells Abraham that he must not be so locked into his entrenched view that
he is incapable of conceiving of its being wrong or different from what he
now thinks. The purpose of the *Aqedah*, then, is to *break* paradigmatic
thinking. The greatness of Abraham at the *Aqedah* cannot be understood,
then, apart from Abraham having prayed for Sodom. At the *Aqedah*,
Abraham does not learn a new paradigm. He learns to transcend
paradigmatic thinking altogether.

This does not mean that Abraham can never proceed in accordance
with a present conviction. There is a great difference between a person
with an unshakable certainty, wholly in accordance with his present
understanding, and a person who, while accepting of his present view,
attentively listens for what God might now say. Again, what does it mean,
pragmatically and existentially, to attentively listen for what God might
say? It means that in principle the future is open and that we will be ready
to embrace a new future, if it comes to that. In a deep existential sense, this
is what it means to be ever ready to hear the voice of God.

While the contemporary understanding of the *Aqedah* reaches well beyond the issue of morality and religion, openness to the future applies to the moral realm as well. A person of faith may live by moral intuitions, yet live with the consciousness that these are vulnerable to the possibility of revision or even abandonment, no less than other convictions and intuitions. A contemporary person of faith has read Nietzsche and Foucault and therefore knows that moral intuitions are vulnerable to deconstruction no less than are any of our other favorite opinions. Moral intuitions have a history from which they grow and a context in which they thrive. The person of faith is prepared to discover one day that what she has taken to be ultimate moral convictions may require revision because of the degree to which they reflect only the settled values of the prevailing social order. Consciousness of vulnerability does not afford a reason to doubt or hesitate over one's present moral values. It does afford a reason to be ready for any future.

The contemporary person of faith knows that some philosophers of biology want to explain our moral intuitions in evolutionary terms as reflecting brain wiring that has proven apt for survival.[28] The possibility arises that moral intuitions will be modified when evolutionary conditions become different, as they do in current, human exosomatic evolution. The person of faith also knows that his moral understanding stands before an enigmatic world saturated with peril and surprises. Even if his moral principles remain unchanged, matters might change on the ground in undreamed of ways. When I was studying for my undergraduate degree in philosophy, a professor told me that until World War II he had been an absolute pacifist. He could imagine no situation in which war could possibly be justified. Then came the Nazis, and he enlisted in the United States Army.

One's understanding of the world can be so challenged that one feels called on to do what would never had been thought possible. The person of faith is saturated with this awareness. The person of faith also knows that moral intuitions rarely speak uniformly for persons or groups. One group's moral intuitions tell it that abortion is fine, while another group has deeply felt opposite intuitions. One group strongly favors the death penalty, while another strongly opposes it. Moral pluralism is a fact of life. On the theoretical level as well, moral intuitions may clash deeply. Some philosophers have a utilitarian moral sense, the moral sensibility of others is deontological, while for still others, "care" is the fundamental moral category. Some ethicists are situational in their understanding, others not.

Moral disputes are no reason, of course, for any person or group to fail to advance their moral sentiments as they experience them. Moral disputes are, however, reason for living within an existential stance of faith, as I present it here. The person of faith may have deeply felt moral convictions, yet avoids the risk of identifying his or her deepest selfhood with the situated values she presently holds. Pragmatically speaking, to be open in principle to alternative moral futures is what it means to be ready to hear the voice of God. Pragmatically speaking, to be able to change one's moral stance or judgment, if that is what it should come to, is to heed the voice of God.

We should remember that at the *Aqedah* Abraham commits no deed. He does not slaughter Isaac. Were we to learn from this episode total submission to God in fact, the story would be ill suited to the lesson. For that, Isaac would have to have been sacrificed. On the contemporary, metaphorical reading I am advancing, the existential meaning of Abraham's submission to God lies in his letting go of his favorite past understandings. Abraham receives a command and then the command is changed. He has a sacrifice, then suddenly has no sacrifice. Then just as suddenly he has a sacrifice again, in the form of the ram that he releases from the thicket in which it was entangled.

This, I propose, is the contemporary meaning of the *Aqedah*: to act and go forward with what is ours to do, yet not to be so confident in any paradigm that we become at most the person of confidence (the hero of David Hartman) or of resignation (the hero of Yeshayahu Leibowitz), and no more. This contemporary interpretation of the *Aqedah* applies equally to a person of faith and to a community of faith. What fashions our person of faith is an openness to the possibility of a future, different from the past, affecting his/her most cherished plans and convictions. A person without faith is committed to clinging desperately to his or her values, beliefs, and traditions, come what may. Not constant change, but constant openness to the future is what a person of faith lives by. I submit that no less than a person of faith, there can be a community of faith. A community of faith has its convictions and its policies, it traditions and its plans for the future. It lives by a hallowed ethos. At the same time, the community of faith is not committed to clinging to the components of its ethos, come what may. A covenantal community might act on its deepest convictions, yet be prepared to call them into question if necessary. A covenantal community can practice its tradition within its moral intuitions, yet have the authenticity to face the possibility of a new voice calling to it. Not constant change, but an original stance of openness to change marks the stance of faith.

Contemporary spirituality exists when biblical episodes are possibilities, not paradigms.

NOTES

[1] Yeshayahu Leibowitz, "Abraham and Job" (Hebrew) in *Yahadut, 'am Yehudi, u-medinat Yisrael* (Jerusalem: Schocken, 1979), 391-94.

[2] *Ibid.*, 391.

[3] *Ibid.*, 392.

[4] *Ibid.*

[5] David Hartman, *Conflicting Visions: Spiritual Possibilities of Modern Israel* (New York: Schocken, 1990), 79.

[6] David Hartman, "Judaism as an Interpretative Tradition," in *A Heart of Many Rooms, Celebrating the Many Voices Within Judaism* (Woodstock: Jewish Lights, 1999), 12. The two images are discussed at length as opposing images of the covenantal relationship in David Hartman, *A Living Covenant: The Innovative Spirit in Traditional Judaism* (Woodstock: Jewish Lights, 1997).

[7] *Ibid.*, 12.

[8] *Ibid.*, 13.

[9] *Ibid.*

[10] *Ibid.*, 14.

[11] *Ibid.*, 20.

[12] I have offered an earlier understanding of Kierkegaard on the *Aqedah* in Jerome Gellman, "Kierkegaard's *Fear and Trembling*," *Man and World* 23 (1990): 295-304; and Jerome Gellman, *The Fear, the Trembling, and the Fire: Kierkegaard and Hasidic Masters on the Binding of Isaac* (Lanham: University Press of America, 1994), chapter one.

[13] Sylvia Crocker, "Sacrifice in Kierkegaard's *Fear and Trembling*," *Harvard Theological Review* 68 (1975): 127.

[14] *Ibid.*

[15] *Ibid.*, 127-29.

[16] I use "projects" in a double sense. The first sense is the ordinary sense denoting what we set ourselves to do. The second sense is Sartre's, in which the term denotes a "projection' of self toward the future.

[17] See Søren Kierkegaard, *Concluding Unscientific Postscript to Philosophical Fragments* (ed. E. H. Hong et al.; Princeton: Princeton University Press, 1992), and *Fear and Trembling* (trans. W. Lowrie; Princeton: Princeton University Press, 1968).

[18] M. Jamie Ferreira, 'Faith and the Kierkegaardian Leap," in *The Cambridge Companion to Kierkegaard* (eds. A. Hannay and G. D. Marino; Cambridge: Cambridge University, 1998), 207-34.

[19] Kierkegaard, *Fear and Trembling*, 51.

[20] For the history and thought of this Hasidic figure, see Morris M. Faierstein, *All is in the Hands of Heaven: The Teachings of Rabbi Mordecai Joseph Leiner of Izbica* (Hoboken: Ktav, 1989). I have written on the Rabbi of Izbica in Yehuda Gellman, "Abraham and Ambiguity," in A. Sagi, ed., *Religion and Morality* (Ramat-Gan: Bar-Ilan University Press, 1993), 23-39, and in Gellman, *The Fear, the Trembling, and the Fire*, chapters two and three.

[21] *b. Tem.* 14b.

[22] *b. Naz.* 23b and *Hor.* 72a.

[23] Mordechai Joseph Leiner, *Mei Hashiloach* (Brooklyn, 1973), Part I, Parashat Va'yeshev, 14b. All translations from this work are mine.

[24] *Mei Hashiloach*, Part II, 12b.

[25] Martin Buber, "The Suspension of Ethics," *Four Existentialist Theologians* (ed. W. Herbert; Garden City: Doubleday, 1958), 226-27, raises the question of whether one hears the voice of God or of an imposter, in connection with the *Aqedah*.

[26] *Mei Hashiloach*, Part II, 32.

[27] *Mei Hashiloach*, Part I, 8b.

[28] For a basic reader in evolutionary ethics, see M. H. Nitecki and D. V. Nitecki, eds., *Evolutionary Ethics* (Albany: SUNY Press, 1993).

Micah 6:1-8
Charles D. Isbell

In 1977, as a young professor of Judaic Studies at the University of Massachusetts, I received a call from the Governor of the State of Louisiana. The Governor, also my mother's brother, was calling to request that I deliver a memorial address for his father, my grandfather, on the fifth anniversary of his death. What had started as a plan for our family to meet as a small and private group soon evolved into a public spectacle, to which all of the public officials in Louisiana would be invited. And the venue was changed from the private home of my grandmother to a church with a sanctuary capable of accommodating what would surely be a large crowd. I was being added to the formal program for my grandfather only at the last minute. Not only was I the oldest of his eighteen grandchildren, but I was also the only one involved in anything remotely connected with faith and/or "religion." Ah! There was the rub. My grandfather had been well known as an agnostic, had made no secret of his lack of trust in religious institutions, and had never attended any religious service.

I had lived with my grandfather for two years (from the age of six to eight), during the severe illness of my own father. Because he spoke no English, my grandfather taught me to speak French, his native language, and became the first person to teach me the rudimentary elements of the Hebrew language. He had taught me about life on a small farm in South Louisiana. He had even spoken to me about God and religion. I was too young to know then what an agnostic was, but I could sense that grandfather's feelings about religion were quite different from everyone else I knew. Eight years after I left his home to move back with my parents, he moved to "town," where at sixteen I was assigned to be his driver and translator. This time, I listened even more carefully to his views about life and God and religion and people. Largely because of him, I studied religion in college and graduate school and became a teacher of religion.

But now I was being asked to memorialize him in a quasi-religious setting attended by scores of public officials who needed to be seen at a service for the father of the Governor. I had only two days to prepare; thus, while seated on the plane from Massachusetts to Louisiana, I was still trying to figure out what I could possibly say. Everyone in attendance would be at least outwardly religious, for virtually every official in the state belonged to a church (mostly the Catholic Church). I would have to say more than that I had loved my grandfather and was proud to be his grandson. But I could not honestly speak about "religion," much less about Judaism, for everyone also knew that my grandfather had not been a religious man. And then I thought of something else. My audience of public officials would consist almost entirely of attorneys. That is when I recalled the short biblical book of Micah and thought that I might be able to shape one of his greatest sermons into a format that could perhaps capture the attention of an audience of lawyers and public officials. With only a Hebrew Bible in hand, I scratched out by hand the address given below. A short time ago, the now former Governor asked me if I had a copy of the remarks I had made about his father almost 25 years ago. I found the faded yellow pages of airline stationary on which I had first written my remarks, and, using a word processor that had not yet been invented in 1977, I typed out my address for the first time. Here is what I said.

Note: Almost no one knew my grandfather's real name. Everyone called him "Beau Boy," a Cajun-English mix of the expression, "Pretty Boy." So my title was:

"THE TRUE CHILDREN OF BEAU BOY"

We are the most litigious society in the world. America produces more lawyers per capita than any nation in the history of civilization. I won't tell whether I think that is good or bad. But it seems that our national motto is no longer, "In God we trust," but "I'll see you in court." Now, I realize how perilous it is for me to broach such a subject in the presence of my audience this morning. Most of you senators and representatives are lawyers by profession. You, Mr. Lieutenant Governor Lambert, are a well-known attorney. And you, Governor Edwards, were known as the boy wonder of lawyers long before you entered the field of politics.

So I think that all of you who are lawyers and honorable public servants may be interested in the biblical passage that forms the basis for my address to you this morning. You see, Micah 6:1-8, to which I will refer throughout my address, is the official record of a lawsuit. That's correct. It is a biblical lawsuit that is quite similar in format to a modern civil suit in which all of you have doubtless been involved numerous times.

Biblical scholars have long recognized that ancient Israel was organized as a "covenantal" society, but few persons fully realize just how much ancient Israel borrowed from her pagan neighbors, especially the numerous details of political reality that are necessary for a new political organization. And just to make it interesting, I should remind you that the biblical word usually translated "covenant" could very easily and accurately be translated as "contract."

It was common in ancient Near Eastern societies for small kingdoms to be conquered and administered by large empires headed by an emperor, who often designated himself as the "Great King," among his many other titles. Shortly after his large empire had conquered a smaller state, the "Great King" or his representative would appear to negotiate terms of coexistence between the large conquering power and the small, conquered state. As you might guess, these agreements were nothing like a bilateral contract of the sort that might be hammered out between two relatively equal parties. Rather, these arrangements came to be called "suzerainty" treaties, describing a contractual agreement offered unilaterally by a greater to a lesser party. In other words, the small state was in no position to demand concessions from its conquerors. Whatever the "Great King" wanted, he would have.

The Bible apparently uses several parts of the basic format of these international suzerainty treaties to describe the covenantal relationship between God and Israel. As I noted, the God-Israel relationship was not perceived as a contract between two equal parties. It was clearly a relationship between a greater (God) and a lesser (Israel) party. Nevertheless, the Bible is very clear that all of the contractual terms and obligations incumbent upon Israel had been willingly accepted by Israel. True, the relationship had been offered at the initiative of the greater party, but the acceptance of the relationship by the lesser party made Israel liable for all the terms of the contract between God and the people who would come to be known as Israel.

The author of the passage that we are considering today was a prophet, a religious spokesman who felt it his duty to remind people in Israel about their obligations to God under the terms of the covenant or contract to which they had agreed and by which they were bound. And so, as any good preacher would do, or any good lawyer giving an opening statement, our biblical prophet becomes quite dramatic the moment he senses that he has latched onto an arresting topic. "Israel is guilty of breach of contract!" That should certainly get everyone's attention. And then Micah proceeds to present his "sermon" in the style of a court reporter who is chronicling the details of a lawsuit.

Let us start at the beginning of his sermon and notice that the first speaker quoted by the prophet Micah is what we would call the "bailiff," that official whose responsibility it was to call court into session. And the case announced on the docket is one in which God is suing Israel for breach of contract. The bailiff speaks:

[1] "Please listen to what the LORD is saying. Arise, plead your case with the mountains and let the hills hear your voice.

[2] "Listen, mountains and everlasting foundations of the earth, to the lawsuit of the LORD, because the LORD has a legal case against his people and he is going to debate with Israel."

Here we have the bailiff identifying several of the major players in the drama or lawsuit. The Lord himself is the plaintiff, Israel is the defendant, and the jury called to hear the case includes the mountains, the hills, the eternal foundations of the earth. They are not an ordinary jury, but are called in this case because of their long history of observing the work of God in the world. In fact, their qualification to be jurors is the fact that they have observed the entire drama being played out between the two parties in the case now before the court: God and Israel.

As is still the custom in legal procedures today, it is the plaintiff who presents his case first. And so, with the case called before the court and the jury chosen, we are asked to hear the case against Israel as argued by the Lord, acting as his own attorney. As God begins his case, it appears that he has called Israel herself to the stand as his own first witness for the plaintiff. Listen to these questions to Israel from God, the answers to which he believes will prove his case: [3a] "My people," says God, using the form of direct address, "What have I done to you?" We might even want to translate the question like this: "Have I done anything wrong to you?" Like any good attorney, God is at pains to demonstrate that his side is without blame in the matter before the court. And it is very significant that there is no answer to this first question. In other words, the defense will be forced to stipulate that God has done nothing wrong.

Plaintiff's question number two now follows: [3b] "How have I exhausted your patience? Answer Me." What a question! God asking his human partners if he has made them tired! But yet a second time the witness can produce no evidence, no answer that would damage God's case, and so a second stipulation by the defense must be made.

The divine examiner presses on, now not asking questions, but doing what we might call "leading the witness," being "argumentative": [4] "I brought you up from the Land of Egypt. I redeemed you from the house of slavery. I sent into your presence Moses, Aaron, and Miriam." We must remember that this format was one that was widely followed when a human "Great King" was introducing himself to new subjects. Before making his demands upon them, the conquering king would typically review all of the great benefits that his reign over them had already provided to them. Today, we are quite familiar with this format in the average campaign speech. Using what was clearly a common formula, the prophet Micah has God review for Israel some of the great benefits that had come to them since the inauguration of his rule over them. And what greater social benefit could have been cited? According to the testimony being given in court, God had taken a motley, disorganized, and dispirited band of slaves and provided political and social, as well as spiritual, freedom for them. Once again we must note that the defense objects neither to the question nor to its form as "leading" or "argumentative."

So God presses further: [5] "My people, remember now what Balaq the King of Moab advised and how Balaam the son of Beor answered him. [Remember my guidance] from Shittim to Gilgal. [Remember] in order that you might know the righteous deeds of the LORD." Now God is taking credit for having controlled even the enemies of Israel, of having protected her from harm at a time when she had not been strong enough to stand on her own military might. And God takes credit also for having sustained Israel physically during her formative years, when she had lived in a wilderness and produced no crops to feed and sustain herself. Yet again, the plaintiff demands that the legal correctness of his actions (the word "righteousness" is a technical forensic term) be stipulated. And yet again, Israel is forced into a silent stipulation that what God says is true.

This is the end of the plaintiff's case. As he rests, the defendant begins his presentation. If you are like me, you probably think that God has made quite an airtight case for himself. And are you curious, as I am, about how the defense attorney will attack such a masterful presentation? How can he argue with history, the interpretation of which his own star witness has already stipulated? We may rest assured that, like any good defense lawyer, this one will argue his version of the facts vigorously. Because he had been forced to stipulate to so much of the evidence, the defense attorney makes two bold and surprising maneuvers. First, the defendant decides to represent himself. And second, he makes the argument that, although God had indeed fulfilled his legal contractual obligation, God had unfairly failed to accept the validity of Israel's actions in return. This stance has led God to become unreasonable, making it impossible for Israel to please him. In other words, in the presentation of this attorney, Israel can never hope that God will deem them to be in compliance with his demands. Notice the sarcasm that drips like acid from his words: [6] "With what should I come into the presence of the LORD or bow down to the exalted God? Should I come into his presence with whole-burnt offerings? With one-year old calves? [7a] Does the LORD want 1,000 rams? 10,000 rivers of olive-oil?"

Can't you almost see the veins bulging in the neck of this indignant lawyer as he presses his argument more and more into the arena of the ridiculous? "Why, your Honor," he seems to be saying, "I cannot be expected to pay what God is demanding. 1,000 rams! 10,000 rivers of olive-oil!" Completely overlooking the fact that nothing of the sort is demanded by God, our self-assured defense lawyer pushes ever harder to buttress his contention that God is guilty of an unreasonable demand that surely cannot be supported on the basis of this flimsy contract we call a covenant.

OK. Not a bad job, given what he had to work with. And the sarcasm was great. But wait! Our attorney can do even better: [7b] "Should I give my 'heir' for my transgression?" Truly, this question was intended to sting. When Israel had been trapped in Egyptian slavery, the Lord had specifically called the Israelites his "heir," using this very word. Standing before the court of the entire world, our clever lawyer is flinging God's own word back in his face. It is as if he were to ask, "How can the God who in Egypt rescued the 'heir' of his promises, now realistically expect that my client should sacrifice that 'heir' just to comply with some extremist notion of covenantal faithfulness?" Our impassioned attorney knows well that if the jury will only accept his defense theory, they will be forced to rule that God does in fact demand too much from his contractual partner, Israel.

Now, of course, the case must go to the judge. In our passage, the prophet himself is the one who will speak as the judge, and his verdict will be the heart of the sermon he has intended for Israel to hear all along. Therefore, the way in which he frames the issue is very significant: [8a] "Man has told you what is good." Elsewhere in his book of prophecy, in what we may recognize as additional documents filed with the court, the human defendant, "man," has advanced the argument that God is concerned only with external issues: how Israel bows for prayer, how expensive are the gifts being brought to him, how loudly his people sing in religious worship. In other words, God may be seen as unreasonable because all he cares about are material things, external forms of worship. The defense needs the judge and the jury to believe that God worries about style rather than about substance. Based on these supporting documents, when the defense falls silent, it appears confident that it has painted God into a corner by portraying him as too stern, too strict, unreasonable.

But the prophet Micah, now the judge speaking on God's behalf, rejects the case for the defense on the grounds that it is based upon a false understanding of the contractual demands being made by God upon Israel. Those demands, as Micah the judge will now state them, become a classical expression of true religion. "What does the LORD require from you?" According to Micah, God seeks only three things from Israel, no one of which is at all complicated, or material, or external.

The first contractual obligation is "to practice *mishpat*," a word usually translated, "justice." God was expecting simple societal justice and ethical living, but Micah knew his audience. Turning to facts he had filed with the court elsewhere in his book, he cites damning evidence against the defendant. Storekeepers were using crooked scales to cheat unwary shoppers (6:11). Rampant real estate fraud by wealthy developers had deprived many ordinary folk of their homes (2:2). Judges could easily and cheaply be bribed (3:11a). Even priests and prophets would say just about anything for the proper fee (3:11bc). Lying, deceit, and acts of lawlessness were widespread (6:12). According to Micah, "the good person has perished from the earth, there is no one righteous among men. They all crouch in waiting for blood, every person hunting his friend with a net. They practice evil well with both hands. The best of them is like a briar, the most upright one like a thorn bush" (7:2-4a). These are the acts that constitute the basis of God's lawsuit against Israel, his claim that they had breached their contract with him. And the legal remedy being sought for such behavior was nothing spectacular, just ordinary, everyday justice—*mishpat!* No, God was not suing on the grounds that Israel was displeasing to him on Shabbat. Rather, he was pointing to their conduct during the other six days of the week. The entire argument of the defense had missed the central point of the suit.

Contractual requirement number two, "love *hesed*." This word, *hesed*, is difficult to express in English. It really means, "treatment one has the right to expect under the terms of a contract," and so it is almost a synonym for *mishpat* here. But this second contractual requirement adds a surprising element. Not only does God expect a society of justice and ethical behavior, he argues that his agreement with Israel calls for Israel to love and to enjoy such behavior. According to this requirement, God apparently thinks that justice and ethical living should come from the heart! To sharpen his point, Micah elsewhere describes the Lord himself as a God who "delights in *hesed*" (7:18)! In other words, God had not only kept his contractual obligations with Israel, but doing so had been a source of joy for him. This is why God can make this second demand upon his covenantal partner: "Practice justice. And love doing it." What we do is important, of course, Micah would argue, but why we do it counts as well. The proper combination God expects is ethical behavior flowing from a loving heart.

Micah now identifies requirement number three: "Walk humbly with your God." The Hebrew word "humbly" is also quite difficult to render here into English. Scholars are divided about whether Micah intends to say "humbly," "carefully," or even "modestly." In the Dead Sea Scrolls, this word is used to describe the obligation for a member to accept the rank to which he has been assigned without vaunting himself ahead of a superior officer. This much at least is clear. For Micah, the "walk" of the Israelite individual meant an entire way of life. The contract between God and Israel was not an agreement between equals, but one that had become possible only at the sovereign initiative of God. Because Israel had no legal standing at all to demand a relationship with God, she could only respond (or not) with gratitude to whatever God might choose to offer. Israel needed to remember her true status in the partnership she shared with the sovereign God of the universe. Such awareness should produce a constant spirit of humility and modesty about her role.

This, then, is the decision of Judge Micah in the case of God vs. Israel. The verdict is for the plaintiff.

When Governor Edwards asked me to preach a memorial sermon in honor of his father, my grandfather, I at first thought he had given me an impossible task. Beau Boy Edwards was not a religious man. In fact, he thought religion rather foolish, and the idea of honoring such a person in a church seemed a bit off base to me. What kind of a sermon can one preach about such a man? I hope you are able to agree with me that the sermon Micah preached almost 2700 years ago is more relevant than anything I could write today. Based on Micah's verdict, it seems fair to conclude that Beau Boy Edwards both understood and actually lived the kind of life that, according to the prophet, God expects everyone to live. Ethical and just behavior was truly a way of life for him, and he seemed genuinely comfortable and delighted about living the way he did. No one ever accused him of lying, of cheating, of cutting corners in any deal. No one could count the sick folk for whom he cooked a special meal or the debts he forgave at his tiny country grocery store because he knew the people who owed him were having a tough time of it. These were not things Beau Boy talked about. But since his death five years ago, Beau Boy's children have received numerous letters and calls from people who simply wanted to say thank you for his acts of kindness that no one had ever heard about. Simple, anonymous people who wanted to talk about deeds of kindness that were themselves simple and unheralded.

I believe that the prophet Micah would have loved and respected Beau Boy. I'm quite certain that God did.

Are we not then privileged to have known one man who lived the way that, according to Micah, God expects all of us to live? To be sure, we could make the argument that his external observance left much to be desired. But according to Micah, his life exhibited the core values that underpin the reasons, the purpose for all religious observance. It surely follows, then, that truly to be the children and grandchildren of Beau Boy Edwards means that all of us must find ways to practice justice daily, to discover the delightful in the ethical, and to maintain the true humility that comes from knowing that we are walking—living—with a Partner far greater than are we.

May it be God's will.

SUGGESTIONS FOR FURTHER READING

Brief surveys of the book of Micah are available in three standard Biblical dictionaries:

Hillers, Delbert R. "The Book of Micah." Pages 807-810 in vol. 4 of *The Anchor Bible Dictionary*. Edited by David Noel Freedman. 6 vols. New York: Doubleday, 1992.

Leslie, E. A. "Micah the Prophet." Pages 369-372 in vol. 3 of *The Interpreter's Dictionary of the Bible*. Edited by G. A. Buttrick. 4 vols. Nashville: Abingdon, 1962.

McComiskey, T. E. "The Book of Micah." Pages 343-346 in vol. 3 of *International Standard Bible Encyclopedia*. Edited by Geoffrey W. Bromley. 4 vols. Grand Rapids: Eerdmans, 1979-1988.

Commentaries:

Allen, Leslie C. *The Books of Joel, Obadiah, Jonah, and Micah*. New International Commentary on the Old Testament. Grand Rapids: Eerdmans, 1976. Allen emphasizes the theological content of the book of Micah as he perceives it, but tends to Christianize far more than explain the text at hand. Nonetheless, the volume is strong in its presentation of the historical backdrop of eighth century Judah.

Mays, James L. *Micah: A Commentary*. Vol. 7 of The Old Testament Library. Philadelphia: Westminster Press, 1976. This work is a solid study of the historical and archaeological evidence that bears on the book of Micah. Mays is particularly good at treating the way in which a series of individual prophetic oracles became a coherent book; he also gives adequate attention to the formal characteristics of individual literary units.

Goldman, S. "Micah," in *The Twelve Prophets: Hebrew Text, English Translation, and Commentary*. Book 8 of Soncino Books of the Bible. Edited by A. Cohen. Bournemouth: Soncino, 1948. Goldman provides a nice balance to Allen, treating the book of Micah from a Jewish perspective. His comments are brief; the strength of the work lies in the citation of parallel or related verses from other biblical books, with a fair sprinkling of rabbinic sources included.

Wolff, Hans W. *Micah: A Commentary*. Translated by G. Stansell. Minneapolis: Augsburg, 1990. This volume is excellent from a form critical as well a text critical perspective. Wolff offers numerous insights into the complexities of the Hebrew text of Micah, as well as many observations about the literary structure of individual oracles and their relationship to the whole.

Special Studies:

Anderson, G. W. "A Study of Micah 6:1-8." *Scottish Journal of Theology* 4 (1951): 191-97.

Hyatt, J. P. "On the Meaning and Origin of Micah 6:8." *Anglican Theological Review* 34 (1952): 232-39.

Willis, John T. "The Structure of the Book of Micah." *Svensk Exegetisk Årsbok* 34 (1969): 5-42.

Between Simeon's Pillars:
Religious Prioritization Between Ethics
and Torah in *Avot de-Rabbi Natan*

Steven D. Sacks

The inheritance of rabbinic tradition is a negotiation between spirituality and the dictates of tradition. Tradition formulated an indwelling of the sacred that is perpetually tested and challenged through the alteration of historical and social circumstances of the Jewish people. The impetus of historical discord induced an adaptation and assessment of these sacred realms and concepts, and hastened a process of prioritization and articulation of principal spiritual ideals. The evolution of historical and social conditions, therefore, demanded an appraisal of emergent spiritual articulation and provided a path of negotiation in which these motive ideals have been tested in the manifold of human circumstance.

The present study examines an illustrative case within rabbinic literature in which polarization and negotiation of spiritual ideas are expressed within a context of reflection upon formerly articulated principles. The case presented here exposes the internal tension of the rabbinic revolution in paradigm and practice. Through a close examination of a passage in which charged and condensed language reveals a world of spiritual contention, this paper details the expression of ideals and demarcation of boundaries within a case that is illustrative of the rabbinic expression of movement and negotiation in transformative spirituality. The passage in question stems from the fourth chapter of *Avot de-Rabbi Natan*, a third century extracanonical tractate of the Babylonian Talmud that is a commentary on *Pirke Avot* [Chapters of the Fathers].[1] It personifies an early reflection upon the transformations and contemporary expression of spiritual and ethical ideals in rabbinic Judaism. Consequently, it is within the context of the language and imagery of this passage that the study of spiritual transformation is conducted, to provide for greater reflection on the negotiation of tradition, the reformulation of spiritual conceptions, and ontological opposition to them.

Avot de-Rabbi Natan (hereafter ARN) confronts the spiritual ideals of its time within a unique assessment of developing spiritual values and cultural ideals. The first chapter introduces a theme that haunts ARN's expansion of *Pirke Avot*. In this initial section, the principal theme of the discussion emerges in which supererogatory ethical acts are posited as a paradigm of opposition to Torah study as the principal form of spiritual expression. From the beginning of the work and throughout, ARN poses a striking question that hastens an investigation into the realms of spiritual boundaries and practice: How may practical ethics survive when a dominant religious obligation demands the continual study of Torah?

The following once occurred with R. Josiah and R. Mattiah ben Heresh who had been sitting and engaging [יֹשְׁבִין ועסקין]² in Torah. R. Josiah departed from study in order to perform an act of kindness [דרך ארץ]. R. Mattiah ben Haresh said to him, "Master, why forsake the words of the living God and let yourself get carried away by kindness? Now, although you are my master and I am your student, it is not good to forsake the words of the living God!"³

This initial passage, therefore, presents the tension between the vertical bond of Torah and practical ethics as a product of a rabbinic revolution in cultural and religious ideas. R. Mattiah ben Haresh's challenge to his teacher represents a perspective that develops out of a historical emphasis on Torah, yet is also a sign that, as a paradigm of practice, Torah study threatens to encompass religious activity all together. ARN, therefore, is characterized by a contradiction that simultaneously asserts "men⁴ were created only for the purpose to engage themselves in the study of Torah"⁵ and protests (as with R. Josiah) that, within the contemporary religious ideals, the ethical dimension must find representation in religious practice.

This challenge of practical ethics to the dominance of Torah study exemplifies the negotiation of spiritual ideals and is most prominently articulated in the primary passage of this study, ARN's commentary upon Simeon the Righteous' statement that the world is founded upon Torah, Temple service, and acts of loving kindness [*gemilut hasadim*]. The reiteration of Simeon the Righteous' traditional ideals stimulates ARN to articulate both the contemporary prominence of Torah study and the conflict of religious priorities. The analysis of Simeon's "pillars" is a reflection upon the development and reformulation of his religious ideals with respect to the destruction of the Second Temple. Consequently, due to the transition from Temple to Torah alone, Simeon's proclamation evokes an immediate theological difficulty which must be confronted and resolved: Temple service, a "pillar" of the world, no longer exists as a foundational religious practice. The contemporary religious ideal contrasts with Simeon's practical ideals and thus presents the commentary with a unique opportunity for meditation upon the rabbinic transformation of Temple-centered Judaism as well as consideration of whether or not contemporary religious values are in harmony with traditional practice. The historical practice of Temple service is eclipsed by the religious paradigms that emerge out of the moment of rabbinic reformulation. The rabbi's ritual simulation of the high priest may supplant the sacrificial obligations of the priest: "A sage who sits and interprets [the Torah] before the assembly, Scripture accounts it to him as if he offered blood and fat upon the altar."[6] Nonetheless, although the chapter underscores the primacy of Torah,[7] the negotiation of spiritual boundaries emerges as an explicit principal concern.

The sublimation of Temple service to Torah study, therefore, not only emphasizes the primacy of Torah study in religious practice, but also evokes within Simeon's system the aforementioned questions about Torah and ethics and their spiritual justifications; the sublimation of one pillar to Torah study raises questions about the contemporary role of the third pillar, acts of loving kindness. Due to the necessary substitution of Temple service by Torah study, ARN revisits the conflict between vertical bond and practical ethics mentioned in the first chapter. The ritual simulation of Temple service reinforces a sense of Torah study's dominance over religious practice. Consequently, one could assume that Torah study may equally supplant the third pillar and thus negate the necessity for practical ethics completely. ARN, however, responds in order to negotiate limitations upon the extent of Torah as the principal ideal. The dominance of Torah study as a spiritual occupation, which was reinforced through substitution of Temple service, is qualified in this chapter through an example of conflicted religious obligations, Torah and ethics, thus upholding the conditional supremacy of ethics. The discussion of this central passage turns from the centrality of Torah study to an instance in which Torah study must be suspended in favor of acts of loving kindness or practical ethics; this represents a negotiated limitation to Torah study.[8]

Two students[9] of sages sitting and occupying themselves in Torah [יושבין ועסקין], and a bride passes before them, or a funeral bier of the dead—if there are enough present [כדי צרכן] to fulfill the obligation, they should not depart from their studies [אל בטלו משנתן]. If not, let them stand, cheer and rejoice in the bride and attend to the deceased.[10]

As in the first example, this passage reiterates a challenge to the paradigmatic dominance of Torah study. Simultaneous religious obligation clarifies in more concrete terms the extent of conflict and the place of ethics. Through the ritual supersession of Torah in this singular example, the passage asserts that attendance to the bride and the deceased are exceptions in which ethics may limit the dominance of study. The challenge of choosing among simultaneous obligations requires the students to choose between an assumed obligation to Torah study and these ethical acts. In language and expression, these acts are immediate and explicit exceptions in which Torah study does not subsume all religious practice. In the conflict of obligations, attendance to the bride and deceased presents an instance of ethics' primacy over Torah study. Therefore, the exception not only creates space for practical ethics over an assumed dominance of Torah, but also reaffirms the historical presence of *gemilut hasadim* and begins a clarification of spiritual expression and obligations within the shift of paradigms.

The language and expression of the passage, however, belie a simple reaffirmation of practical ethics. Rather, the case of supersession of Torah in the passage is characterized by expressions that reveal a more dynamic tension within Simeon's model between the principal paradigms of ethics and Torah study and negotiate new boundaries of sanctification. Consequently, the course of discussion below first elucidates the factors of legal conditioning that define the paradigm with respect to this exception and then pursues the spiritual motivation that underscores the rationale within this example. In the pragmatic and legal sense, the primacy of attendance to bride and deceased in this case is based upon a degree of merit relative to Torah study and conditioned on the narrow scope of the ethical action. The passage asserts a place for ethical action against the monolithic obligation to Torah study, but the language and expression delineate the case as a narrow and well-negotiated exception to the rule. To begin with, an implicit assumption of the passage is that this case is unique among ethical acts. Although practical ethics supersede a simultaneous obligation to Torah study here, all other acts of *gemilut hasadim* and expressions of practical ethics surely do not supersede the obligation to Torah study.[11] Beyond the narrative structure and linguistic hints of the chapter, a superficial assessment of these cases reveals a cautious limitation to the suspension of study. This case, therefore, demands further arbitration as an initiation into the complexity of the exception.

The primary source of tension and description in ARN's negotiation of ethics and study remains buried in the language and reference of the passage. In the narrative representation of the passage, attendance of bride and deceased are acknowledged as exceptional cases of practical ethics that are alone able to suspend Torah study.[12] Nonetheless, the language and reference of the passage indicate both a greater reservation on the subordination of Torah study for even these exceptional ethical activities and a deeper significance to the decisions which deem particular acts as practically more relevant. This passage mysteriously conditions a demand that one "must depart from study" at the appearance of a procession of a bride or the deceased upon a stipulation that is reflected in the phrase "such that there are enough." If "enough" people attend to the bride or deceased, then the supersession of study as a conflicting religious obligation is invalid. According to this assessment, the sublimation of study by ethical practice is conditioned upon the fulfillment of communal, and not necessary individual, obligations. As an undefined phrase, this addition substantially weakens the power of ethics to remove an obligation of Torah study.

Nonetheless, although ARN thus introduces doubt into the practical application of attendance to bride and deceased in opposition to Torah study, later tradition sheds light upon the tension of practical dynamics outlined in ARN. Accordingly, the Babylonian Talmud stems the possible eradication of ethical participation and indicates a framework for the boundaries of action and spiritual obligation within this case:

Our rabbis taught: The study of Torah may be suspended [מבטלין] for escorting a dead body to the burying place and a bride to the canopy....When does this rule apply? When there are not sufficient numbers; but if sufficient numbers are available, [the study of Torah] is not suspended. What numbers are sufficient? R. Samuel b. Inia said in the name of Rab: Twelve thousand men and six thousand trumpeters or according to another version twelve thousand men of whom six thousand have trumpets. Ulla said: enough to make a procession extending from the burying ground to the town gate.[13]

In consideration of this linguistic challenge, the vast number of participants who must fulfill the practical implications of this Talmudic interpretation of the phrase removes the conditionality of ARN's ethical prescription; the thousands and thousands of participants necessary to fulfill the obligation of the Talmud weakens the negative implications of the phrase "such that there are enough." The phrase indicates a necessity for ethical action rather than further caution against foolish departure from a primary obligation towards Torah study; the Talmud's assessment transforms the cautionary connotation of the phrase. Consequently, the paradoxical shift in interpretation of this phrase magnifies the tension and negotiation between Torah study and ethical action within this passage as well as the caution of rabbinic opinion and efforts to preserve the vitality of these exceptions.

Similarly, the Talmud's legal decision in this specific case further elucidates the tension between Torah's dominance and the separation of religious space for ethical conduct. As a definitive resolution of the issue, the Talmud concludes, "One interrupts the study of Torah [מבטלין] for the sake of a funeral procession and the leading of the bride."[14] The legal authority of the Talmud removes doubt from the negotiation of religious sensibility. The structure of religious practice dictates that these acts of ethical conduct supersede the conflicting and continual obligation for Torah study. Nonetheless, by virtue of the legal authority of this decree, the Talmud institutionalizes these ethical acts, thus distancing ethical practice from the supererogatory ethical expression implicit in the original statement by Simeon the Righteous. The legal decree, therefore, cuts both in favor and against the supersession of ethical action over study. Although these ethical activities supersede Torah practice, the ethical exceptions require the force of legal prescription in order to succeed. As a further attempt to resolve the tension raised in the ARN passage, these efforts of the Talmud testify to the nature of the tension inherent in the negotiation of a place for practical ethics which sets the foundation for a discussion of the spiritual negotiation occurring within the articulation of practical principles.

The vital linguistic sensibility of the ARN passage, therefore, not only provides fodder for the practical negotiation of religious duty, but, more importantly, also indicates the foundations and rationale for spiritual negotiation between the principles of ethics and study through a polarity of language which signifies engagement [עסק] in spiritual activity as opposed to departure [בטל] into secularity. The terms עסק and בטל are focal indicators in the expression of the passage that ground the nature of the conflict between study and ethics as well as express the spiritual rationale of its practical resolution. In the narrative course of the passage, the terms stand in immediate opposition to one another. The first word within our central passage, עסק, refers to a sanctioned occupation with the sanctified activity of Torah as well as occupation with the bride and deceased for an intentional purpose.[15] The passage reinforces the centrality of the term in a subsequent elaboration of the issue by R. Judah bar Ill'ai: "Another time

[R. Judah bar Ill'ai] sat and taught his students and a bride passed before him. He asked his students, 'What was that?' They answered him, 'A bride that has passed.' He said to them, 'My sons, stand and occupy yourselves [עמדו והתעסקון] in the bride."[16] The passage reflects moral intent through the repetition of language: the transition of religious occupation is equal in the transfer of spiritual merit, and thus the departure from study is justifiable. The students who have "occupied" themselves in the study of Torah are encouraged through this similar expression to transfer their "engagement" from study to an act of *gemilut hasadim*. The parallelism of language evokes a notion of religious justification by means of similar terminology, since religious occupation with the bride is indicated to be as worthy as Torah study.[17] Therefore, those who engage in Torah may garner spiritual benefits from a transfer of religious occupation to ethical conduct. The spiritual value of each "occupation" ultimately dictates the framework and negotiation of spiritual prioritization. Torah study, as the primary occupation of religious worth, is temporarily suspended in order to participate in an activity of equal worth.

The balance of spiritual benefits in this case, however, is not merely founded upon an ideal of religious merit, but is also derived from an implicit conception of spiritual necessity. Consequently, ARN's use of the term בטל signifies both an inverse relation to religious occupation such as Torah study and an indication of a defined field of spiritual practice, in which a negative spiritual force supplies the rationale behind the negotiation between Torah study and these acts of practical ethics. Through the use of בטל, the passage evokes a conception of "departure" as opposed to "occupation." As much as the answer—namely, that when in conflict, one may transfer one's occupation from study to attendance of bride and deceased—is elucidated by the repetition of עסק, so the question of relative spiritual worth is raised by the use of the term בטל. In our central passage, and within rabbinic literature as a whole, בטל signals an interruption of occupation with sanctified activity and the possibility of severance from the source of spiritual occupation that is an inherent tension in any ethical act:

> Once as R. Simeon ben Yohai went about visiting the sick, he found a certain man, afflicted and laid up with bowel sickness, uttering blasphemies against the Holy One blessed be He. R. Simeon said, "Wretch—you should be asking for mercy for yourself and you are swearing!" The man said, "May the Holy One blessed be He remove my illness from me and place it upon you." R.

Simeon replied, "It is beautiful that the Holy One blessed be He
has done this with me for I neglected the words of Torah and
engaged in idle matters" [מתעסקין בדברים בטלים].[18]
The opposition of בטל to עסק in this passage, as well as in ARN as a
whole, represents the encoded terminology of the passage and elucidates
the spiritual foundations behind the later legal clarifications of opposition
between the pillars of Torah study and ethical conduct. The vitality of the
continual obligation to Torah study is based upon its function as a religious
occupation, as indicated by עסק and in opposition to activities indicated
by בטל. The innate opposition of the terms appears elsewhere in rabbinic
literature with similar results, thus indicating an opposition between fruitless
secular concerns and sanctified occupation.[19] The opposition between the
activity of engagement [עסק] and common activity [בטל], therefore,
implies a deeper kinship in ARN between these particular acts of ethical
activity and the spiritual utility of the study of Torah. עסק indicates a
justifiable direction of religious occupation, whereas בטל emphasizes a
questioning and cautious attitude towards ritual supersession and
substitution which border on secular occupation

The tension between these two focal terms in the passage underlines
the challenge of ethical conduct to the dominance of Torah in spiritual
terms that dictate the framework of spiritual boundaries within the
evolution of past spiritual ideals. Throughout ARN's discussion of
conflicted obligations, two foundational questions remain: On what basis
does ARN distinguish these particular ethical acts from others?
Furthermore, on what basis does ARN negotiate the spiritual value of Torah
study as opposed to these ethical acts? In both regards, although the literature
is elusive, the oppositional connotation of these terms in ARN as well as
rabbinic literature as a whole is instructive. The notion of continual
"occupation" in religious activity, as indicated by the conflict of this passage,
is a peculiar assumption, yet one consistently indicated by the use of the
term עסק. ARN's insistence upon consistent occupation in sanctified
activity is prevalent throughout the work and is frequently characterized
by the term עסק:

> "If one sits and does not occupy himself with words of Torah he
> will surely settle into foolishness:
>
> [אם ישבין ולא עסקין בדברי תורה מושבתם לצים]."[20]

The notion of consistent occupation in religious activity is derived from
the opposition of בטל, a term which signifies the secular, unstructured,
and unsanctified realm of בטלה, in which spirituality is plagued by the

secular forces of contest:[21]"Why do scholars die young? It is not because they are adulterous and not because they rob, but because they break off from studying Torah and engage in idle conversations, and then do not begin where they left off."[22] עסק and בטל, therefore, indicate a conflict between consistent religious occupation and its spiritual protection and actions defined by their secularity as embodying the danger of exposure to negative forces.

The continual obligation towards Torah, which is the foundation for this relevant passage from ARN, therefore reveals the terminological as well as spiritual considerations in the negotiation between Torah study and practical ethics. Through the language of עסק and בטל, ARN evokes a consistent trope of religious opposition in which sacred activity is opposed to secular activity; this is similarly stated in the Babylonian Talmud, "If [one] ate in a company celebrating a religious act...he does not become a rebellious son thereby...since they were engaged [עסק] in a religious act, he would not be led astray."[23] According to the explicit assumption of ARN, Torah study is a paradigm of religious activity that stands in opposition to the dangers of the secular realm: "[You should] toil in the words of Torah and not occupy yourself in idle matters."[24] The dangers of departure are, in the explicit words of ARN, inherent in the destructive and evil nature of humankind: "The evil inclination is like iron which one holds in a flame: just as long as [iron] is in the flame one can make of it any implement he chooses, so it is also with the evil impulse; and the only remedy is in the words of Torah."[25]

The act of Torah study as a protective occupation is similarly indicated in the words and phrasing of the passage from ARN, there defined as a sacred occupation. Torah study is considered as a complete and vital standard of religious occupation; it defines the boundaries of spiritual expression, since it alone is known to eradicate the dangers of the secular realm and preserve the sanctity of the scholar. ARN does not consider the dominance of Torah study over all other "occupations" merely on the basis of its foundational theological strength and character, but also as a spiritual principle that defends against the rabbinic fears of secular occupations. Consequently, ARN uses a linguistic indicator of a spiritual principle through the term עסק, to interrogate ethical activity in the reformulation of religious paradigms, as well as evaluating the status of these activities as a sanctified occupation. ARN, by using these terms, asks whether these acts of ethical conduct safeguard against the evil inclination, like Torah through עסק, or whether there is a danger that this departure [בטל] is not an act that may fulfill this necessary requirement. Through the repetition of the עסק root in reference to attendance to bride and deceased, ARN answers the foundational questions by indicating that these ethical acts are indeed also capable of protecting the participant in this regard. In response to the justification of occupation and transference that occurs in this passage, the Babylonian Talmud articulates the fundamental conceptions of the passage's terse and meaningful language:

> What is the meaning of the verse "Blessed are you who sow beside all waters, that send forth the feet of the ox and the ass?" (Isaiah 32:20) [It means this:] Blessed is Israel when they occupy themselves with Torah
>
> [בזמן שעסקין בתורה בגמלות חסדים יצרם מוסר בידם]
>
> and *gemilut hasadim*, for their inclination is mastered by them, and not they by their inclination.[26]

The negotiation of spiritual concerns is therefore isolated in the passage within the field of rabbinic language, yet indicative of a range of spiritual movement and consideration. The negotiation of past spiritual practice, which is inherent to the discussion of the fourth chapter of ARN, occurs within the arbitration of a singular circumstance of practical ethics. The singular form of expression, which occurs within this passage, reflects a range of spiritual and practical conceptions in which present notions evolve in conversation with prior ideals.

CONCLUSION

In the negotiation between ethics and study that personifies the character of *Avot de-Rabbi Natan*, a struggle of prioritization and internal indications of moral efforts yield a rabbinic reflection upon the status and spiritual justification for religious occupation. In this case, the reformulation of historical spiritual practice in rabbinic literature exposes the extension of the spiritual realm in opposition to a secular realm in which spirituality is undermined by the inclination to do evil. The development and expression of spiritual prioritization have been discussed here in terms of the practical and spiritual resonance of rabbinic negotiations. The expression of legal and spiritual representation has been found to be dormant within the inflection of rabbinic language. The confrontation and transformation of the spiritual present emerges out of the language and ideals of the rabbinic heritage.

ACKNOWLEDGMENTS

I would like to express my gratitude to Professor Michael Fishbane for his insightful guidance in my studies and instruction these past years. His work and advice have been invaluable to me. Similarly, without the patience and advice of Maria Rethelyi and my family, this product of my efforts would have been impossible.

NOTES

[1] *Avot de-Rabbi Natan* exists in two versions, A and B, which were presented in an excellent edition by Solomon Schechter *Avoth de-Rabbi Natan* (New York: Jewish Theological Seminary, 1997). A good English translation of version A is available in Judah Goldin, *The Fathers According to Rabbi Nathan* Yale (New Haven, 1983) and a translation of version B into English is in A. J. Saldarini, *The Fathers According to Rabbi Nathan Version B: A Translation and Commentary* (Brill; Leiden, 1975). For a basic introduction to the history of the material and reference to secondary literature, see H.L. Strack and Günter Stemberger, *Introduction to the Talmud and Midrash* (trans. M. Bockmuehl; Fortress: Minneapolis 1992), 225-27.

[2] The use of the terminology עסק and בטל is particularly important in the consideration of this question throughout ARN. These terms will be noted throughout and clarified later in the paper.

[3] ARN (A) 1.

[4] Men, indeed, are solely intended throughout the discussion of these issues. Women and others who are not in rabbinic circles are not considered subject to these religious concerns or to their consequences. The discussion of Torah obligations for the common person is most thorough and interesting; see *b. Men.* 99b.

[5] ARN (A) 14.

[6] ARN (A) 4.

[7] More famously, the later portion of the chapter asserts that the third pillar, acts of loving kindness, is an adequate replacement for the atonement offerings of the Temple service. Nonetheless, this is the first response, consistent with the themes and language of ARN; it sets up a particular tension between Torah study and *gemilut hasadim*.

[8] The danger of Torah study's possible dominance over all other expressions of religious practice is most explicitly raised in *b. Avot Zar.* 17b: "R. Huna said, He who only occupies himself with the study of Torah is as if he had no God, for it is said 'Now for long season Israel was without the true God [2 Chr 15:3].' What is meant by 'without the true God'? It means that he who only occupies himself with the study of Torah is as if he had no God."

[9] The mention of two who study together is neither coincidental nor irrelevant for this case. The act of studying alone as less than desirable is reflected in statements of ARN (A) 8 and supported by *b. Ber.* 63a. The benefit of a study partner is

crucial to the success and worth of religious occupation, since the partner "returns" his companion to a correct view.

[10] ARN (A) 4.

[11] The alternative application of the term *gemilut hasadim* described in more detail later in the chapter of ARN is inclusive of the duties of adorning the bride and pleasing her, accompanying the dead, giving a *perutah* [money] to the poor and praying three times a day (ARN [A] 4). Therefore, attending the bride or deceased is classified within the category of *gemilut hasadim* and also unique in its capacity as *gemilut hasadim* that suspends Torah study.

[12] There are other instances introduced in rabbinic literature, not exclusive to this case, where the obligation to study is suspended due to "religious errand" (*b. Sukkah* 25-6a) or occupations of the mind. Nonetheless, the substitute act of religious practice is often, as in described below in ARN, considered as equivalent in some measure to the act of study (*b. Yebam.* 109a).

[13] *b. Meg.* 29a

[14] *b. Ketub.* 17a; *b. Meg.* 29a; *b. Ber.* 18a.

[15] There are terminological distinctions for the act of studying Torah that are relevant, but beyond the scope of this exercise. Nonetheless, it is worthwhile to note that the B version of our text in ARN (B) 8 uses the term שנה instead of עסק. In the context of the definition of this term in ARN (B) 13 such a term refers particularly to the study of the oral law. This distinction in terminology does not disturb our analysis; although the expression of the B version is distinct, the conceptual assumption is quite similar.

[16] ARN (A) 4.

[17] The notion of assessment of an action's merit by the standard of Torah study is prevalent in rabbinic literature. See, for example, the saying, "whoever is observing is regarded as if he was studying, but whoever is not observing is not regarded as if he were studying," from *b. Sukkah* 25a.

[18] ARN (A) 41.

[19] For example, in *b. Ber.* 20b, the Talmud's assessment of the legal prohibition against participating in Torah study by the *ba'al keri* due to his impurity reflects an oppositional use of these terms: he should recite silently, "so that he should not be doing nothing while everyone else is engaged in the Shema."

[20] ARN Hosfa Bet to (A) 7.

[21] In regards to בטל, see also *b. Shabbat* 30a.

[22] ARN (A) 26.

[23] *b. Sanh.* 70b.

[24] ARN (A) 41.

[25] ARN (A) 16.

[26] *b. Avod. Zar.* 5b.

Spirituality, *Kavannah*, and Ethics: Ancient Wisdom for a Modern World

Zion Zohar

INTRODUCTION

Several times over the course of Jewish history the subject of spirituality has emerged as a weighty issue within Jewish theology and philosophy. Unprecedented numbers of books and articles in the last several decades have been written on aspects of spirituality,[1] and clearly interest in this issue (as attested by the choice of "Spiritual Dimensions of Judaism" as the topic of a Klutznick-Harris Symposium) is ongoing. Yet one must properly ask: What is spirituality? What is the object of the spiritual search in these millennial times?

Arthur Green defines spirituality as "a striving for the presence of God and the fashioning of a life of holiness appropriate to such striving."[2] Precisely how one strives for the presence of God and exactly how one fashions a life of holiness have engendered many answers throughout Jewish history. Yet, as Green attests in a different article, "what all these have in common is a commitment to the life of holiness, a faith in the power of Israel's ancient code to embody that holiness, and a knowledge that such a life fulfills God's intent in creation and in the election, however understood, of His 'kingdom of priests,' the people Israel."[3] That commonality lasted until modern times, when we find "Jews in search of the spiritual life who can no longer accept its premises as classically outlined by Judaism."[4] Indeed, despite unprecedented levels of prosperity, life expectancy, food supply, and material wealth achieved by the citizens of modern industrialized nations, a spiritual malaise seems to suffuse Jewish life for many.

In *Spiritual Judaism*, David Ariel assesses the spiritual status of North American Jewry when he writes:

> Many of us do not find our faith to be a significant factor in our lives or a compelling guide to life today. We search, often in vain, for a spiritual home in Judaism. Our spiritual aspirations are often quite high, but Judaism does not seem to be sufficiently spiritual. Many of us have turned outside Judaism—to New Age religions,

Buddhism, and elsewhere—in our search. We value our own inner experience and look for a spirituality that can be expressed in how we live our lives.[5]

Nor is this search for spiritual meaning limited to Jews on the more liberal end of the denominational spectrum. Aryeh Kaplan, a prolific author of books on Jewish spiritual practices and a prominent Orthodox rabbi, noted:

If finding spiritual meaning is difficult for the uncommitted Jew, it is sometimes difficult for the Orthodox Jew as well. I have been approached by yeshiva students who are committed to observing the rituals of Judaism but fail to see how these practices can elevate them spiritually. Even more troubling is the number of Orthodox Jews who are involved in disciplines such as Transcendental Meditation. Most of them express uneasiness about these practices but feel that the benefits outweigh the dangers. When asked why they do not seek this type of experience within Judaism, they give the same answer as uncommitted Jews: they are not aware that such an experience can be found within Judaism.[6]

CHALLENGES TO JUDAISM TODAY

A dual phenomenon is taking place with challenges to Jewish life from within and from without. As Ariel points out, Jews today are exposed to other religious traditions and cultures and have the freedom to both learn from and practice them at will. Moreover, the vast majority of Jews do not live in ghettos anymore, self-imposed or otherwise, and as a result are increasingly knowledgeable about (and potentially attracted to) the spiritual offerings of other faiths.[7]

At the same time that Judaism is being confronted by outside forces, it is also experiencing challenges from within. A. James Rudin characterizes the situation as follows:

American Jewish life today is somewhat similar to the arrows going in two directions that are found in chemical equations. One arrow leads out of the American Jewish community.... Indifference and those intermarriages where the children are not raised as Jews act as a hemorrhage on the Jewish demography.... While one arrow leads to an "Exit" sign for some American Jews, the other arrow leads to religious renewal or first time commitment to Judaism.... The Orthodox Jewish community is not only retaining its own young people but is attracting many Jews who have had little or no contact with traditional Judaism. These newcomers to the faith are called in Hebrew, *baalay teshuvah* [or masters of repentance or return]. Nicknamed "BTs," these born again Jews are increasing in number....But a renewal of Jewish spiritual life is also taking place within the Progressive or non-Orthodox branches of Judaism.[8]

Finally, Judaism in contemporary America is experiencing internal struggles, as denominational politics and sharp rhetoric increase concerning which movement provides the best path for a Jewish future.[9] Within those denominations, Jews who have elected to remain active in the Jewish community, through synagogue membership for example, are seeking answers and searching for a spiritual home inside Judaism. At the same time, Judaism faces challenges from the outside, since the modern Jew is exposed to, and often actively seeks information about, the beliefs and practices of other religions and spiritual traditions.

PARALLELS TO THE GOLDEN AGE OF SPAIN
Intriguingly, our current situation in North America, with its attendant spiritual searching, contains remarkable parallels to another era in Jewish history, known as the Golden Age of Spain. From roughly the tenth through the thirteenth century, a golden age flourished in various provinces of Spain when for the most part Islamic forces ruled it.[10] The tenth century Jewish statesman Hasdai ibn Shaprut described the material wealth of medieval Andalusia in details that parallel the prosperity Jews in contemporary America enjoy:

> The land is rich, abounding in rivers, springs, and aqueducts; a land of corn, oil and wine, of fruits and all manner of delicacies; it has pleasure-gardens and orchards, fruitful trees of every kind, including the leaves of the trees upon which the silkworm feeds....There are also found among us mountains...with veins of sulphur, porphyry, marble and crystal. Merchants congregate in it and traffickers from the ends of the earth...bring spices, precious stones, splendid wares for kings and princes and all the desirable things of Egypt.[11]

Beyond material advancement, Jews in Muslim Spain also achieved a cultural flowering due to a profound synthesis between Jewish culture and foreign elements that was virtually unrivaled until modern times. Similar to the condition of Jews in modern Western Europe and America, Spanish Jewry was culturally integrated into the society in which they lived, speaking the same language and generally sharing the same cultural values as the surrounding majority. Joseph L. Blau details the atmosphere under which Jewish philosophy realized new heights:

> The Umayyad family of Caliphs who ruled Muslim Spain were men of liberal spirit. They recognized and rewarded intellectual and cultural activity regardless of whether it came from Muslim or non-Muslim sources. In this atmosphere, Jewish intellectual life opened a glorious period of flourishing creativity....Jews carried on work in the medical sciences and astronomy, wrote poetry, began studies in the grammar of the Hebrew language which had far-reaching effects on Bible study, and even started a Talmudic academy in the city of Cordova. Some Jewish leaders rose to positions of prominence and influence in court circles and used their wealth to support learning among their co-religionists.[12]

The medieval synthesis of Jews and Arabs in Spain, particularly in the province of Andalusia, is remarkably similar to the pattern of modern Western Europe and America and very different from the situation of Jews under Christian rule.[13] Historian of Islam Bernard Lewis notes, "As Professor Goitein has pointed out, this symbiosis produced something that was not merely Jewish culture in Arabic. It was a Judeo-Arabic, or one might even say a Judaeo-Islamic, culture."[14] In addition, a fluidity of social intercourse existed among Muslims, Christians, and Jews "who, while professing different religions, formed a single society, in which personal friendships, business partnerships, intellectual discipleships, and other forms of shared activity were normal, and indeed, common."[15]

Yet for all its glory, Judaism and its adherents were tested in the early years of Islamic rule by numerous challenges from within and without that led to the development of new philosophical, ethical, and spiritual works. In *Jewish People, Jewish Thought*, historian Robert M. Seltzer aptly describes the forces operative upon medieval Jewry:

> Medieval Jewish philosophical literature first emerged when Judaism sought other intellectual tools besides a direct appeal to received tradition and talmudic hermeneutics to justify and strengthen loyalty to the Jewish religion among questioning members of the expanded Jewish middle class in the Islamic world—a middle class that was actively participating in general trade and commerce, and that because it spoke Arabic, was absorbing the cultural riches, especially from ancient Greece, increasingly available in Arabic. A significant body of Jews was now becoming knowledgeable in sophisticated scientific and

philosophical concepts and very much aware of the intellectual ferment going on outside Judaism.[16]

In this atmosphere, rabbinical Judaism faced challenges from several groups:

First, some of the Karaites had taken an interest in philosophical concepts and had gone beyond attacking talmudic law to criticize the anthropomorphic view of God in talmudic and midrashic literature. Not only did the Rabbinites have to defend the legitimacy of the rabbinic tradition against Karaism, but they had to show that these anthropomorphic expressions did not detract from the rationality of their concept of God. Second, Muslims asserted that Muhammad's revelation in the Koran superseded Judaism. The question of which was the true revelation involved the reliability of all historical traditions....Third, Zoroastrianism and Manichaeans attacked the monotheistic faith that Judaism, Christianity, and Islam shared....Fourth, there was the challenge to religion of the Greek scientific and philosophical world view, which explained the origin and structure of the universe without recourse to the supernatural, personal, creative God who guided history and revealed his word to the prophets.[17]

Thus, just as medieval Jewry in Andalusia reached a high point of cultural achievement and assimilation, it faced numerous dangers, largely stemming from this very same cultural achievement. Since ideas flowed freely among the different faith communities of the Iberian Peninsula, Jews had to learn to engage in religious polemics, which had achieved a new level of sophistication.[18] Moreover, as Abraham S. Halkin attests, "The encounter with Greek thought was a profoundly disturbing event in the life of the Jews under Islam. The modern world offers a parallel. Then, as now, the exposure to new winds of doctrine produced confusion and perplexity at the same time that it stimulated a rethinking of old problems."[19] Assimilation sometimes took the form of social breakdown or intellectual floundering, and voluntary conversions from Judaism were hardly unheard of.[20]

Exposed to so many conflicting forces, Spanish Jews, who were citizens of the two worlds of Jewish tradition on the one hand and Islamic culture on the other, were shaken by doubts, uncertainties, and conflicts. Dissensions within the Jewish body, combined with challenges from without, inspired much soul-searching and introspective thought that led to a prodigious quantity of writings, much of which was motivated by a desire to answer questions posed by internal and external critics.

In sum, we have discerned that many of the same challenges—both the difficulties and the opportunities—Jews face today in the modern era are quite similar to those faced by their predecessors during the period known as the Golden Age of Spain. Then as now, Jews were divided by internal dissent from sectarians who posed troublesome questions. Then as now, Jews delighted in their close social and intellectual contact with people of different faiths, yet as a result they were confronted, actively or passively, with the need to answer the contentions of the Other. Finally, then as now, those who wished to remain among "the community of Jewish believers" were forced to address their own doubts and spiritual uncertainties.

THE GUIDE TO SPIRITUALITY OF RABBI BAHYA IBN PAKUDA
One of the masterpieces of spiritual literature produced during the period known as the Golden Age of Spain, the *Book of Guidance to the Duties of the Heart* [*Kitab al-Hidaya ila Fara'id al-Qulub*] of Rabbi Bahya Ibn Pakuda, may serve as a beacon of light for our own times as it did for Bahya's generation nearly one thousand years ago. Because the circumstances of our time and his are so similar, Bahya's literary classic, which attempted to "spiritualize" Judaism, might still be relevant as a model for those seeking spirituality within Judaism today.

Bahya ben Joseph ibn Pakuda (late eleventh century) appeared within the ferment of the Golden Age, functioning as a well-known rabbi and *dayyan* [religious judge]. Little was recorded about the details of his life except that he lived in Muslim Spain, possibly in Saragossa.[21] What we do know, however, is that he produced one of the seminal works of spiritual-ethical literature in Jewish history; *Duties of the Heart* (as it was known by its shortened title) was designed as a manual seeking to intensify the inner devotional life of the Jew. Written in Arabic around 1080, it was translated into Hebrew in 1161. Very few books in the Jewish world within the genre of spiritual literature were as popular as Bahya's *Duties of the Heart* throughout medieval and early modern times. In fact, this book is still studied by students in ultra-Orthodox yeshivot.

BAHYA'S PROFICIENCY WITH THE RELIGIONS
AND CHALLENGES OF HIS DAY
Before we enter into a detailed analysis of the text, we should first ascertain that Bahya, living in the Golden Age, is indeed a product of that era with all of its parallels to our own time. Only in this way may we trust that his

words and wisdom have something to offer us. Once we have established Bahya as a thinker whose breadth of vision, despite his medieval origins, can address the crises of our day, we shall allow Bahya himself to delineate the historical background of his time, which, as he explains, required him to undertake the process of spiritualization within Judaism.

In writing *Duties of the Heart*, Bahya clearly exhibits a grasp of the times in which he lived and the various internal and external influences that operated upon the educated Jew of his era. In fact the very title of his book is borrowed from Muslim theology, which referred to inward spirituality as "the duties of the heart" in contrast to outward observances that were characterized as "duties of the limbs."[22] But beyond his title, Bahya was indisputably a product of his epoch, thoroughly steeped in the social, cultural, and intellectual cooperation that characterized the Golden Age. One small illustration should suffice to illustrate his facility with the cultural and intellectual proceedings of his day:

> There is a chapter in one of the theological writings of the great Muslim theologian al-Ghazali (1059-1111) that is almost identical to a chapter in a work by his near contemporary, the Jewish philosopher Bahye ibn Paquda. The connection between the two has puzzled many scholars. At one time it was assumed that Bahye must have taken the contents of the chapter from al-Ghazali, since, while Bahye could read Arabic, al-Ghazali could not have read the Hebrew script in which Bahye's work was written. When it was shown that there was no way in which Bahye could have seen or read al-Ghazali's work, the problem seemed insoluble until the late Professor Baneth found the answer. An earlier text, previously unknown, was the common source of the relevant chapters in both al-Ghazali and Bahye, and accounts for the striking resemblances between the two. What makes the case still more remarkable is that this earlier work was written by a Christian. We thus have a Christian who writes a theological treatise, presumably intended for Christian readers, which is then studied and, so to speak, borrowed by two subsequent theologians, one Muslim and the other Jewish, each writing a work of religious instruction for his own coreligionists.[23]

That such intellectual appropriation from members of other faiths extended into the realm of philosophy and theology demonstrates the extraordinary degree of symbiosis even among theologians, where one might naturally expect far more estrangement. Such fluency in the religious writings of surrounding cultures makes Bahya and his work exceedingly helpful for our times, as he clearly shows that he is as conversant with the numerous philosophical challenges of his era as would be any educated theologian of ours.[24] Moreover, in the introduction to *Duties of the Heart*, Bahya himself admits:

> I quoted also the saints and sages of other nations whose words
> have come down to us; hoping that my readers' hearts would incline
> to them, and give heed to their wisdom. I quote for example the
> dicta of the philosophers, the ethical teachings of the Ascetics,
> and their praiseworthy customs.[25]

Bahya was keenly aware of the void within Jewish literature regarding a systematic presentation of how to achieve spirituality. In the introduction to *Duties*, Bahya explains that he was motivated to write his guide because the inner life of the Jew had been largely neglected by his predecessors and contemporaries, whose writings had focused almost exclusively upon what he called "the Duties of the Limbs" or the bodily, visible precepts:

I studied the books of the ancient writers who flourished after the Talmud and who composed many works dealing with the Precepts [mitzvot], in the expectation of learning from them the science of inward religion.

I found however that all that they intended to interpret and expound does not go beyond one of three objects: The first of these was to expound the Pentateuch and the Prophetical Books, and this in one of two ways, either explaining the words and subject matter...or elucidating the language and grammar....The second was to give accounts of the Precepts [mitzvot], in summary form...or of the laws that are now in force...or of special topics, as the Geonim did in their Responses on practical duties.... The third was to confirm our faith in the contents of the Torah by logical demonstrations and by refutation of heretics.[26]

This text testifies to Bahya's view of the state of religiosity in his times. He characterizes Jewish literature until his day as seeking to answer the needs of people who wished to better understand the meaning of Scripture, to live their lives practically in accordance with halacha (Jewish law delineated in practical precepts), and to confirm their faith in Torah and its contents (probably owing to challenges from philosophers and heretics). Nowhere, however, did he find, to his great surprise, "a treatise specially devoted to Inward Duties. This department of knowledge, the science of the Duties of the Heart [*Hokhmat Hovot haLevavot*], had, I saw, been entirely neglected. No work had been composed, systematically setting forth its principles and divisions."[27]

THE STRUCTURE OF HOVOT HALEVAVOT OR DUTIES
OF THE HEART AND THE EMPHASIS ON *KAVANNAH*

Because so much had been written, according to Bahya, on what human beings should do, while hardly any literature existed delineating what they should believe in and feel, Bahya sought to address this deficiency by fashioning a step-by-step guide, one which was clearly modeled after works of Muslim mysticism that attempt to lead the reader through various stages of a person's inner life towards spiritual perfection.[28] In *Duties of the Heart* he constructs a system of ten basic spiritual "duties of the heart" or "commandments," which he declares should be central in a Jew's religious life. When performed, these duties are designed to help the practitioner create a life of holiness that is distinguished by being totally inner directed— totally of the soul and spirit—without any reference or recourse to external, bodily practices or activities involving the senses.

As the name of his book implies, these "Duties of Heart" stand at the center of the program of spirituality that Bahya has proposed we follow, and thus to grasp his spiritual vision we must properly understand these duties. What we shall find is that directing the soul towards God and reaching the highest duty of the heart (the love of God) is inextricably bound up with the concept of *kavannah* or intention. This concept of purposeful, directed concentration on the acts that we perform, mental or physical, is in my opinion at the heart of his theology.[29] To fully appreciate the role of *kavannah* in Bahya's thinking, I first set out the structure of his work, noting where *kavannah* is mentioned in his chapters. Then I proceed to a more concentrated analysis of various textual quotations from his work in order to demonstrate that the religion of "inwardness" (termed "Duties of the Heart") and *kavannah* is central to Bahya's notion of spiritual quest and attainment. After that, I interpret how inwardness and *kavannah* affect his conception of ethics. Finally I offer some general thoughts as to how Bahya's spiritual insight may serve as a useful tool for spiritual seekers in our day.

For Bahya, the knowledge of God's existence and of his unity is a prerequisite for not only understanding but embracing the devotional life. Therefore, the first chapter of *Duties of the Heart*, the Treatise on Unity [*sha'ar hayichud*], is a philosophical and theological treatment of these two subjects, since, to paraphrase Bahya, the wholehearted acceptance of the Unity of God is the root and foundation of Judaism and whoever has deviated from it will neither practice any duty properly nor retain any creed permanently.[30]

In the second chapter, the Treatise on Examining [*sha'ar habechinah*], Bahya seeks to reveal the various means by which God's existence can be demonstrated and finds that the most direct way to recognize the reality of the Creator is by examining the divine order and benevolence present in the universe. By examination, Bahya here means meditation or contemplation [*hitbonenut*] of God's creatures and the marks of divine wisdom manifested in all created things, from contemplating how orderly each element in the universe functions to observing the incredible complexity of the human body. To Bahya, such recognition would seem to be natural. However, in a marvelously contemporary-sounding critique of his era, he notes that there are three reasons preventing human beings from comprehending God:

1. Their absorption in secular affairs and pleasures...their neglect to contemplate the benefits God bestows upon them because the sole hope on which their hearts are fixed is the satisfaction of their desires and fulfillment of their wishes; whatever stage of success they attain, they seek to proceed higher and further; the numerous benefits enjoyed by them are, in their view, but few. The great gifts already conferred on them, they deem small, so that any advantage gained by another person, they look upon as having been taken from them.

2. [Human beings] grow up surrounded with a superabundance of Divine favors which they experience continuously, and to which they become so used that they come to regard these as essential parts of their being...and do not consider the obligation of gratitude for Divine beneficence.

3. Human beings are subject in this world to various mishaps and damage in person and property....They are resentful when His judgment is visited upon them, but they do not praise him when His mercy and loving-kindness are manifested to them.[31]

After examining the world as detailed in the second chapter, a person should understand the benefits received from God and assume the obligation of serving God in gratitude for what he has received. Thus, the third chapter, the Treatise on the Worship of God [*sha'ar avodat ha'elohim*], concerns the type of service one owes God and the way in which human beings might be motivated to serve God.

To attain one's maximum spiritual potential, a person must, according to Bahya, diligently embrace a number of virtues, one of which is trust in God, which constitutes the fourth chapter, the Treatise on Trust [*sha'ar habitachon*]. A further advantage is that those who trust in God rejoice in whatever situation they are placed because they always trust that God will do nothing but what is for their good in all things. The reward of such trust is an internal transformation—tranquility of the soul, ease of the mind, and diminishing anxieties in regard to secular interests.

Next Bahya turns in the fifth chapter, called the Treatise on the Unity of Action [*sha'ar yichud hama'aseh*], to the obligation of performing all of our activities with a sense of wholehearted devotion to God, by which he means "that every act, public and private, the aim and purpose should be service of God for His Name's sake, to please Him only, without thought of winning the favor of human creatures."[32] Moreover, in keeping with his prior explanation of the distinctions between the visible physical duties and the duties of the heart, he notes that it is possible to observe the former with a *kavannah* that is distinctly ungodly in nature, as when one is motivated by a desire to seem virtuous or by the expectation of receiving praise for fulfilling one's duties. With the duties of the heart, by contrast, there can be no hypocrisy nor any expectation of mortal praise, since the duty takes place within one's inner life and thus is entirely invisible to other human beings. Bahya further cautions his readers to be vigilant in monitoring their thoughts, reflections, and feelings and again stresses his earlier theme that the quality of one's inward intention [*kavannah*] is of the utmost import, rather than the quantity of one's outer deeds.[33]

Since Bahya feels that pride in the actions we do for God is perhaps the most injurious influence operating upon the one who seeks to practice wholehearted devotion, he immediately offers the reader an antidote in the sixth chapter, aptly titled the Treatise on Humility [*sha'ar hakeniah*]. He defines humility as "lowliness of the soul" and declares that the primary condition for the service of God is for the worshipper to avoid all forms of domination, such as pride and haughtiness. Since one must serve God and such service can be rendered only if one is humble and lowly before God, Bayha concludes that humility is the most important of all the moral qualities. In fact, without humility before God, no moral quality can possibly exist within a person.

The next chapter, the Treatise on Repentance [*sha'ar hateshuvah*], follows immediately after humility because Bahya perceives humility as the root and beginning of repentance. Repentance is defined as the resumption of service to God after having withdrawn from it and sinned. Of the three kinds of repentance that Bahya outlines, the first and least describes a person who repents, but, lacking true *kavannah,* continues to be overcome by the evil inclination (i.e., temptation) and thus repeats the offense again and again. Such a person is described as one who "repents with his mouth but not with his heart" and thus merits the Creator's punishment. Pure repentance, on the other hand, contains the proper *kavannah* and is thus likely to be successful in truly transforming the individual.

Bahya perceives the subject of the eighth chapter, the Treatise on Spiritual Accounting [*sha'ar cheshbon hanefesh*], as important in achieving true repentance and thus addresses it straightaway. For him, spiritual accounting means "striving to consider one's religious and secular concerns, so that one may know what he possesses and what is due from him."[34] Of the many ways of performing a spiritual accounting, Bahya lists thirty as illustrations of how one might utilize the accounting process to reorganize and refocus one's spiritual life. The completion of the process results not only in an improvement of the soul, but also in an entirely new level of spiritual development in which "your understanding will be illuminated. You will then obtain insight into great themes and see profound secrets, because your soul will be pure and your faith will be strong....the gate to high degrees will be opened to you; the curtain that interposes between you and the Creator's wisdom will be rolled away from your vision."[35]

One of the methods of spiritual accounting that is presented in the eighth chapter–abstinence from worldly interests–forms the nucleus of the ninth chapter, titled the Treatise on Abstinence [*sha'ar haprishut*], which Bahya views as an especially helpful method of spiritual improvement. For him, abstinence means "bridling the inner lust, voluntarily refraining from something that is in our power and which we have the opportunity to do";[36] by so doing, we restore our equilibrium in inner tendencies as well as outer forms of living. Since abstinence helps us overcome the strength of the evil inclination, Bahya feels that there should be some individuals who dedicate themselves to especially zealous abstinence in order to serve as spiritual role models for the majority. Yet he is careful to promote a level of abstinence within the limits of the Torah by concentrating on inward abstinence (regarding thoughts or inclinations) and not by separating physically from the community and its norms (for example, living like a hermit, entirely abstaining from sexual intercourse, or fasting during days on which it is prohibited to fast). In keeping with his hatred for those who do not act with a whole heart, he especially excoriates those who practice abstinence to gain some sort of advantage—a reputation for piety, for example—calling them hypocrites in faith, "the worst of all classes of human beings, being further removed from truth and more despicable in their mode of life than anyone else."[37]

The final section of Bahya's book concerns the end goal of all that he has written about thus far; namely, the love of God. He introduces this tenth chapter, titled the Treatise on the Love of God [*sha'ar ahavat hashem*], with this counsel:

> It is proper, my brother, that you understand and know, that all that has been mentioned in this work on the duties of the heart, on morals and spiritual nobility, are rungs and steps leading to the supreme object which it is our purpose to expound in this treatise. It is also proper for you to know, that every duty and every good quality–whether it be rational, found in Scripture or based on Tradition–are all forms and steps by which [human beings] ascend to this, their ultimate aim for there is no degree above or beyond it.[38]

He notes that once the believer's heart has been emptied of love of this world and freed from lusts by following the path recommended in the chapter on abstinence, then the love of God can be established in the heart and fixed in the soul, which is the ultimate aim of life and the climax of the process of self-development delineated throughout the *Duties of the Heart*.

As one might expect, Bahya expresses concern, as he has throughout his work, that the believer must come to love God with a "perfect heart" and a "genuine purity of the soul." Once again, motives are important to him; he cautions the reader not to "be like the servants who minister to their master upon the condition of receiving a reward,"[39] but instead to love God out of awe for his exalted glory and almighty power and to remain in a state of constant consciousness that he knows what is hidden within and what is seen. Bahya exhorts us to read a special prayer he himself has composed for the purpose of rousing our souls, but he hastens to remind us once again what is of utmost value:

> The main thing, brother, is the purity of your soul while you are offering up the prayer, and the *kavannah* of your heart at the time....Let not your tongue hurry before your heart; for reciting a little of a prayer with the heart's devotion is better than the hurried movements of your tongue in reciting much of it while your heart is empty of feeling. A pietist said, "Do not offer praise that is empty because the heart is not in it, but let your heart be ever present."[40]

Thus, throughout Bahya's guide, *kavannah* serves as a central, pivotal focus within the various chapters of the book, each of which constitutes the steps and stages towards the attainment of ultimate spirituality, namely loving God. We also note that Bahya greets with withering criticism any outer or inner duty done for an ulterior motive. For him, the essence of the religious life is genuine unity between soul, heart, mind, and body at all times. Such wholeheartedness is the fundamental requirement and the essential value of the duties of the heart.

BAHYA SEEKS TO "SPIRITUALIZE" JUDAISM

From Bahya's juxtaposition of the types of literature published up until his day, which sought to fulfill various needs, and his own stated desire to find a treatise devoted to the Duties of the Heart, it is clear that he too seeks to fulfill a need in his own day: a systematic work on the inward aspect of religious life, which we would today call "spirituality."[41] Indeed, later in his introduction he explicitly links the Inward Life and the Duties of the Heart with spirituality:

> The wise and sagacious man, when he reads and clearly understands
> [the Torah], will classify its contents under three headings. First,
> he will endeavor to know the subtle spiritual themes *[inyanim
> haruchani'im]* which belong to the science of the Inward Life—
> the Duties of the Heart, the discipline of the soul, and will constrain
> himself continually to fulfill these duties.[42]

He clearly recognizes that by focusing on what he calls "the Inward Life" or "the Duties of the Heart," he will have in effect "spiritualized" Judaism for those of his generation who felt that Judaism was lacking in this area.

For Bahya, Judaism (or the science of Torah, as he calls it in some places) may be divided into two parts. The first aims at the knowledge of practical duties *[hovot ha'evarim,* more accurately translated as "duties of the limbs"] and is the science of external conduct, which includes prayer, fasting, almsgiving, learning the Torah and teaching it, erecting a booth for the feast of Tabernacles, and any other precept which calls for the utilization of the physical organs.[43] Although some of these may be considered "spiritual" in a colloquial sense (prayer, for example), Bahya decisively classifies them as "duties of the limbs" because at least one aspect of their practice involves the observable activity of the body.

The second part of Judaism for him deals with the duties of the heart *[hovot halevavot],* which constitute the science of the inward life.[44] As Bahya understands them, the duties of the heart are entirely rooted in rational principles, as opposed to some of the practical duties that are sanctioned by revelation or tradition alone. Later, when we consider ways in which Bahya's system might help us in our modern era, we shall see the importance of the fact that the duties of the heart are entirely rooted in rational principles. In addition, we again emphasize that these duties are fulfilled by thought and the exercise of the inward faculties, with no recourse to visible physical activities.

Bahya divides the duties of the heart into two types, affirmative and negative, and enumerates them as follows:

Among affirmative duties of the heart are—to believe[45] that the world had a Creator, that He created it *ex nihilo,* and that there is none like unto Him; to accept His Unity; to worship Him with our hearts; to meditate on the marvels exhibited in His creatures, that these may serve us as evidences of Him; that we put our trust in Him; that we humble ourselves before Him, and revere Him; that we tremble and be abashed when we consider that He observes our visible and our hidden activities; that we yearn for His favor; that we devote our works to the glory of His name; that we love Him and love those that love Him, and thus draw nigh unto Him; that we hate His enemies—and similar duties, not apprehended by the senses *[ha'evarim].*

Negative duties of the heart are the converse of those just mentioned. Also included among them are: that we shall not covet, avenge, nor bear a grudge; as it is written, (Lev 19:18) "Thou shalt not avenge nor bear a grudge"; that our minds shall not dwell on transgressions, nor hanker after them, nor resolve to commit them; that we shall abstain from transgressions of a similar character—all of which are purely mental and observed by none but the Creator; as it is written (Jer 17:10) "I, the Lord, search the heart; I try the reins"; (Prov 20:27) "The lamp of God is the soul of man, searching all the inward parts."[46]

As specified, these affirmative duties, all of which are centered within the heart or mind, to some extent form the outline of his book, in which he elaborates upon each one in the ten chapters that follow his introduction. Overall, Bahya's work emphasizes the affirmative duties rather than the negative. However, we must remember that the idea of dividing up Jewish religious practice into inward and outward duties was not only novel in Bahya's day, but in a subtle way quite radical. By dividing the duties of the heart into positive and negative categories, he probably sought to defuse possible criticism of or resistance to his work by utilizing a structure that was already familiar and comfortable to the people of his time, who were well acquainted with the traditional division of the practical precepts [mitzvot] into positive and negative categories. In addition, we recognize that the ultimate goal of the affirmative duties as set out in *Duties of the Heart* is "to draw nigh unto him," which falls squarely within the definition of spirituality, "a striving for the presence of God," as offered by Arthur Green above. Thus, through his step-by-step guide to the affirmative duties of the heart, Bahya seeks to propel his reader by stages on an ascent towards spiritual mastery.

THE CENTRALITY OF THE DUTIES OF THE HEART

Following his enumeration of the affirmative duties, Bahya then records his attempt to determine if the Duties of the Heart are obligatory or not. After "a careful examination by the light of Reason, Scripture, and Tradition,"[47] he concludes: "We are under the obligation of inward as well as external duties so that our service [of God] shall be perfect and complete, and shall engage mind as well as body."[48] Reason leads him to determine that mankind consists of body, the element of our being that is seen, and of soul, the element that remains unseen. Bahya does not reject the notion that we must fulfill our halachic obligations, as evidenced by his statement to the effect that humanity is "accordingly bound to render the Creator visible and invisible service," which consists of the Duties of the Limbs and the Duties of the Heart respectively.[49] He further notes that Scripture frequently mentions the Duties of the Heart, as in "To love the Lord, thy God, to hearken unto His voice and to cleave unto Him" (Deut 11:13).[50] Finally, he investigates the oral tradition of the sages and discovers numerous instances in which the Duties of the Heart are perceived as important.[51]

Yet, more than being important, more than being as much a part of Judaism as the Duties of the Limbs [practical mitzvot], for Bahya the Duties of the Heart are a fundamental, foundational component of faith, without which one is a less than perfect Jew. As he puts it regarding the Duties of the Heart, "The believer's faith will not be complete unless these duties are known and practiced."[52] In contrast to virtually all of the normative Jewish literature that came before him, Bahya clearly predicates observance of the practical mitzvot [*mitzvot ha'evarim*] upon observance of the Duties of the Heart, which to him are more essential and more primary than the practical mitzvot—as when he asserts, "they [Duties of the Heart] indeed form the foundation of all the Precepts and if there is any shortcoming in their observance, it would be impossible for us [to fulfill] even one deed out of the external duties."[53] Bahya writes further:

> I am certain that even the practical duties [*hovot ha'evarim* or Duties of the Limbs] cannot be performed completely without the willingness of the heart and the desire of the soul to do them. If it should enter our mind that we are under no obligation to choose and desire the Service of God, our bodily organs would be released from the obligation devolving upon us, of fulfilling the practical duties, since no action is completed without the assent of the soul.[54]

Thus we see that Bahya considers the obligation to observe the Duties of the Heart as of primary importance and that no deed can be performed without the cooperation of the inner self, heart and mind. In the next section, I demonstrate that the Duties of the Heart cannot exist without *kavannah* or intention.

THE SIGNIFICANCE OF *KAVANNAH*

Kavannah is the key to spirituality in Bahya's guide, which he wrote to counsel those of his generation. The correlation between *kavannah* and the Duties of the Heart can be demonstrated in several ways, of which I will mention only two. First, I show that *kavannah* is the essential tool necessary to achieve the Duties of the Heart, "the heart," so to speak, of the Duties of the Heart. Second, I seek to define *kavannah* and place Bahya's perspective on it in the context of the Jewish literature that preceded him.

As noted above, for Bahya it is not enough to practice the bodily mitzvot of Judaism to be considered a "righteous Jew"; as he states, unless the Duties of the Heart are known and observed, one's faith is incomplete. Similarly, he maintains that "if the sentiments of our heart [*kavannat levaveinu*] contradict our words, and the actions of our body contradict our inner state of mind, the service we render God will not be perfect, for He does not accept service that is spurious."[55] Clearly, just as the Duties of the Heart are crucial to the right practice of Judaism, one's *kavannah* or mental state must coincide with deeds of the body for those deeds to be acceptable to God.

The correlation between the Duties of the Heart and the *kavannah* of heart and mind can be established immediately when we compare two of Bahya's statements, one which relates to the Duties of the Heart and the other to *kavannah*. What we will find is an almost complete correspondence between these two terms. As noted above, Bahya testifies that he searched prior Jewish literature for a treatise devoted to the Inward Duties, and "a careful examination, however, by the light of Reason, Scripture, and

Tradition, of the question of whether the Duties of the Heart are obligatory or not, convinced me that [the Duties of the Heart] indeed form the foundations [*yesodai*] of all the Precepts." He concludes with the key words that follow:

> and where there is any shortcoming in their observance,
>
> [*ve'im ye'erah behem shum hefsed*],
>
> it is impossible for us [to fulfill] even one deed of the external duties.
>
> [*lo titachen lanu mitzvah mimitzvot ha'evarim*].[56]

Each word here is important for the comparison we are making between this quotation, concerning the centrality of the Duties of the Heart, and the quotation that follows below, regarding the centrality of *kavannah*. Virtually identical words are used: "It accordingly became clear to me that each of the roots of the deeds performed for the sake of God, may His Name be blessed, they are founded [*hem miyusadim*] upon purity of the heart and singleness of the mind."[57] And then Bahya continues with the words that are so crucial to our comparison:

> And where there is any shortcoming in *kavannah*
>
> [*ve'im ye'erah al ha'kavannah hefsed*],
>
> the deeds will not be accepted,
>
> [*lo yehiyu hama'asim mekubalim*]
>
> even if they are numerous and continuous.[58]

If we accept the Hebrew translation of Ibn Tibbon as faithful to Bahya's original work in Arabic, then we must conclude from this comparison that *kavannah* is closely correlated (in fact nearly identical) to the term "Duties of the Heart." Or, more precisely, we should say that *kavannah*, as an independent concept, serves as a tool as well as an indispensable, fundamental characteristic of the Duties of the Heart. In conclusion, whereas the Duties of the Heart encompass the totality of the specific spiritual duties, *kavannah* relates to the mental act that is required of the one who performs these spiritual duties, termed "Duties of the Heart."

THE ROLE OF *KAVANNAH* IN JUDAISM PRIOR
TO BAHYA AND WITHIN BAHYA'S SYSTEM

To fathom the status of *kavannah* in rabbinic literature, we need to make a distinct division between two kinds of sources—the legalistic (halachic) sources on the one hand and the non-legalistic (non-halachic) on the other. In the non-legalistic sources (where legal determinations are not present), one may find a wide variety of references to *kavannah* in different contexts, such as principles of faith, ethics, sermons, biblical commentary, stories, and legends. In these sources, one finds unanimous agreement that *kavannah* plays a very important role within the framework of belief and religious life.

The other group of sources is devoted totally to the pragmatic, legalistic (halachic) practice of the Jew. In the context of *kavannah*, this group also may be divided into two subgroups. Within the first subgroup, which consists mainly of Tannaitic literature such as the Mishnah, *kavannah* is required while one is performing commandments or physical religious actions.[59] Within the second subgroup of legalistic sources, which includes mainly Talmudic literature, *kavannah* is given weight but is not required in the performance of the commandments. As Isaiah Tishby aptly characterizes it, these two approaches "are indicative of two different and sometimes contrary tendencies in Judaism: the external ritualistic approach, which emphasizes above all the correct fulfillment of the practical commandments; and the internal spiritualistic approach, which places the highest value on the intellectual and spiritual striving to achieve emotional or rational contact with supernatural elements."[60] Interestingly, both of the approaches mentioned above concerning *kavannah* occupy respected positions within Jewish thought. However, from the point of view of daily behavior, this second subgroup, the Talmudic literature, became operative as the normative religious standard of practice expected of the Jew.

In sum, from the analysis of the various Tannaitic and Talmudic sources[61] that deal with the concept of *kavannah*, the following picture emerges. Although the Tannaitic literature requires *kavannah* during the performance of the mitzvot, or commandments, the Talmudic literature evidences considerable effort in removing the obligation of *kavannah* during the performance of mitzvot—except during some parts of the prayer service, for which even the Talmudic scholars required *kavannah*. On the whole, one may say with a large measure of certainty that for legalistic and practical purposes, it was determined that mitzvot do not require *kavannah*, meaning focused mental concentration on the act while performing it.[62]

BAHYA'S QUIET ETHICAL-PHILOSOPHICAL REVOLUTION

In light of these conclusions, one may discern the enormity of the religious revolution that Bahya posed to the Jewish world. Prior to Bahya, distinctions were made between duties to God, known as the ritual or ceremonial obligations [*mitzvot bein adam lamakom*], and duties towards one's fellow man, known as the ethical obligations [*mitzvot bein adam l'havero*].

However, in Bahya's ethics the focus is entirely God-centered, starting with one's relationship to God and only from that relationship proceeding towards humanity. Bahya's classic was also the first medieval Jewish work to evolve an ethical system rooted in Jewish thought, as it tried to come to grips with the most challenging question to Judaism at that time: the inner quality of religious life.[63] Joseph Dan describes the philisophico-historical situation in Bahya's time as follows:

> Judaism had come to be seen as a materialistic religion, based on practical deeds and actions, and not on spiritual attitudes which, to the medieval scholars, seemed the essence of religious life. Jewish moralists were therefore confronted with the problem of reconciling the contemporary Jewish concept of religious life which was practically oriented and consequently seen as inferior, with the new ideas which saw religion almost exclusively in a spiritual light.[64]

While Bahya does not minimize the significance of the ethics of human relations, one of his major innovations was to place moral actions on a level secondary to the higher spiritual plane of maintaining the correct religious attitude. Thus, Bahya introduces another entire category of systematic ethics into Judaism; namely, an ethics of purely internal, invisible duties. Within this system, actions derive their ethical value only insofar as they reflect the underlying intention of the heart.

By taking this position, he was in effect advocating a near reversal of values in Judaism, departing radically from the position taken by the Talmudic sages.[65] According to Bahya, the commandment or religious action performed without intention is like the body without a soul. Such a performance of the mitzvot has no validity; certainly such a person has not for Bahya fulfilled his religious obligation, as we see in such quotations as "Where *kavannah* is lacking, deeds are not acceptable to God, numerous and consistent as they may be" and "If the *kavannah* of our heart contradicts the profession of our lips...the service we render to God is not perfect."[66]

For a post-Talmudic Jew living at the beginning of the second millennium, the belief in the superiority of the practical commandments in religious life over any inner sentiments or motives was a given, an undeniable certainty. Bahya, on the other hand, explicitly dismisses the value of a deed performed without *kavannah*:

> Hence a single precept, depending upon the spirit and *kavannah* with which it is performed, may outweigh the performance of many precepts, and one transgression, many transgressions. Even

meditation/thought on a commandment and the longing/desire to carry it out prompted by reverence for God, even if he proves unable to do so, may outweigh the performance of numerous commandments that lack them [reverence for God and *kavannah*].[67]

He also dared to assert an alternative system of religious values—the fulfillment of the Duties of the Heart—as superior to performance of the normative religious values—the Duties of the Limbs or the bodily commandments—as when he maintains: "And since every act hinges and rests on *kavannah* and the hidden sentiment of the heart, a System of the Duties of the Heart should naturally take precedence over a System of Duties of the Limbs."[68]

Thus, for Bahya, the *kavannah*—one's directed and reverent intention—to perform a commandment, even if the commandment is not realized, may be worth more than the accomplishment of a commandment executed precisely, but lacking spiritual motivation. Moreover, according to Bahya, the system of the Duties of the Heart he proposes is superior to the traditional system of commandments, which is designated by him as Duties of the Limbs, including (but not limited to) prayer and study of the Torah, even though these last two are generally considered key "spiritual" commandments within the traditional system of mitzvot.

Joseph Dan, the Gershom Scholem Professor of Kabbalah at the Hebrew University of Jerusalem and a scholar of Jewish ethical literature, summarizes his remarkable originality:

In many respects Bahya's ethics can be regarded as the most radical and revolutionary in Jewish ethical-philosophical literature. When discussing the "duties of the limbs," in contradistinction to the "duties of the heart," he clearly states that the performance does not include any religious value if they are not coupled, at least, with a spiritual "intention" which gives them value. When they are performed with such an intention (*kavannah*), the source of their meaning is the spiritual intensity and not the deed itself. As the "duties of the limbs" include all the traditional commandments, precepts, and ethical, social, and ritualistic demands of Judaism, Bahya in fact denies the existence of an intrinsic religious value in the performance of the basic Jewish rituals, such as prayers and the observance of the Sabbath and holy days, and social commandments, such as charity. They may have some value only if a spiritual experience accompanies them, but this spiritual experience does not have to be coupled with the physical deed. It is even more perfect if it stands alone, without any connection with the physical or the sensual parts of man, and then it becomes a "duty of the heart," the supreme element of religious life. As Jewish life is totally dependent on the performance of the physical commandments, Bahya's book could very easily be regarded as heretical, preaching a secondary status–if any–of everything that was regarded as of paramount importance in Judaism.[69]

Bahya's daring looms even larger when one takes into consideration the fact that he served as a *dayyan* or halachic judge for the Jewish community and thus was a personage to whom the Jewish authorities entrusted the determination of halachic or legalistic matters. Here was a man whose very professional life was rooted in the Duties of the Limbs, the practical commandments, and yet, despite his circumstance, he emphatically disagreed with the accepted views of tradition as well as those of his own time. Perhaps in this very fact lay the reason for the popularity of his work and the unprecedented influence it exerted within the ethical literature of Judaism from the time it was written until this very day: that is, his total command of the Jewish tradition (especially the legal tradition), his liberal use of quotations from traditional Jewish sources, and his prominence as a *dayyan* [judge] doubtless gave him the immunity to criticism that very well might not have been given to another person lacking Bahya's background and standing.

CONCLUSIONS FOR OUR TIME

As a student of philosophy and history, my role is not to provide spiritual counseling or specific practical suggestions to ameliorate the contemporary crises of our day. That I leave to spiritual teachers and practitioners. What I can do, however, within the confines of my role as I understand it, is to offer the historical research and my findings as a possible basis for anyone wishing to expand upon them and pursue detailed solutions. Therefore, what is proposed below should be seen as merely alluding to solutions in a very general way rather than fully fleshing them out.

In terms of finding solutions to the spiritual crisis of our time, what then are the points that one ought to pay attention to when reading *Duties of the Heart*? At the outset, it must be emphasized that Bahya's wisdom may in essence serve people of any religion or even a person who lacks religion, since what makes Bahya's thought Jewish are the proof texts he constantly cites from Jewish sources. His message, however, is universal.

I would suggest three areas Bahya touches upon for further examination. Most of the written spiritual guides today seem to emphasize what I would term "emotional spirituality." In these guides, the author seeks to provide the reader with a path for spiritual fulfillment that moves him emotionally so that he or she will have a "spiritual experience." Though many people seem to find this a suitable solution, the problem with this method for others is that it does not address the many individuals who identify or perceive themselves as "rational" and who use their intellect as the primary tool for examining their reality. For these people, the existing "spiritual" guides may not be at all attractive. On the contrary, they may arouse feelings of rejection and alienation, since they are perceived as too emotional. For these people, Bahya's guide may offer an acceptable spiritual approach (or at least a tolerable one) due to its extensive emphasis on exercising the intellect to reach spiritual fulfillment and that the duties of the heart are entirely rooted in rational principles.

Secondly, Bahya's accentuation of the role of *kavannah* might lead one to think that *kavannah* leads directly to spirituality. While not all intention is spiritual, for Bahya no true spirituality exists without intention—namely, *kavannah*—that stems from a wholehearted devotion to God. The role that *kavannah* might play in contemporary spiritual life is a subject that deserves a great deal more thought and research.

Finally, it would seem that what is called New Age Spirituality relies heavily upon different methods of meditation, most of which have been borrowed from Eastern religions, especially Buddhism. Generally, this kind of spiritual practice is carried out in a closed, or at least semi-controlled environment. Often the best way to practice these types of meditation are in mental and physical isolation or with at least enough mental detachment that the practitioner can concentrate throughout the spiritual exercise. Bahya is familiar with this kind of spiritual discipline and in fact refers to it quite positively in his book. However, he offers not only a spirituality of isolation and detachment, but another kind of spirituality, which I would call "cosmic spirituality." In the second chapter of *Duties of the Heart*, he suggests that we examine the universe, the world created by God, as one of the fundamental steps in the ladder of ascent towards the attainment of peak spirituality. The implications of this suggestion are tremendous. In a modern world that demands from us an active engagement with the environment, often surrounded by people, Bahya's proposal to infuse spiritual intent into it could be spiritually transformative. His rejection of the hermit's path of isolated spirituality, coupled with his emphasis on the inward state, turns the cosmos (and every element in it) into a giant cathedral of spirituality:

> You will never leave God out of your thoughts; He will never depart from before your eyes. He will be in your company when you are alone; He will dwell with you in the deserts. A place full of people will be in your sight as though it were not full, and a place that is empty will appear as if it were not empty.[70]

ACKNOWLEDGMENTS

I wish to thank two wonderful colleagues, Stephen Sapp and Henry Abramson, for their most useful critical reading of my paper. I would also like to acknowledge my wife, Rabbi Efrat Zarren-Zohar, who devoted many hours of her time to this project and who helped me with some of the research, editing, and typing. Finally, I would like to dedicate this paper to Moshe Kadoch z"l, who was a man of ethical and spiritual virtues, always acting with good intention [kavannah]. May his memory be for a blessing to us all.

NOTES

[1] Several publishing houses, such as Jewish Lights Publishing and SkyLight Paths Publishing, both established within the last ten years, perceive as their mission the printing of books relating to spirituality. Jewish Lights describes itself in this way: "Given our name and subject matter, the tendency is immediately to pigeonhole us as 'another publisher of Jewish books.' [However,] our books really focus on the issue of the quest for the self, seeking meaning in life....They deal with issues of personal growth. They deal with issues of religious inspiration." SkyLight Paths is even more explicit: "Through spirituality, our religious beliefs are increasingly becoming a part of our lives rather than apart from our lives. Nevertheless, while many people are more interested than ever in spiritual growth, they are less firmly planted in traditional religion."
[2] Arthur Green, "Spirituality," in *Contemporary Jewish Religious Thought* (ed. A. A. Cohen and P. Mendes-Flohr; New York: The Free Press, 1972), 903.
[3] Arthur Green, *Jewish Spirituality: From the Bible Through the Middle Ages* (World Spirituality 15; New York: Crossroads, 1986), xiv.
[4] *Ibid.*
[5] David S. Ariel, *Spiritual Judaism: Restoring Heart and Soul to Jewish Life* (New York: Hyperion, 1998), 2.
[6] Aryeh Kaplan, *Jewish Meditation: A Practical Guide* (New York: Schocken, 1985), vii.

[7] See the catalogue of SkyLight Paths Publishing, which was recently established to reach people who want "to learn from their own and other faith traditions, in new ways" in order "to deepen their relationship to the sacred." It goes on to say, "SkyLight Paths sees both believers and seekers as a community that increasingly transcends traditional boundaries of religion and denomination. Many people want to learn from each other, walking together, finding the way." See also Howard A. Addison, *Show Me Your Way: The Complete Guide to Exploring Interfaith Spiritual Direction* (Woodstock: Jewish Lights Publishing, 2000), in which the author, himself a Conservative rabbi, reveals that a Catholic nun is his spiritual director. In this book, the author tries to demonstrate the effectiveness of finding guidance and inspiration from people of other faiths, ponder the contemporary trends leading to an increased interest in seeking guidance from another faith, and analyze what interfaith spiritual direction means for the future of religion and spirituality in our modern world. Though "interfaith spiritual direction" is called a modern phenomenon, this paper will show that is not entirely true in light of the cross-religious study and sharing that took place during the Golden Age of Spain, in particular.

[8] A. James Rudin, "American Jewry in a Multi-Religious and Multi-Ethnic Society," in *Amerikanisches Judentum heute* (Trier: Paulinus, 1999), 87.

[9] Jerome A. Chanes, *A Primer on the American Jewish Community* (New York: American Jewish Committee, 1999), 10: "The growth of an Orthodox triumphalism that is dismissive of the other movements, and the radicalization of the liberal denominations on such issues as intermarriage, homosexuality, and the criteria for defining Jewishness, have both played a part in this polarization. The breakdown of relations has been marked by a new sharpness of rhetoric and an unwillingness to seek common ground. There have been harsh statements from all sides on the issue of religious pluralism, with the non-Orthodox calling the Orthodox ghetto Jews, and the Orthodox denying the Jewish authenticity of the other branches."

[10] Robert M. Seltzer, *Jewish People, Jewish Thought: The Jewish Experience in History* (New York: Macmillan, 1980), 346. Strictly speaking the major Golden Age existed in the tenth and eleventh centuries, perhaps coming to an end in 1086 with the Almoravide invasion against Christian kingdoms to the north. Literary productivity, however, continued apace until 1146, when the fanatical Almohade invasion commenced. Even then great literature, especially in Kabbalah but also in philosophy, was introduced in Christian Spain through the end of the fourteenth century.

[11] Jane S. Gerber, *The Jews of Spain: A History of the Sephardic Experience* (New York: The Free Press, 1992) 31.

[12] Joseph L. Blau, *The Story of Jewish Philosophy* (New York: Random House, 1962), 154.

[13] Bernard Lewis, *The Jews of Islam* (Princeton: Princeton University Press, 1984), 77.

[14] *Ibid.*

[15] *Ibid.*, 56.

[16] Seltzer, *Jewish People*, 375.

[17] *Ibid.*

[18] Gerber, *The Jews of Spain*, 75.

[19] Abraham S. Halkin, "Revolt and Revival in Judeo-Islamic Culture," in *Great Ages and Ideas of the Jewish People*, ed. Leo W. Schwarz (New York: Random House, 1956), 260.

[20] Gerber, *The Jews of Spain*, 74.

[21] Steven T. Katz, *Jewish Philosophers* (Jerusalem: Keter, 1975), 55.

[22] Blau, *Jewish Philosophy*, 168.

[23] Lewis, *The Jews of Islam*, 57.

[24] Isaac Husik, *A History of Mediaeval Jewish Philosophy* (Philadelphia: The Jewish Publication Society, 1940), 86: "Bahya was indebted for his ideas to the ascetic and Sufic literature of the Arabs, and Yahuda, who is the authority in this matter of Bahya's sources, has shown recently that among the quotations of the wise men of other nations in Bahya's work are such as are attributed by the Arabs to Jesus and the gospels, to Mohammed and his companions, to the early caliphs, in particular to caliph Ali, to Mohammedan ascetics and Sufis." See also Katz, *Jewish Philosophers*, 56: "Bahya drew a great deal upon non-Jewish sources, borrowing from Muslim mysticism, Arabic Neoplatonism, and perhaps also from the Hermetic writings. From Muslim authors he borrowed the basic structure of the book as well as definitions, aphorisms, and examples to illustrate his doctrine."

[25] R. Bachya ben Joseph ibn Paquda, *Duties of the Heart*, trans. Moses Hyamson (vol 1; Jerusalem: Feldheim Publishers, 1962), 45. Throughout this paper, I will be selectively using Hyamson's translation. Often I offer my own translation, which more accurately reflects the Hebrew text of Judah Ibn Tibbon.

[26] *Ibid.*, 19-21.

[27] *Ibid.*, 21.

[28] Katz, *Jewish Philosophers*, 56.

[29] Some other definitions of the term *kavannah* are given by Rabbi Aryeh Kaplan, one of the foremost expositors of Jewish mysticism and spirituality, as "directed consciousness"; David Ariel as "intention or mystical consciousness"; and H. Elchanan Blumenthal as literally meaning "directed intention," observing that in rabbinic literature the term denotes a state of mental concentration and devotion. The concept of "intention" itself is defined as "an act or an instance of determining upon some action or result" as well as "the end, or the object intended, or the purpose." In philosophy, "intentionality" is a term revived in 1874 by Franz Brentano for "the direction of the mind on an object," displaying "the mark of the mental since all and only mental states are intentional." For a fuller treatment of the entire subject of *kavannah*, see Zion Zohar, "The Concept of *Kavannah* (Intention) in Jewish Thought During the Middle Ages and its Roots in *Sifrut Hazal* (Rabbinic Literature)" (Doctoral dissertation, The Hebrew Union College-

Jewish Institute of Religion, 1998).

[30] *Duties of the Heart*, Introduction, 55.

[31] *Ibid.*, Volume I, Chapter 2, 127-129.

[32] *Ibid.*, Volume II, Chapter 5, 11.

[33] *Ibid.*, 65, where he states, "Strive therefore with all your might that your deeds shall be pure [in intention], even though they be few, rather than many but not pure. For that which is small in quantity and pure in quality is much, while what is much in quality, but impure is little and useless."

[34] *Duties of the Heart*, Chapter 8, 187.

[35] *Ibid.*, 279-281.

[36] *Ibid.*, Chapter 9, 291.

[37] *Ibid.*, 305.

[38] *Ibid.*, Chapter 10, 339.

[39] *Ibid.*, Chapter 10, 363.

[40] *Ibid.*, 371.

[41] *Duties of the Heart*, Introduction, 39, where Bahya explicitly states that he feels he must write this treatise not only for the instruction of others but for his own needs as well.

[42] *Ibid.*, 51.

[43] *Ibid.*, 21.

[44] *Ibid*, 17.

[45] When Bahya here utilizes the words "to believe," he means by this "to know" rather than "to accept what has been received through tradition," which is the usual sense of "to believe." Bahya's sense of "believe" is obvious upon examination of his first chapter concerning the Unity of God.

[46] *Duties of the Heart*, Introduction, 19.

[47] Reason (logic and philosophy), Scripture (the Bible or Written Law), and Tradition (Oral Law as delineated by the rabbinic sages) are the three main means God has given humanity for evaluating knowledge of Torah and Judaism, according to Saadiah Gaon. *Duties of the Heart*, Introduction, 17.

[48] *Ibid.*, 21-23.

[49] *Ibid.*, 21.

[50] *Ibid.*, 23.

[51] *Ibid.*, 23-25.

[52] *Ibid.*, 27.

[53] *Ibid.*, 21.

[54] *Ibid.*

[55] *Ibid.*, 37.

[56] *Ibid.*

[57] *Ibid.*, 35.

[58] *Ibid.*

[59] Isaiah Tishby, *The Wisdom of the Zohar: An Anthology of Texts* (vol. 3, Introduction to "Prayer and Devotion"; Oxford: Oxford University Press, 1961), 942 : "The

question of whether 'the commandments required intention' or not applied to all
the practical precepts in general. But the essential meaning of 'intention' (*kavannah*)
in this argument is bound up with the correct fulfillment of the commandments.
It means simply the intention to carry out one's religious obligation through an
understanding of its import, and it is contrasted with the performance of what
appears to be a commandment for non-religious purposes, or at least not for the
purpose of fulfilling the commandment....The insistence on *kavannah* in this sense
does not therefore imply a desire for inner religious spirituality, although if one
does not demand this simple kind of *kavannah*, one adopts an extremely formalistic
view, dispensing with the most elementary kind of consciousness, and regarding
as valid the most perfunctory kind of religious acts."

[60] *Ibid.*, 941.

[61] *b. Pesah.* 114a and 114b; *b. Ber.* 13a, 28a and 28b; and *b. Eruv.* 95b, among
others.

[62] See Tishby's comment above on formalistic performance of the mitzvot as well
as Zohar, "The Concept of *Kavannah* (Intention)," chapter two. See also Ephraim
Orbach's treatment of the subject in *The Sages* (Cambridge: Harvard University
Press, 1975), 394-99: "The problem confronting the Sages is known in every
religion and in every system of ethics. What significance can a man's conduct
have, if he observes the laws of ethics and religion as stereotyped, conventional
acts without giving them an inner meaning? Some people declare: These are
'precepts learned by rote', and actions that are merely external and unaccompanied
by inner feeling—inward devotion—only do harm, and it is better to dispense
with them. On the other hand, it is realized that not everyone is capable of being
constantly in that high state of tension requisite to action intentionally and
consciously performed for its own sake" (397-98).

[63] *Encyclopaedia Judaica* CD-ROM, "Ethical Literature" by Joseph Dan.

[64] *Ibid.*

[65] Tishby, *Wisdom of the Zohar*, 943.

[66] *Duties of the Heart*, Introduction, 35-37.

[67] *Ibid.*, 37-39.

[68] *Ibid.*, 25.

[69] Joseph Dan, *Jewish Mysticism and Jewish Ethics* (New Jersey: Jason Aronson,
1986), 26-27.

[70] *Duties*, Chapter 10, 353.

From Kabbalist to Zaddik: R. Isaac Luria as Precursor of the Baal Shem Tov

Morris M. Faierstein

The small Galilean town of Safed became the center of a spiritual revolution that transformed Jewish life and religious practice in the sixteenth century. Kabbalistic concepts and rituals, previously the preserve of a small mystical elite, came to be at the center of Jewish life through the influence of the Safed kabbalists.[1] The ritual of welcoming the Sabbath [*kabbalat Shabbat*], which culminates with the hymn *Lekha Dodi*,[2] is one of the best-known rituals popularized by the Safed kabbalists. Unknown outside of Safed in 1550, it had become an accepted part of the liturgy in all of Jewish communities not long after 1600.

The most influential figure in the Safed revival was Rabbi Isaac Luria [Ari].[3] Luria came to Safed from Egypt in 1570 at the age of 36. He died only two years later at the age of 38, in the summer of 1572. In his short time in Safed he gathered together a group of disciples and created a new school of kabbalistic thought that revolutionized the Jewish mystical tradition and put mysticism at the center of Jewish life and thought.

Stories about Luria's abilities as a "holy man" began to circulate shortly after his death. Not only was he a great mystic, but was also credited with the ability to heal the physically and mentally ill, expel evil spirits, and foretell the future. Tales of his magical abilities began to be collected and retold. The popular image of Luria led to the creation of a new type of Jewish leader, the *zaddiq*. The *zaddiq* is a charismatic leader who derives his authority from his mystical knowledge and magical abilities to effect cures and resolve the spiritual and ordinary problems of his adherents.

After Luria, the most important figure in defining the image of the *zaddiq* is Rabbi Israel Baal Shem Tov [Besht], the founder of Hasidism.[4] Great strides have been made in recent years in our understanding of the life of the Besht.[5] The historical Besht has come into sharper focus as a result of these efforts. At the same time, new questions have arisen about the nature of the Besht's role in East European Jewish society. Was he primarily a *baal shem*, a writer of amulets designed to heal and exorcise demons, or was he a charismatic mystic and spiritual teacher who attracted rabbis and mystics as disciples? The image of the Besht that emerges from hasidic hagiography, particularly the hagiographic biography *Shivhei ha-Besht*,[6] is that the Besht combined aspects of both types, but is not a pure example of either type.[7]

Scholars of Hasidism have recognized parallels between the hagiographic biographies of the Besht and the Ari, but they have not explored the full implications of these parallels.[8] For the most part, scholars have seen the Ari as the founder of Lurianic Kabbalah, a mystic who founded one of the most esoteric schools of Kabbalah. At the same time, they de-emphasized the other image of the Ari, that of the healer, miracle worker, and exorciser of demons. The reason for this is the overwhelming influence of Gershom Scholem and his intellectual agenda. Scholem saw the importance of Lurianic Kabbalah in its esoteric messianic theology and its role leading up to the rise of Sabbatai Sevi. Scholem saw this false prophet as one of the major figures in Judaism and his movement as a major turning point in Jewish history. Anything that did not fit this paradigm was irrelevant to Scholem. In addition, Scholem had an antipathy to the magical aspects of Kabbalah.[9] However, in the early modern period, it was the second, popular image of the Ari that had the most influence. Moshe Idel has shown that only a small mystical elite knew the details of Lurianic Kabbalah.[10] On the other hand, the popular image of the Ari was well known and highly influential.

The popularization of the image of the Ari began with the letters sent by Shlomel Dresnitz[11] from Safed not long after the death of the Ari. The letters were first published in 1629, but were also circulated and quoted in a wide variety of sources. The two main sources for the transmission of the Lurianic hagiography in the seventeenth and eighteenth centuries were collections of stories and religio-ethical [*musar*] works written in Hebrew and Yiddish.[12] The dissemination of the hagiographical stories about the Ari culminated in the 1785 publication of *Shivhei ha-Ari* in Koretz.[13] This collection became the standard biography of the Ari. The stories were also translated into Yiddish and thus reached the widest possible audience.[14]

Ma'ase ha-Shem, by Simeon Akiva Baer,[15] was among the more popular collections of kabbalistic stories. In his introduction he explains his intentions and the sources of his collection:

Within are told God Almighty's great miracles which he did through the sages Rabbi Shimon bar Yohai[16] and his father-in-law R. Pinhas ben Yair and also stories of R. Isaac Luria and his pupil R. Hayyim Vital. You will certainly enjoy reading it for you will hear many new tales. You should spend your Sabbath time with it and abandon trivialities. I have transcribed from *Shalshelet ha-Qabbalah*[17] many beautiful new stories for men and for women, as well as a great many from the *Zohar* and from the *Etz Hayyim*[18] and other holy books. I also drew much from the *Zohar Hadash* and the *Emek ha-Melekh*[19] a lot. Such a book in Yiddish has never been printed.[20]

An examination of the stories contained in this collection and others like it shows that there are no discussions of kabbalistic concepts or ideas. The heroes, Rabbi Shimon bar Yohai and the Ari, derive their significance from their status as important mystics, but in the stories they are portrayed as ethical exemplars or miracle workers. The Ari, in particular, is seen as a miracle worker, healer, and exorcist. Prophetic powers and even the ability to understand the speech of animals were also attributed to the Ari. The stories in *Ma'ase ha-Shem* and stories about the Ari in other genres of literature ultimately derive from the image first presented in Shlomel Dresnitz's letters.

The other genre that played an important role in the dissemination of the legend of the Ari is the religio-ethical [*musar*] literature written in the seventeenth and eighteenth centuries, in both Hebrew and Yiddish. Zvi Hirsch Koidanover's *Kav ha-Yashar*[21] is one of the classics of this genre. Moshe Idel, in his study of this work and its relation to Kabbalah, also concludes that the Ari is a major figure and role model in this work. He writes:

> The name of Luria recurs tens of times in the book and it is second only to the Zohar as a source of many passages. However, also in this case, Koidanover has been very selective. Out of the numerous quotes in the name of Luria, the great theological mythologoumena are negligible. In lieu of the famous concepts that a modern scholar would expect to find in the name of the great kabbalist, *zimzum*, *shevirat ha-kelim*, *parzufim*, or *yihudim*, we find time and again, legends which are intended to inculcate a certain mystical *modus vivendi*, rather than a theological *modus_cognoscendi*. The Luria who appears in *Kav ha-Yashar* is the great occultist, the ideal figure, or type, whose religious behavior should be imitated, but a great

kabbalist whose metaphysics remains, nonetheless, in deep shadow.[22]

Other contemporary works of this genre, like Jehiel Michel Epstein's *Derekh ha-Yashar le-Hayyei Olam ha-Ba*[23] and Elchanan Kirchan's *Simhat ha-Nefesh*,[24] present the same model in their portrayals of the Ari. All of these books were quite popular and often reprinted. The average eighteenth-century Jew would know that the Ari was a great mystic, but would have no idea of his mystical teachings with the possible exception of the concept of transmigration [*gilgul*].[25] On the other hand, they would have known that he expelled demons and had many other powers that can only be described as magical. He also had prophetic powers and was worthy of visits by Elijah, who was also his teacher.

The Besht as he is portrayed in *Shivhei ha-Besht* appears to be a combination of several distinct modes of religious leadership. He appears as a *baal shem*, a healer who utilizes amulets with divine names; a kabbalist who can exorcise spirits and is a miracle worker; and as a mystical teacher and leader of a new religious and social group. In recent years scholars have debated the extent to which these images conform to historical reality.[26] However, our concern is not with the merits of the historical arguments, but only with the image of the Besht as portrayed in *Shivhei ha-Besht*.

It is almost a truism that in traditional Jewish societies continuity with the past was more desirable than novelty and innovation. Thus, the Besht needed to be presented as a link in the chain of tradition rather than as a new type of leader who was different from those who preceded him. Part of the problem was that the Besht was indeed a new type of leader. Though he contained within himself aspects of earlier models like *baal shem* and mystical teacher, a role model was also needed who combined these characteristics as did the Besht. The Ari, as he was presented in the popular religious literature, is the figure that comes closest to the Besht in combining the same qualities within one person.

There is a pattern underlying these stories and they reflect an old and well-known tradition. It is a pattern already found in the Talmud, in which we find some connection and comparison between earlier and later figures who are seen as seminal. One of the best known Talmudic examples is the comparison of Rabbi Akiva with Moses in tractate *B. Menachot*, 29b. In the *Zohar* we find a significant number of deliberate comparisons between Rabbi Simeon bar Yohai and Moses. In some of these comparisons the author hints that Rabbi Simeon may have been even greater than Moses in some respects.[27]

In the same way, the editors of *Shivhei ha-Besht* tried to establish a clear and unambiguous linkage between the Besht and the Ari. The Besht is more than a follower of the Ari. He was the *gilgul* [transmigration] of the Ari for his generation. R. Aaron of Starosselje, the leading disciple of R. Shneur Zalman of Liadi, makes this point clearly. He argues that Hasidism was continuous with and based on the secret teachings of the Ari. In every generation, according to him, there was a central figure who was the chief teacher of his generation. This teacher's primary qualification was his association with his predecessor.[28] The connections between the Ari are both explicit and implicit, as we shall see. What makes R. Aaron's views particularly relevant is the association of the editors of *Shivhei ha-Besht* with the same Habad school of Hasidism.[29]

The printer of *Shivhei ha-Besht*, in his introduction, makes explicit the connection that he sees between *Shivhei ha-Besht* and *Shivhei ha-Ari*. He writes, "I realized all the benefits that would result from this printing. And as we know, the book *Shivhei ha-Ari*, God bless his memory, was also printed. There his disciple Rabbi Hayyim Vital, God bless his memory, also testified that it did not contain even a thousandth of his greatness."[30] Thus the very idea of collecting and printing the hagiographical biography of the Besht is justified because a similar biography had been written about the Ari.

Gedaliah Nigal lists almost thirty parallels between what is found about the Ari in *Shivhei ha-Ari* and about the Besht in *Shivhei ha-Besht*.[31] Some of these parallels are general ones that can be found regarding many figures and are not distinctive to these two heroes. For example, the announcement of the hero's birth by Elijah is a theme that can be traced back to the angel's announcement to Abraham and Sarah of the birth of Isaac. Many other parallels can also be considered standard aspects of Jewish hagiography. However, there are also some stories that connect the Ari and the Besht that cannot be attributed to standard motifs. These stories are designed to help the reader make the "connection" between the Ari and the Besht.

Several stories about the Besht illustrate this attempt to present him as the reincarnation of the Ari. First is the story about Rabbi Adam Baal Shem and the secret writings. Chone Shmeruk has shown that this story is based on a tale published in Prague in the seventeenth century and is not the invention of the editors of *Shivhei ha-Besht*.[32] That still does not explain why the story is included. The answer becomes apparent when we look at the legendary biography of the Ari.

According to the legends that crystallized in *Shivhei ha-Ari*, the hagiographical biography of the Ari, the Ari's mystical insights were based on a book of secret teachings. A merchant from a distant land came to Egypt, where the Ari was living. The merchant needed some help with the payment of customs duties, and in return for the Ari's father-in-law's absolving him of payment, he gave the Ari the mystical writings that he had in his possession. These turned out to be the *Zohar*, which the Ari then spent years studying alone in a hut by the Nile, coming home only for the Sabbath.[33] The story of the Ari's isolation in the hut should be familiar to the reader of *Shivhei ha-Besht*: like the Ari, the Besht spent many years in isolation studying the esoteric holy books that had been entrusted to him, although in his case the hut was in the deepest woods rather than along the banks of the Nile.[34]

The parallels between these stories are clear. Both men gained their insights from a mystical text and in both cases they had a heavenly mentor. Elijah appeared to the Ari and guided his studies; similarly, the Besht was visited by Ahijah the Shilonite, an obscure prophet who in rabbinic tradition was considered the teacher of Elijah.[35]

Ze'ev Gries has recently pointed out another important connection between the Besht and the Ari related to the R. Adam Baal Shem legend. *Shivhei ha-Besht* relates that the Besht sealed these writings in a stone in a mountain. As the story recounts, R. Aryeh Leib of Pollnoye revealed in his old age that he knew where these manuscripts were, but would not disturb them out of respect for the Besht. He also stated that these writings had been revealed only five times, and that they were in the hands of Abraham and Joshua ben Nun, but that he did not know who the others were.[36] It has been assumed that the Joshua ben Nun mentioned here was the biblical figure. However, Gries has suggested an alternate explanation. As he pointed out, there is no tradition of the biblical Joshua being a carrier of mystical traditions. There is another Joshua ben Nun, who does play an important role in the transmission of kabbalistic writings in sixteenth century Safed. Hayyim Vital, the custodian of the Lurianic literary corpus, guarded these writings jealously and would not share them, regardless of inducements. Once when Vital was very ill, Joshua ben Nun, who was very wealthy, bribed Vital's brother to obtain access to the writings and also paid for scribes to transcribe them. Thus, Gries argues that the Joshua ben Nun in the *Shivhei ha-Besht* story was the one from Safed. This also greatly strengthens the argument that the secret writings of the Besht were indeed Lurianic writings.[37]

Several stories directly connect the Besht with the Ari by attributing to the Besht theurgic powers that had previously been associated only with the Ari. Among the Ari's unique attributes was the ability to know a person's sins and to hear heavenly decrees.[38] Similar abilities were attributed to the Besht.[39] Both the Ari[40] and the Besht[41] were also able to provide a *tikkun,* a spiritual repair for a sin that prevented a person's soul from ascending to heaven after death. Another story that connects the Besht and the Ari is that of the frog in *Shivhei ha-Besht.* The Besht met a frog that was the transmigration of a scholar being punished for sin. Since this frog lived in an uninhabited place, his soul had not been redeemed by the Ari when he redeemed many others. The outcome of the story is that the Besht redeemed the frog, thus finishing the task begun by the Ari.[42] It also confirms that the Besht had the same theurgic powers as the Ari and was his worthy successor.

There is one further noteworthy connection between the Besht and the Ari. Both of them became public figures at the age of thirty-six. There are several versions of how the Besht's theurgic powers were revealed. According to one story, when the Besht and several others entered the room where a possessed woman was found, the spirit possessing her greeted each according to his deeds and status. However, the spirit said to the Besht that it is not afraid of him because it knew that he had been forbidden by heaven to utilize holy names and to practice as a *baal shem* before his thirty-sixth birthday.[43] In another story, the Besht was living in Tlust and earning a living as a teacher of small children. People began to sense that he had magical abilities, and sick people came to him for healing. Once a madman was brought to him, and he refused to see him. That night he was told in a dream that it was his thirty-sixth birthday. In the morning he made the calculations and discovered that the dream was correct. He cured the madman, left his teaching post, hired a scribe, and set out on his career as a *baal shem.*[44]

The turning point in both stories is the age of thirty-six. The Besht was restrained by heaven from starting his career before that age. What is the significance of thirty-six? Why not forty, an age with a long and distinguished pedigree as the age of transition?[45] The answer again is the Ari. Thirty-six is the age at which the Ari was told by Elijah to leave Egypt and go to Safed. It is only in Safed that the Ari becomes a public figure and spiritual teacher.

It is reasonable to assume that the editors of *Shivhei ha-Besht* expected their readers to be familiar with the allusions to the Ari in these stories and the connections they were trying to make between the Ari and the Besht. Stories about the Ari as healer and miracle worker were widespread in both the Hebrew and Yiddish literature of the period. Thus, we see that the stories about the Besht need to be taken seriously and not merely tossed aside as legends and folktales.

The identification of the Besht with the Ari fits the recent consensus of scholars of Hasidism that the Besht was a *baal shem* and a mystical teacher. However, there is one crucial difference between the Besht and the Ari. The Ari was a mystical teacher whose teachings were restricted to a small group of distinguished disciples and were not originally intended for public dissemination. The Besht, on the other hand, founded a movement that ultimately was able to unite all spiritual levels of Jewish society from the mystical elite to the simplest unlearned Jew.

NOTES

[1] The most informative overview of Safed in the sixteenth century remains S. Schechter, "Safed in the Sixteenth Century" in *Studies in Judaism* (second series; Philadelphia: Jewish Publication Society, 1908), 202-306. L. Fine, *Safed Spirituality* (Classics of Western Spirituality; Ramsey: Paulist, 1984), is also useful.

[2] *Lekha Dodi* was written by Rabbi Solomon Alkabetz (1505-1584), who introduced it to the Safed kabbalists.

[3] Ari is an acronym for R. Isaac Luria (1534-1572), and this is how he is referred to in the traditional sources.

[4] Besht is an acronym for "Baal Shem Tov" (1700-1760), and is the way he is usually referred to in hasidic sources.

[5] The two recent biographies—Moshe Rosman, *Founder of Hasidism: A Quest for the Historical Ba'al Shem Tov* (Berkeley: University of California Press, 1996), and Imanuel Etkes, *Ba'al ha-Shem: Magia, Mystica, Hanhagah* (Jerusalem: Merkaz Zalman Shazar le-toldot Yisra'el, 2000)—reach somewhat different conclusions about what we can know about the Besht and his teachings. However, collectively they have significantly advanced our understanding of the Besht and his milieu.

[6] First published in 1815. An English translation is Dan Ben-Amos and Jerome Mintz, eds. and trans., *In Praise of the Baal Shem Tov* (Bloomington: Indiana University Press, 1970).

[7] G. Nigal, "New Light on the Hasidic Tale and its Sources," in A. Rapoport-Albert, ed., *Hasidism Reappraised* (London: Vallentine Mitchell, 1996), 349.

[8] Among the scholars who have noted the parallels are Joseph Dan, *Ha-Sippur ha-Hasidi* (Jerusalem: Bet Hotsa'ah Keter Yerushalayim, 1975), 68-74; Gedalyah Nigal, *Ha-Siporet ha-Hasidit* (Jerusalem: Y. Markus, 1981), 26-27; and Ada Rapoport-Albert, "Hagiography with Footnotes: Edifying Tales and the Writing of History

in Hasidism," in *Essays in Jewish Historiography* (ed. A. Rapoport-Albert; Middletown: Wesleyan University Press, 1988), 123.

[9] Moshe Idel, *Hasidism: Between Ecstasy and Magic* (Albany, 1995), deals with this issue extensively.

[10] Moshe Idel, "Perceptions of Kabbalah in the Second Half of the Eighteenth Century," *Journal of Jewish Thought and Philosophy* 1 (1991): 55-114.

[11] He was an immigrant to Safed from Moravia who wrote several letters to a friend in Krakow during 1602-1609. These letters were first published in Joseph Solomon Delmegido, *Ta'alumot Hokhmah* (Basel, 1629).

[12] Many of these stories can now be found in English translation in two volumes by Aryeh Wineman: *Beyond Appearances: Stories from the Kabbalistic Ethical Writings* (Philadelphia: Jewish Publication Society, 1989), and *Ethical Tales from the Kabbalah* (Philadelphia: Jewish Publication Society, 1999).

[13] On the history of this literature and its dissemination, see Meir Benayahu, *Sefer Toldot ha-Ari* (Jerusalem: Makhon Ben-Tsevi be-Universitah ha-'Ivrit, 1967). An English translation of *Shivhei ha-Ari* can be found in A. Klein, *Tales in Praise of the ARI* (trans. J. Machlowitz; Philadelphia: Jewish Publication Society, 1970).

[14] Meir Benayahu, "Shivhei ha-Ari be-Yiddish," *Areshet* 4 (1966): 481-489.

[15] *Ma'ase ha-Shem* was first published in Frankfurt am Main, 1691, and republished several times in the next century. On the author, see *Encyclopedia Judaica* (*EJ*) (vol. 2; Jerusalem: Keter, 1970), 492-93.

[16] A second century tanna. Authorship of the *Zohar* was traditionally ascribed to him.

[17] Venice, 1587. One of the most important Jewish chronicles, by Gedalia ibn Yahyah. See, *EJ*, vol. 8, 1,208-209.

[18] The primary text of Lurianic Kabbalah.

[19] The *Zohar Hadash* is part of the Zoharic corpus. *Emek ha-Melekh* (Amsterdam, 1648) is a kabbalistic treatise that contains many stories about the Ari.

[20] Chava Turniansky, "Yiddish Literature in Frankfurt am Main," in *Juedische Kultur in Frankfurt am Main* (ed. Karl Erich Groezinger; Wiesbaden: Harrassowitz, 1997), 276.

[21] It was first published in Hebrew in Frankfurt, 1705. It was translated into Yiddish and published in 1709. Subsequently, it was reprinted many times in both languages and remains in print to the present day.

[22] Moshe Idel, "On Rabbi Zvi Hirsh Koidanover's Sefer Qav ha-Yashar," in *Juedische Kultur*, 125.

[23] Frankfurt, 1704, and several reprints.

[24] Frankfurt, 1707, and several reprints.

[25] Idel, "Qav ha-Yashar," 125.

[26] See the biographies mentioned above, n. 5. See also the review essay by Ze'ev Gries, "Demuto ha-Historit shel ha-Besht," *Kabbalah: Journal for the Study of Jewish Mystical Texts* 5 (2000): 411-46.

[27] Boaz Huss, "Hakham Adif mi-Navi: R. Shimon bar Yohai ve-Moshe Rabenu ba-Zohar," *Kabbalah: Journal for the Study of Jewish Mystical Texts* 4 (1999): 103-39.

[28] Rosman, *Founder of Hasidism*, 190.

[29] *Ibid.*, chapter 12, analyzes this connection.

[30] *In Praise of the Baal Shem Tov*, 2.

[31] Nigal, *Ha-Siporet*, 26-27.

[32] Chone Shmeruk, "Ha-Sippurim al R. Adam Baal Shem ve-Gilguleihem be-Nushaot Sefer Shivhei ha-Besht," *Zion* 28 (1963): 86-105.

[33] *Shivhei ha-Ari* (Jerusalem, 1998), 3-4 (chap. 2).

[34] *In Praise of the Baal Shem Tov*, 34.

[35] Abraham Rubenstein, "Al Rabo shel ha-Besht ve-al ha-Ketavim she-Mehem Lamad ha-Besht," *Tarbiz* 42 (1979): 146-58.

[36] *In Praise of the Baal Shem Tov*, 32.

[37] Ze'ev Gries, "Bein Sifrut le-Historia: Hakdamot le-Diun ve-Iyyun be-Shivhei ha-Besht," *Tura* 3 (1994): 162-65.

[38] *Toldot ha-Ari*, 157.

[39] *In Praise of the Baal Shem Tov*, 231-33.

[40] *Toldot ha-Ari*, 236.

[41] *In Praise of the Baal Shem Tov*, 96-98.

[42] *Ibid.*, 24-26.

[43] *Ibid.*, 34-35.

[44] *Ibid.*, 36.

[45] Among the important figures for whom forty was the transitional age were Moses, Rabbi Johanan ben Zakkai, and Rabbi Akiva.

Spirituality Into a New Millennium:
Mysticism in Jewish Art

Ori Z. Soltes

SACER AND PROFANUS

Religion presupposes an opposition between the life of the everyday—the safely circumscribed, the familiar and knowable, the human—and a realm beyond the human: unknowable, fraught with both hope and fear, with both positive and negative possibilities. That realm, so rigorously separated from the profane of the day-to-day is referred to in English as the "sacred."

Our understanding of the opposition between sacred and profane is better served if we use the Latin antecedents of these terms, *sacer* and *profanus*. For, whereas "sacred" and "profane" tend, particularly when juxtaposed, to offer positive and negative connotations, it is critical to the understanding of mysticism to recognize the intrinsic neutrality of these concepts.

Indeed, the *profanus*, as the Romans used the term, is simply the realm of the familiar—the known and/or knowable—the everyday in all its aspects. *Sacer* is the unknown and/or unknowable, the intrinsically unpredictable. Wilderness, night, sleep, dreams, death, and divinity are all aspects of the *sacer*. When we sleep, will we have a sweet dream, a nightmare, or none? In death, will we go to heaven, to hell, or nowhere? Will the gods bless us, curse us, or not respond at all? Religion addresses the most disturbing aspect of the *sacer*, divinity. It is disturbing because, having created us, it can destroy us (or so we assume) and it cannot be fathomed. It is inherently unpredictable.

It is the purpose and province of religion to address the *sacer*. Religious rites and rituals regulate our traversal of the boundaries between *profanus* and *sacer*, structuring the process with minutely detailed care so as to insure a positive response from that realm towards our own. Priestly beings—sacerdotes—are those who are assumed by their constituents to possess the knowledge of what rituals, rites, and behavior to prescribe. Every tradition is guided by such individuals: Abraham, Moses, Jesus, Muhammad,

Buddha, the Baha'ullah are all exemplars; so, too, the priest in the Jerusalem Temple, in the Sumerian Ziqqurat, or in the Temple to Jupiter in Rome.

The *sacer* is boundless and shapeless. Nonetheless, we address it in precisely bounded and shaped spaces (a Temple, an altar, a Ziqqurat, a synagogue, a church, a mosque), at precisely bounded and shaped times (sunset, sunrise, noon, midnight), and by way of precisely prescribed rituals. It is as if, in so defining these aspects (times, places, methods) of addressing the *sacer*, we might render its unfathomability accessible; as if its intrinsic unpredictable chaos might be ordered to our limited understanding of it.

Every religion prescribes precise times within precise spaces for the precise rituals that define the relationship between the *profanus* (in this case, the community of each such religion) and the sense of *sacer* that it addresses. Thus, for Judaism, Shabbat begins precisely at sunset and ends precisely when, after sunset, three stars appear in the sky. One enters and exits this *sacer* time, celebrated within *sacer* space (the synagogue or the home) by means of precisely prescribed ritual: candle-lighting, wine, bread of a special sort.

Moreover, the centered *sacer* spaces that one enters to celebrate religious ritual are all analogues of, and connected to, an ultimate centering point for the cosmos. The far-flung *profanus* (in the sense of community) of Judaism centers around synagogues as surrogates of the destroyed Temple in Jerusalem. When that edifice still stood, the *sacer* space of the Temple was the bounded and prescribed center of the Israelite-Judaean community. They understood it to be connected to the centering point found within the boundless, centerless *sacer*. As the Holy of Holies in the Temple in Jerusalem was for Israelite-Judaeans, so the Omphalos at Delphi was for Greeks, and so the Great Ziqqurat with its temple of the moon god, Sin, for Sumerians. They are all, within their traditions, centering points connecting *profanus* (the community) to *sacer* (its god or gods).

RELIGION AND MYSTICISM

Religion, then, presupposes a complex of ideas asserting the existence of a *sacer*. Mysticism may be understood as a particularly intense aspect of religious experience, a particular means of traversing the boundary into relationship with the *sacer*. The term "mysticism", related to the word mystery, derives from the Latin *mysterium,* that in turn derives from the Greek *mysterion*, rooted in the Greek verb *mystein* meaning "to close" or, by extension, "to hide." The *mysterion* is the closed, hidden center of the *sacer* that the mystic seeks to enter and to which the mystical method offers access. That method is itself intrinsically hidden: the mystic hopes to travel hidden paths, to absorb hidden knowledge of how to interpret and understand the world by transcending its bounds into communion with the *sacer* that engendered our world.

Mysticism, then, presupposes that, within the deep recesses of the *sacer*, its ultimate essence is hidden. This ultimate unknown is the wholly transcendent, wholly other that is beyond the intelligible and beyond normative religious ritual. It can be sought only by carefully and precisely prescribed methods particular even within precisely prescribed normative religious method and sensibility.

Mysticism, moreover, implies a personalized communion with the *sacer*, as opposed to normative religious experience with its emphasis on the group—particularly in Judaism. The mystic who succeeds achieves ecstasy—*ek stasis* in Greek, meaning "out of (an ordinary state of) being." Such a person stands outside the normal, *profanus* being, bursting boundaries via a method that carries beyond the normative patterns of logic and intuition.

Mystics, if they would merge with the center of the *sacer*, must be in perfect equilibrium within themselves, centered as the cosmos is, a pivot that spins without wobbling, so that, traveling beyond *profanus* self, they are able to return to that self without being harmed by the experience. One of the salient features of Jewish mysticism is the obligation of mystics to return to the *profanus* and to benefit the community of which they remain a part with whatever insights have been gained in communion with the unknown.

JEWISH MYSTICISM

As Judaism evolved, the God of Israel came to be understood as ubiquitous, all-powerful, all-knowing, singular, invisible, indescribable, and ineffable. The issue, for Jewish mysticism, of addressing and merging with such an utterly other *sacer* engages obvious and emphatic paradoxes. Since the God of Israel, the *sacer* of Judaism, is by definition seamless, singular, indivisible, then Jewish mysticism engenders a contradiction in supposing that there is a center within the *sacer* with which the mystic may aspire to merge.

But several distinctly paradoxic features characterize Jewish mysticism. In large part because of the heavy communal emphasis within Judaism, we find the obligation to the *profanus* previously referred to, even for the mystic. We rarely find within Jewish mysticism images of mystics alone on a mountaintop in never-ending, isolated personal communion with God.

Central to Judaism is the sense of covenantal relationship between *sacer* and *profanes*—between God and Israel as a sacred community, Israel as a *sacer-profanus*. This sense naturally extends even more intensely to the relationship between God and the Jewish mystic. Thus there is strong emphasis, within Jewish mysticism, on the idea that the mystical initiate, at the *profanus-sacer* border, is pulled over at the moment of mystical revelation. The initiate prepares himself for that moment, but the moment comes from the *sacer*. The aspirant to contact with the inner hiddenness of God prepares himself according to the proper method, with awe, love, yearning, concentration, but—and this is the paradox—ultimately the choice is God's to pull him into that center.

The guide for proper preparation, effectively the bridge between God and Israel, is the Torah, the Five Books of Moses. All matters regarding the prescribed patterns of behavior for a community that wishes to exist in a covenantal relationship with the *sacer*, to be a *sacer profanus*, will be found there. So will the answer to the ultimate question: how is it that an invisible, intangible, singular, seamless, inaccessible, transcendent, all-good God engendered a reality—our world—that is visible, tangible, multifarious, seamed, accessible, immanent, a mixture of good and evil?

The long history of Jewish mysticism is the history of an intense and varied response to this ultimate question. It is the history of an intense superrational inquiry into the *sacer*. It is, in a fundamental sense, an ongoing exploration of the Torah that holds the answer to all questions. The Torah, after all, reports to us the process of Creation: "In the beginning, God created...and God said, 'let there be...' and there was." Yet that answer gives us only the surface; the mystic seeks the center of the centerless or centered *sacer* hidden deep below the surface of the text.

THE SIGNIFICANCE OF LETTERS AND NUMBERS: *MERKAVAH*

The roots of Jewish mystical writing are, not surprisingly, in the Bible itself. Moses stands on *sacer* ground before a bush that burns but is not consumed and that exemplifies the paradoxic nature of the *sacer*: it is the symbol of his intense, elemental confrontation with a God who identifies itself as pure Being. Isaiah experiences the *sacer* as strange, indescribable beings intoning "Holy, holy, holy is the LORD of Hosts." Ezekiel, in a vision by the riverside, sees an extraordinary, extraterrestrial "something" that subsequently comes to be thought of as a Throne-Chariot [*merkavah*]. Within the normative prophetic experience of contact with the *sacer*, these individuals in these moments experience something even more intense, more abnormal. Their experiences of *sacer* become the paradigm for the mystical experience in the generations that follow, long after the prophetic experience is assumed to be no longer possible.

It is in the era of post-prophecy, of post-Temple destruction, and of the crystallizing of Judaism that questions of existence, beginning from and returning to the question of Creation, engender the first formal Jewish mystical texts. To no less a figure than Rabbi Akiva is ascribed the *Sefer Yetzirah* [The Book of Creation, or, more precisely, The Book of Formation], wherein a solution to the problem of how a singular God engendered a multifarious universe is offered. That text suggests that God created the universe through thirty-two conduits—namely, the ten numbers and twenty-two Hebrew letters.

Contemplation of the letters and numbers can lead towards the *sacer*, provided it is undertaken with the utmost concentration and according to carefully prescribed methodology. Because God is unknowable, God's name, ineffable since the destruction of the Temple, is somewhat less unknowable. Yet God's name is made up of knowable letters, as is the entirety of the Torah, God's word to us intermediated by Moses at Sinai. If we concentrate on the letters in a particular, properly prescribed manner, we may come to understand the inner, hidden recesses of the words that comprise Torah wisdom. We may even enter into an understanding of God's name and ultimately approach the outer edge of the surface of God itself.

In the earliest phase of Jewish mysticism known as *merkavah* mysticism (named for Ezekiel's vision of the so-called *merkavah* and extending in its development perhaps from the fifth to the tenth centuries), the awesome qualities of God, that is to say, God's transcendence, are emphasized by a further focus on "ten-ness." Specifically, *merkavah* mysticism speaks of the ten heavens or *hechalot* [chambers] through which one passes in ascending towards contact with God or in descending from the *mysterion* into touch with our reality.

KABBALAH

By contrast with *merkavah* mysticism, the later, better-known phase of Jewish mysticism called Kabbalah emphasizes the paradoxical closeness to us of God, God's immanence. The God more distant than the most distant star is as close as our own breathing. The most famous text of Kabbalah is the *Zohar* [Book of Splendor], in which the love relationship between God and Israel is emphasized. This text is an extensive and meandering six-volume collection of midrashim on wide-ranging subjects, not a systematic presentation of a doctrine. Thus we extract its principles, issues, and ideas by reaching here and there within it.

The *Zohar*, ascribed by tradition to a contemporary of Rabbi Akiva, Shimeon bar Yohai, was no doubt authored or collated in the early thirteenth century by Moses de Leon.[1] To the paradoxically male aspect of the genderless God of Israel, the Zohar offers the concept of the Shechinah, the paradoxically female aspect. To the absolutely singular God, the Shechinah suggests an unexpectedly divisible aspect. God. In God's male *elohim* aspect, God drives Adam and Eve from the Garden of Eden and allows the exile of the House of Israel from its Land; in God's female Shechinah aspect, God goes out into exile with Adam and Eve and with their descendants. The meaning of the Hebrew term Shechinah is "indwelling"; it emphasizes the closeness of God to us even as it presents that aspect of ever-presence.

The *Zohar*, as with *Sefer Yetzirah* and *merkavah* mysticism, is concerned with creation, with the relationship between humans and the world and between the world and the God that made it. The "ten-ness" of the earlier doctrines is transformed into ten qualities, called *spherot*. The doctrine of the *spherot* (ten entities, concepts, or ideas), from *malchut* [kingdom] below to *keter* [crown] above, suggests the divine creative process through a series of lightning-like flashes from God through the *spherot* to ourselves. But they also suggest a bridge between God and ourselves: the center around which the universe revolves, connecting heaven and earth. Furthermore, we also ascend through the *spherot*, arriving at the uppermost reaches of *keter* to find ourselves at the lowest reaches of the *eyn sof* [the endless], the outermost fringe of the outermost edge of the most distant veil of the most hidden recess of God. *Malchut* only touches our reality; once we have begun the ascent through the *spherot* to *keter*, we have already begun the ascent through the tenfold aspects of the aspectless God itself.

These different understandings of what the *spherot* represent coexist: it is not one understanding or another; it is all simultaneously. Their coexistence is another symptom of the paradox defining the attempt at contact between *sacer* and *profanus* as it is set forth in Jewish mysticism.

The *spherot* are sometimes represented in the image of a tree and sometimes superimposed over the image of a man. One might say that Jewish mysticism inherently lends itself to the possibilities of visual imagery: the *spherot* are the macrocosmos of the world consonant with the microcosmos of humanity, creation on the grand scale and the human scale. These features are ranged in threes, left and right, around a central axis of four *spherot*. Left and right are often described as representing female and male aspects of reality, of humankind, and of God. Yet God is aspectless and genderless. Further, the *spherot* must be understood as swirling and spinning at such a rate that there is no discernable right and left, no male and female. This perfectly spinning concept is like that forever spinning yet steady and perfectly centered pivot that not only connects earth and heaven, but must also define the mystics who would contemplate these concepts if they are not to go mad.

The dangers of mystical contemplation are indeed many: madness, apostasy, even death. If one succeeds in losing one's self entirely within the utterly other, subsuming one's self completely into that alien realm, crossing over into the *sacer* with one's entire being, will one ever be able to come back? If one returns with mind, soul, and body intact, will one then be able to communicate the ineffable experience of that realm? It is no wonder that, throughout most of Jewish history, Jewish leadership has discouraged most seekers from engaging in mystical study and contemplation.

In the sixteenth century, Kabbalah found two new directions in far-separated Safed and Prague. In Safed, Rabbi Isaac Luria, known as the Ari,[2] evolved an esoteric system including the idea that the primordial goodness was smashed the moment when Adam and Eve disobeyed God's word and scattered like tiny sparks throughout creation. Those sparks are embedded in every human soul as the God-ness within it; when we die, our souls are reincarnated again and again. Therefore, an individual whose purity and righteousness is such that he is called a *tzadik* [righteous one] is inspired by God in a particular manner to perceive that spark in everyone. He can recognize our past lives and know us in a way that we cannot even know ourselves.

Judah Loew, living in Prague at approximately the same time, was also evolving more and more esoteric systems of Kabbalah. He is said to have used his extraordinary esoteric knowledge to emulate God itself, in creating a golem, an anthropoid formed out of formless earth. The Golem of Prague became a gigantic protector of the Jewish community and a piece of Bohemian folklore shared by Jews and non-Jews into our own time.

MASTERING THE GOOD NAME: HASIDISM

One of the essential features of Jewish mysticism is the necessity of absolute aloneness. Mystics must ultimately abandon even their own selves to accomplish union with the *sacer*. Surely, then, disconnection from everyone else would seem to be another requisite. Yet the Jewish mystic is obligated to return to the *profanus*, the community, to share with others whatever esoteric knowledge was gained through communion with that other realm. In this way, the group benefits from the accession into the *mysterion* of the one. Moses, Akiva, Shimeon Bar Yochai, Moses de Leon, Isaac Luria, Judah Loew, Israel Ba'al Shem Tov, each had to bring that realm into ours, to infuse the *profanus* with the *sacer*.

One with the power to connect with the Name to effect positive results for his community was the Master of the Good Name or Ba'al Shem Tov. This phrase attaches itself most commonly to Israel ben Eliezer, founder of the latest phase of Jewish mysticism, *hasidut,* begun in Eastern Europe nearly two and a half centuries ago. The Ba'al Shem is the paradigm of the *tzadik* or righteous leader, who possesses all the esoteric knowledge of communion with the *sacer* that centuries of mystical tradition can possibly have yielded, and at the same time is more down-to-earth than a next-door neighbor. In one sense *hasidut* represents the ultimate development of Jewish mysticism, not merely historically, but conceptually: it is the ultimate form of the multi-layered paradox of dualistic monotheism and social esotericism.

Hasidut teaches that its leader can ascend to the throne of heaven at will, yet remains rooted at all times in the community. He ascends through the most esoteric of properly prescribed, ineffable, formulaic means, yet his rootedness makes him the humblest of leaders who imbues the smallest act, even tying his shoe, with sacred significance. When he speaks to his followers, each feels as if he speaks to him or her alone. The *tzadik,* intermediary between God and the Hasidic community, is both like the *profanus*, humble and impoverished, and the *sacer*, God itself. Indeed, to his constituency the *tzadik* is the ultimate meeting point of *sacer* and *profanus*. He is the pole connecting heaven and earth, spinning perfectly without wobbling.

In his presumed ability to enter into and commune with the innermost essence of God, the *tzadik* offers the ultimate in esoteric accomplishment. The relationship that he achieves with the Center of all being, conveyed by his mastery of the ineffable Name of God, makes it possible for him to accomplish miracles. He does so for those needful within the community (the *profanus*) of which he is a part, for the *tzadik* has no meaning apart from the community of his Hasidim. Like God itself, he is simultaneously distantly apart from and a part of that *sacer profanus*. *Hasidut* offers Jewish mysticism as a discipline held together by the flame of enthusiasm and concentrated intention [*kavannah*] that connects the Hasid to the Other and transforms his interior world from a muddy gray reality into a glorious Kingdom of God.

The *tzadik* teaches that God may be found throughout creation, but this is neither polytheism nor pantheism; rather, it is panhenotheism, the one God found in all of creation, in every person, animal, tree, rock. The tricky part is to recognize and worship the divine presence [Shechinah] within all the elements of creation without worshipping the elements themselves.

The instruments of connection and transformation are often the letters that comprise God's Name and, by extension, all the letters that make up the words of the Torah, which letters take on a life and character of their own. They become flesh-and-blood concepts, their very shapes part not of abstract arbitrariness, but of divine intention [*kavannah*]. They become inflamed umbilical tissue connecting heaven and earth, shaped and reshaped by the soul of the *tzadik* and the souls of his Hasidim.

MYSTICISM AND JEWISH ART

Jewish mysticism, then, has developed over the course of Jewish history, never leaving the ground upon which it began, the question of how God created the universe and all the ramifications of that question, yet ever soaring toward new conceptual heights. The most important of these ramifications is why God created us and what our God-given purpose is. Jewish mysticism seeks the center of Godness in pursuit of the answer. It is fraught with all the paradoxes derived from the essential paradox of the Jewish sense of God, that God is simultaneously distant and near. As Jewish mysticism evolved in ever more esoteric directions, it turned ultimately down to earth, while pushing up towards heaven. The *tzadik* pushes further and further out into the reaches of the *sacer* as he is obligated with greater and greater assertiveness to remain rooted within the *profanus*.

The Other, with which religion in general and mysticism in particular wrestle, is both unfathomable and ultimately inaccessible, and yet it is entered in its oxymoronic accessibility through different doorways. One of the obvious entryways is language, but words, even as they extend us, are also limited. Words offer an instrument for apprehending the world, but there are many aspects of our world for which words prove inadequate. Within the human realm, they obfuscate as much as communicate. As a uniquely human instrument, they will by definition not be overly useful in addressing realms beyond the human.

Art is another means with which humans have long sought to communicate and with which we seek to understand, to fathom, the Other. Music, dance, and visual art can transcend words, carrying both their maker and their audience towards that super-verbal realm of the Other that is addressed by religion generally and mysticism in particular. Visual art has been, through most of human history and across most of human geography, a handmaiden of religion. Art has functioned as a visual concomitant of the verbal instruments of religion (such as myth and prayer) in addressing, describing, and seeking to apprehend divinity. Both kinds of instruments seek to represent divinity, to explore its relationship with humanity, and to point out what it is that the creative forces wish from us to assure that we are furthered rather than destroyed by them.

In the course of religious history, the artist has been a figure whose position is analogous to that of the priest and the prophet. An artist functions as a *sacerdos* in mediating between humanity and divinity, in representing and interpreting that other realm. From Neolithic fertility figurines and Sumerian priest-figures to medieval sculptures and Baroque paintings, art has addressed the other realm. This role has acquired a different nuance in the art of the West over the past three centuries or so. With increased secularization in western society, increased secularization of subject matter for artists has also become apparent. That change accelerated during the past century, as western art has moved from narrative to landscape to cubist breakdown to absolute abstraction.

Yet artists remain sacerdotal in the sense that they may be viewed as inspired (in-spirited) from that other realm (even as the Other is increasingly construed as internal rather than external, mind-derived rather than God-derived). They remain intermediaries, guiding the viewer to see with eyes not limited by ordinary reality, creating, as God creates, by transforming reality into a new microcosmic formation on the canvas or in the sculpted form. On the other hand, in our own time—perhaps, in part, in response to the spiritual emptiness that secularization offers to many—there have evolved many artists who choose as their explicit subject matter the Other and its concomitants. Such artists return to that centuries' long tradition of art as a handmaiden of religion, albeit often by way of radically untraditional visual routes.

The role of the artist as *sacerdos* becomes even more intense when his or her subject is that central aspect of the Other addressed by mysticism. For a Jewish artist, the attempt to address that hiddenmost center of the invisible Other in visual terms is an absolute oxymoron. It challenges the capacity to visualize the invisible as it focuses on the center of a centerless Other that cannot be located even as it may be found. There is further paradox in the fact that visualization can be and in some ways has been a consistent part of Jewish mystical thinking throughout history.

CHARLES STERN AND THE SACRED LETTERS

Charles Stern offers the Hebrew letters grown to gigantic proportions, pulled off the page, and transformed into massive sculptures of Texas cream limestone. The notion, fundamental to Jewish mystical thinking, of the relationship between macrocosm (the universe) and microcosm (all of the universe's constituent parts, but particularly the human body and soul) is concretized by these works.

By way of the *Sefer Yetzirah* each letter may be seen to contain the potential universe in microcosm. Each letter has power and possibility beyond its presence as a series of marks in the Torah scrolls. Each sets forth the Creation and defines the relationship between the Creator and the created, but how can one look beneath the surface of the letters to find the hidden meanings that they contain? For Stern the answer is clear: lift them from the text and magnify them, so that one metaphorically turns the Torah, with its words, letters, and their meanings, around and around in an attempt to understand them. The letters as three-dimensional sculptures are thus encircled and encircling as the viewer tries to see them from all angles.

Each letter contains more than itself: *Aleph* [fig. 1], the first letter of the Hebrew alphabet, proclaims God's unity because it is the first letter of the Hebrew word *ehad* [one]. More than that, it is the beginning of the beginning. God's unity, which precedes Creation and is most essential to our reality, begins the beginning of reality by creating the Torah. According to the Jewish mystical tradition, Torah precedes reality; the Torah, in turn, is written in the Hebrew alphabet, in which *aleph* is the beginning. Thus, *aleph* proclaims beginning-ness that is God's One-ness.

Bet [fig. 2], the second letter, is offered as "Blessing." Its "head" inclines on a horizontal, as if in prayerful recitation of a blessing, and it is the first letter of the Hebrew word *bracha*, which means "blessing." That in turn is related to *berech*, meaning "knee"; while a blessing is what, when we are fortunate, we receive as a gift from the *sacer*, it is also a description of our act of acknowledgement of the power of the *sacer* as we bend our knee in prayer. Together, of course, *aleph* and *bet* became their Greek counterparts, *alpha* and *beta*, and the basis, subsequently, for the term we use to refer to

fig. 1 *Aleph*

fig. 2 *Bet*

all the letters together: alphabet. As such, they are the beginning of that essential aspect of human development. They offer the blessing of immortality to words and ideas that might die with their speakers were they not written down.

Lamed [fig. 3] is the first letter of the root of words pertaining to "learning." The secret it contains is that of learning, of studying the Torah and all its concomitant literatures and interpretations in order to fathom its depths, to understand how to live one's life in the shadow of the covenant set forth in the Torah, and to maintain a connection with the ultimate source of blessing and curse—and be blessed thereby.

Each letter of the alphabet hides its own gigantic secrets, and all of Stern's letters are adorned with the crowning nodules with which particular letters in the Torah are decorated. For we don't merely read the Torah, we chant it. We sing its words in melodies, the notes for which are hinted at in the particulars of such adornments, the antiquity of which sweeps Jews back across history. The letters are not, then, merely letters, any more than in Stern's hands they are merely sculptures. They are the concretization of the abstract relationship between *sacer* and *profanus*. They are thick ropes of connective tissue between God and Israel.

JANE LOGEMANN AND LETTERS/WORDS/IDEAS

Jane Logemann's work is constructed with layers and with layers of letters. The rows of letters or words over which subtle pigments are washed may be viewed as simple abstractions and plays of line and color (objective art for its own aesthetic sake), while at the same time they may be read in terms of their content and message (subjective art connected to issues outside the canvas frame). As the works themselves are diversely evocative to the viewer, the sources of inspiration to the artist are diverse.

In scale, Logemann's work is the opposite of Stern's: much of it is contrived of tiny Hebrew letters or whole words repeated again and again across a page. Three issues are apparent in this. First, the word has become image—in two-dimensional, subtly colored format, rather than the sculpted format of Stern's work. At the same time, it offers entire words or even whole texts, broadening the idea to play on the notion of the people of the text (the People of the Book) as a people of the image. Letters and the words that they comprise become patterns: vertical, horizontal and diagonal strokes, rectilinear and curvilinear forms within a visual context of subtle pigment.

fig. 3 *Lamed*

fig. 4 *Landscape*

Second, the focus on the words and letters in a mesmerizing repetitiousness offers the viewer a visual analogue to the kind of focused concentration on sounds and syllables prescribed for the mystic in several Jewish mystical systems. The words, even as they have meaning that the artist wants to stress, cease to have meaning as they return to where they began as pure pattern and shape. They become non-sense, transcending normative *profanus* sense, pushing the one who focuses on them towards that beyondness the center of which the mystic seeks.

Third, the contemporary secularized and universalized context of these works, recalling as an aural analogue contemporary music such as that of Phillip Glass means that Logemann's work is simultaneously embedded in the Jewish mystical tradition and directed toward much wider circles.

One might say that Logemann's work, *in imitatio dei*, builds from the smallest elements to the larger: she moves from a series on the Hebrew letters to one on particular Hebrew words (which she then intersects in universalist fashion by works using parallel words in other languages and other traditions, notably Arabic, Russian, Korean, and Japanese), to one on a complete text, the Kaddish, to one that is devoid of words or letters and comprised of pure color and form.

Words that are simply part of our world may be viewed as reconceived according to the tenets of Jewish mysticism. The *"Plant-life"* series, for example, which uses Hebrew, Russian, Korean, and Japanese to create abstract word-patterns of plants, acts on the impulse that the letters are the conduits of Creation and are therefore the essence of the words. The words in turn contain the essence of the objects to which they are attached. In the case of plants, this is, of course, the natural world itself, which, as opposed to the technological world of human contrivance, is God-created and apprehended by humans by means of the words and names that we attach to it.

Word, image, and idea intersect in the realm of relationship between realms. The word *Landscape* [fig. 4] is repeated against a pale green wash, suggesting grass against which the lettered pattern is the endlessly same yet individualized wind-swept grass stalks. The yellow ground for *Leopard* offers the hint of the animal's silky pelt, with repeating black marks that repeat the name: "leopard." This is at once the mysticism of the microcosm implanted within the macrocosm and the contemporary aesthetic of representation through abstract symbolism. It is thus rooted simultaneously in a specific aspect of centuries-old Jewish thinking and in a specific aspect of current art theory.

Logemann's work is impelled not only by the *sacer* but by the *profanus*, not only by spirituality and aesthetics but by politics: words selected for parallel works in Hebrew and Arabic are clearly laden with implications for the war and peace process of the Middle East in the second half of the twentieth century. *Sea* [fig. 5] intersperses the sinuousness of Arabic script with the blockiness of Hebrew print to imply the motion of the waters. The sea bounds the Middle East, and water, salty and desalinated, defines its continued existence. More direct still is a work called *Co-existence* [fig. 6], in which the Hebrew and Arabic words are serialized side-by-side against pale colors. They coexist on either side of a visual border; the message is simply and straightforwardly set forth by the medium.

Logemann's work makes the viewer aware of the process of creating it: one cannot look at these works without being conscious of the slow, painstaking concentration [*kavannah*] involved. In this sense these works, which identify her as what one might call a meditative devotee of visual *hasidut*, also offer two particular directions of secularized visual thinking, one ancient, the other contemporary. The calligraphic component associates these multi-lingual expressions with cultures in which writing is an old, respected art form (not surprisingly, she has chosen languages whose writing systems relate to that sensibility). So, too, the subtle modulations of color connect them to Paul Klee as well as to Ad Reinhardt; the minimalist gestural quality of the marks that make up the letters and words, as well as the conceptual underpinnings, connects them to Sol LeWitt. This latter aspect of her oeuvre is even more obvious in those works that have no letters at all, but are purely exercises in color and its modulations.

One aspect of the kabbalistic connection for Logemann is the power of the Hebrew letters to connect us, the creation, to the Creator. At the same time, the physical nature of her writing (simple and uncalligraphic) reminds us of the copybooks in which little children learning the alphabet repeat letters whose forms they seek to master. This suggests growth and development of the human from childhood to adulthood, connecting the notion of the growth and development of writing itself to the growth of the universe from the point at which creation began. Paradoxically, there is something intensely kabbalistic in the thinking that underlies her work and something modernist in the presentation of the idea of process as part of the art itself.

The bridge between the *Book of Formation* and the idea of *kavannah* is composed of many planks. Perhaps the most essential is that of the twelfth century Rhineland group of mystics known as the *hasidei ashkenaz*, whose

fig. 5 *Sea*

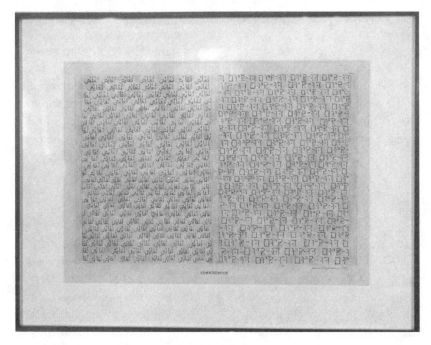

fig. 6 *Co-Existence*

notion of the potency of words and their constituent letters is foundational to the emphasis on concentration on the letters and words that is a centering point of the east European *hasidut* of the eighteenth century. The *hasidei ashkenaz* focused ongoing contemplation and repetitive recitation onto particular combinations of letters, maintained an intense care in the pronunciation of every phoneme in every word of prayer; and prolonged the articulation of the sounds of prayer-words and phrases in the correct order, so as to intensify the inward seeking that connects the devotee to the ultimate celestial reality.

Within Logemann's work, perhaps the ultimate exercise in graduated visual devotion (with its conceptual concomitant of ascent towards the celestial realm) is offered by her stunning series, *Kaddish* [fig. 7]. Here the various elements of her enterprise come together. The text of the Kaddish is repeated in Aramaic letters that sandwich a Latin (English)-letter transliteration, all within a circular frame. The circle, without beginning or end, bespeaks the notion of continuum that is essential to the idea of the Kaddish, both as the mourner's prayer it has become over time and as an affirmation of faith in God's goodness and greatness. This is how it originated and is how and why it came to be used as a mourner's prayer: it pronounces the faith in God and the continuum, even when the moment of grief at the loss of a loved one would undermine that faith.

Logemann's rendition of the Kaddish is framed by a repeating Hebrew alphabet—each line a letter from beginning to end, then beginning again and continuing until the rectangular frame that frames the circular frame of the Kaddish runs out. This sense that it continues, that not only the letters repeat themselves, but that the lines of letters and the entire alphabet repeat beyond the picture frame ad infinitum, is paramount. Moreover, across the ten-image series, the circle within the rectangle shifts, upwards and downwards within the picture plane, as the color (whitish to grey that is almost white, towards grey and grey that is almost black to blackish) modulates in harmony with the shifting of the circular form within the series.

Thus the letters are building blocks to contrive this microcosm, corresponding to the letters that engendered the macrocosm. The ten parts of the series correspond to the ten ascents and descents of the *hechalot* that define the relationship between heaven and earth. They correspond to the ten statements known in English as The Ten Commandments, the heart of the Torah received at Sinai. The concentrated, repetitive focus on the ultimate statement of prayerful connection to God corresponds to the

fig. 7 *Kaddish*

devotional ethos of the *hasidei ashkenaz*, and the concentrated repetition of the letters that frame this statement correspond to the pregnant-with-life focus of the later, eighteenth century Hasidim. The rhythmic graduated color and form shift points to contemporary minimalism in visual art, but also in music and dance. The artist is simple child and sophisticated intermediary between realms. The viewer observes her creation, is aware of the process of creation, and, in focusing intently on her work, is mesmerized, becoming part of the potential communion with the center of the Other that the work offers.

MARILYN BANNER AND LADDERS OF THE SOUL

Marilyn Banner's work touches on letters, too: Hebrew letters occur and recur throughout her work, both in overt, undisguised form and, consistent with the Jewish mystical tradition obliquely addressed by Stern and Logemann, in hidden, disguised form. Letters repeat themselves, obscured as a bird or deer or reconceived as the figure of a woman kindling candles. Again and again she turns in particular to the *aleph* that is the beginning of the beginning, the first letter of the Hebrew alphabet, and to the *shin*, the letter used on *mezzuzot* and in other contexts in which God's protection is invoked. For it stands for the word *shaddai*, that name for God that refers to Its all-powerful, protective aspect. The tradition of Jewish mysticism that looks beneath the surface of words and letters would comment without fail on the combination of these two particular letters in several works, such as *Shin #2* [fig. 8], for *aleph* and *shin* together spell the word for fire [*aysh*].

There are at least three significances to the fact of such combination and to the term that the combination creates. As artists act *in imitatio dei* in creating the microcosm of their work and as the Jewish mystical tradition observes that, by definition, there are hidden meanings buried not only within creation, but within the Torah that is the blueprint for creation, so in this case the artist offers (intuitively, perhaps unconsciously) meanings buried within her work, by selecting these two particular letters to use in concert.

For fire, one of the elements basic to the universe, is also one of those elements that, like letters and numbers, stands between the abstraction associated with the Creator and the concrete reality of creation. We see fire and yet we do not: it flickers so that we can at no time really see it in a visually graspable manner. We can touch it and yet cannot grasp it: to hold it is to feel the pain of its heat, and yet we cannot close our hand around it

fig. 8 *Shin #2*

as around some solid entity. It is part of that vast realm of intermediation that presents a non-answer/answer to the question of how the creation of such a universe as ours took place.

Moreover, to become fire is the goal of the Jewish mystic, as implicitly suggested in the apocalyptic books of Enoch that are part of the foundation of *merkavah* mysticism, and as more explicitly set forth in the principles of *hasidut*. The mystic wishes to be transformed from flesh and blood and the preoccupations of such matter into the substanceless substance that is fire. We see this in the figure of Enoch himself, who becomes flame, yet is not burnt up; we see it in the imagery of the Hasid and above all the Hasidic master, the *tzadik*. The Hasid seeks enthusiastic engagement with the Other. The Hebrew root of "enthusiastic engagement," *lahav*, means flame. The Hasid seeks to burn with connectedness to the spirit of God.

Nor do the possibilities of Banner's intuitive hiddenness end there. For a careful perusal of *Shin #2* reveals the quite distinct form of the Hebrew letter *mem*, half obscured behind the centrally placed *shin*. In this case, she has placed together the three particular letters that are treated by the *Sefer Yetzirah* as the "mother letters," corresponding to the formative elements of creation: air (*aleph*), fire (*shin*), and water (*mem*). They are viewed, within the letter-and-number-conduits of the process, as even more essentially central than the others: these letters dance across the microcosmic spaces of Banner's universe.

But Hebrew letters, alone or in consort, are merely the beginning point for Banner, as they are the beginning point for creation in the *Book of Formation*. We follow her work both through the development of Jewish mystical textuality and away from the specifics of Jewish mysticism into broader spiritual considerations. The broader realms are both embedded within Judaism but not necessarily the mystical tradition; they are attached to other traditions altogether. They are interwoven with her roles as an artist, as a woman (mother and wife), and simply as a person. They are directed into the psyche along its conscious and unconscious paths, which lead her work through her own ancestry and sense of genealogy, while also leading her out into the universe of intuition. Her works, devised so often from the blue and brown colors and textures of heaven and earth, present imagery that leads from one to the other. The Other, with which her work connects us, is both the soaring heavens beyond the outermost edges of the familiar and the deepest, most remote corners of the interior, unconscious mind.

Hava, Mother of All Things [fig. 9], swirls with the colors of earth and sky. A bird-form (a disguised *aleph*) sweeps down from the upper right of the panel, recalling the image, offered in the first chapter of Genesis, of the spirit of God swooping over the deep before the process of creation began with light. The artist, *in imitatio dei*, creates a work whose colors and textures are elemental; the forms echo phrases from the text that describe the setting of the ultimate Creation in motion; the subject is the aboriginal woman, whose Hebrew name, *Hava*, means life and who is the first direct creator of the generations of humans of which we are all part.

A Blessing Over Earth [fig. 10] swirls in the same sort of textures and pigments, but further along on the path of Creation. For here the blacks of the previous image have been replaced by whites, as if light has indeed now swept over the vast formlessness of the *tohu vavohu*, pure No-thingness, pure Is-ness, that preceded the light-induced ordering of things and began to order it. Most noticeable are the hands: spread-fingered, disconnected, and yet overseeing. These are the hands of God, who "saw that it was good" as each phase of Creation proceeded. They are the hands of a Jewish mother, held up to bless the Sabbath candles as, week by week throughout the last thirty-three centuries, we have celebrated the re-creation of our world made possible by the Sabbath. They are literally the artist's hands,

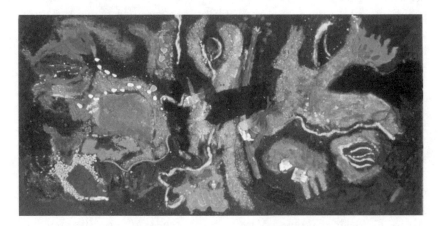

fig. 9 *Hava, Mother of All Things*

fig. 10 *A Blessing Over Earth*

blessing the 2' high x 4' wide microcosm of reality as she has re-visioned it and as it takes shape before the viewer.

Banner's ladder constructions illustrate the principal of connecting heaven to earth by way of the imagery for which Jacob's dream is the obvious paradigm and the imagery of the kabbalistic *spherot* a particular variation and concentration. There are dozens of variations on this theme, which has evolved from "Soul Ladders," dark-hued and sometimes overrun with red, to "Ancestor Ladders," to the "Sky Spirit Ladders" of most recent vintage, light blue and altogether brightly hued.

Her *Woman Ladder/Reaching* [fig. 11] offers a directly human form of intermediation between realms, crowned as it is by upward reaching hands, with feet at the bottom of its vertical planks. The upward-reaching hands suggest striving towards heaven; they also recall the upraised hands of the high priest in the Jerusalem Temple, offering his blessing. His fingers were configured as a double *shin*, a double *shaddai*, as he mediated between God and Israel. But they also echo the imagery, from ancient Phoenicia and her Carthaginian colony, of the priestess of the sun/moon disc/crescent, her arms upraised in veneration, often simply represented in the artwork of those places and time by upraised hands. These hands, literally the artist's hands, also remind us of the upraised hands of a Jewish mother blessing the Sabbath candles. The ladder, therefore, combines personal, Jewish, and universal symbols in its uppermost reaches.

The artist repeatedly hangs skin from these ladders, especially the "Ancestor Ladders." They connote Holocaust, and the usage, by the Nazis, of human skin for lampshades and soap. There is irony in this. For these strange stretchings of flesh recall the crucifix imagery of Soutine, bloody carcasses hung in the slaughterhouse. The recurrent use of skins together with bones also calls to mind the text in Ezek 37, the Valley of the Bones, where God resurrects the righteous in the time to come. We are thus led to the beginning of the text with its vision of the *merkavah*, a starting point for the Jewish mystical tradition. We are further led to the notion of *tikkun olam* [repairing the universe] as set forth later on in the Safed-centered Kabbalah of Isaac Luria. Banner's use of animal skin and bones to evoke the Holocaust has, as part of its intention, to effect a kind of magical resurrection of the dead. That is, the remnants of life have been returned [*t'shuvah*, or "return," also means redemption] and thus redeemed to life as art. Those returned to life in this way are, as it were, the righteous referred to in Ezekiel's vision.

fig. 11 *Woman Ladder/Reaching*

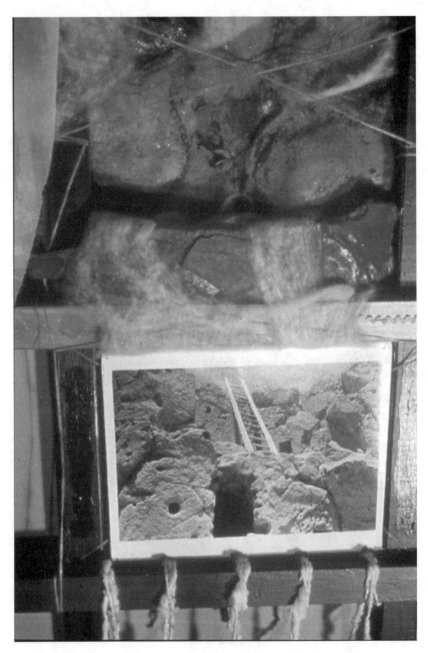

fig. 12 *Marriage Ladder*

For Banner, these righteous are most specifically the members of her own family who perished in the Holocaust; their restoration is a reordering by the artist, who redoes what God originally did. It is she who is the shaman, the guide, the intermediary, the ladder between heaven and earth. The skins that festoon the ladders' rungs weld verbal pun to visual image, moreover. The Hebrew word for skin [*'or*] plays perhaps on the Hebrew word for light [*or*]. This ordering principle of Creation is thus suggested in the artist's reordering, with skins, after Holocaust chaos. The mystical ladder between the celestial and mundane realms is made of light and leads to the "hidden light" [*or ganooz*] sought by Jewish mystics in their desire to ascend toward the divine essence.

The ladders lead from past to future. They extend upward from her *Mother's Grave* ladder, where resurrection is implied, among other ways, by the reversal of coloration: the dark black of the earth is above; the lighter blue of the sky is below. This journey down as up and up as down also recalls the imagery of the *hechalot* literature of early *merkavah* mysticism, where one speaks paradoxically of the descent, rather than the ascent, through the chambers that connect our realm with that of God. The paradox of the Jewish mystical journey is that God "descends" to pull us up as we "ascend" towards contact with the Divine.

The ladders lead to the sky-spirit *Marriage Ladder* [fig. 12]. The fringe that hangs from its lowermost rung suggests the *tzitzit* [fringes] of a *tallit* [prayer shawl], the garment worn during the intense rapture of seeking God through spiritual speech. The strings crossed diagonally between the vertical struts of the ladder's uppermost reaches recall the interconnectedness of the *spherot* delineated in the *Zohar*. As the *spherot* set forth ten aspects of God, ten aspects of the Creation process, ten aspects of the connection between God and humanity, so the interconnectedness of these strings and their diagonal patterns symbolizes the connection between humanity and divinity and the process by which the One engendered the endlessly diverse universe in the beginning of time.

DION KLINER: LETTERS, TEXTS AND POLITICS

Process defines the human experience on all levels, as thinkers from Plato to Martin Buber have observed. God, the forms, gods, the Wholly Other, simply is or are, perfected, fully realized, eternal, and unchanging. We, and the universe of which we are part, are temporary, changing, in a constant state of flux. It is the impossibility of succeeding in the quest to alter that condition that makes it paradoxical, full of ironies, pure madness, heroic.

As a particular quest, the Jewish mystical experience is a complex, esoteric engagement of impossibility built on absolute faith in the certainty of achieving the impossible to achieve. The goal is hidden; the process of reaching the goal (the process is part of the goal) is hidden. The key to everything is the Torah. Buried within its text are keys to the chamber hiding that key. Those keys to the key are the letters, but the keys to those keys are also hidden. They are hidden as the hidden meanings held, according to the Jewish mystical tradition, by the letters.

They are also hidden, according to a parallel strand in the tradition, as an additional, twenty-third letter of the Hebrew alphabet, residing in the empty white spaces between the twenty-two Hebrew letters that we see throughout the Torah. But we can only begin to hope to find that key buried within the deepest recesses of the hidden when we are able to understand that the letters, words, and text that the words yield are other than they appear to us. Within this other understanding is hidden a greater Torah than the one we ordinarily study.

This is the take-off point for Dion Kliner's works. Following the kabbalistic notion of the hidden twenty-third letter, the artist wrote, "I began to think of the possibilities hidden within it." Hhe continued:

Perhaps a text within a text. Perhaps a landscape. Perhaps a drawing. On a trip to Israel, closed in a room with a Torah, I embarked upon an absurd meander to the shoreless sea between the letters. In the absence of fixed navigational points boundlessness swamped my consciousness. Out of this arose the jumbled debris of the entropic state drawings. Literal rewritings of the first five books of the Torah, the entire text of each book is contained within the drawing, but has been pulverized and dumped to form outcroppings of possibility. Far from being permanent formations the drawings are rather temporary precipitations and short-term agglomerations that could at any moment crumble back to their original state or dissolve into something new. They are arrested *clinamens*, "swerves" in the atoms of Lucretian cosmology that makes change in the universe possible.[3]

Thus, we observe two principles in Kliner's five graphite-on-paper works, each offering a different book of the Torah "in an Entropic State." First, the idea of re-visioning reality by way of re-visioning the text that is the blueprint of reality intersects the paradox of restoring order to reality by reducing the apparent order of the text to the purest chaos: ascent has become descent and descent has become ascent. In the purest mystical sense, the artist has transformed the sense of the text to non-sense, forcing the viewer to consider new directions for understanding it; in order to grasp it, he has reconceived it [from Latin *con-cipio*, meaning "to thoroughly grasp"].

Second, the artist's esotericism has, in turn, interwoven Kabbalah with two additional strands. On the one hand, he has added the atomism of Epicurus and Lucretius, according to which all of reality began as two components, empty space and irreducible motes [*a-tomos*, in Greek, meaning "un-cuttable"], falling through that space. Lucretius writes that something unaccountable causes the atoms to experience a "swerve" [*klinamen*, in Lucretius' Greek-based Latin vocabulary] and to hit against and stick to each other, eventually building up to the substances of our world. This is what Kliner has, as it were, done with the letters, allowing them to fall through spiritual space, the empty spaces of the twenty-third letter, and to glom onto each other with apparent arbitrariness.

He has also woven in the strand of contemporary scientific thinking and its vocabulary. It is in thermodynamics that we find the notion of entropy as the measure of the capacity of a system to undergo spontaneous change, but also as the measure of the randomness, disorder, or chaos in a system specified in statistical mechanics by a particular formula. The system there is the universe; the system here is the Torah, which is the universe cast as a text. Kliner has subjected the system to spontaneous change and to randomness, disorder, and chaos, in order to squeeze out the hidden secret(s) of its underpinning(s).

His work moves in yet another logical direction. As the Jewish mystical tradition culminate historically with the social esotericism of *hasidut*, so Kliner's obscure and esoteric *sacer* engagement of the Torah also drives directly back toward the *profanus*, reminding us of the responsibility of Jewish mystics to be engaged in their community. *Profanus* is, in one sense, a Latin term for "community," referring to the realm of the familiar and the everyday; so, too, is the Greek *polis*, from which of course we derive our term "political." We have observed how Logemann's work at times crosses into this realm, most obviously in her Hebrew and Arabic works. We also note that of Kliner's five Torah texts, one, *Numbers in an Entropic State*, is subtitled *The Hypothetic Sub-Continent of Israel*.

The meaning of this becomes clear when we turn to the artist's three-dimensional installation. It was originally conceived at the same time as the *Entropic Drawings*, while he was in Israel, towards the beginning of the 1997 Palestinian Intifada. *The Three Hypothetical Islands of Israel* [fig. 13],

fig. 13 *The Three Hypothetical Islands of Israel*

which, in its originally intended configuration, included the text of the book of Numbers and three dolomite boulders, relates to the delineation of the Israelite borders in the text of that book.

As the Torah contains the universe, so, more simply, the book of Numbers contains the borders of Israel. As Israel and the Palestinians, to say nothing of her Egyptian, Jordanian, Syrian, and Lebanese neighbors, have struggled to define and redefine borders and as the possession of tracts of land and the possession of portions of peace have interwoven each other as concepts in the political arena of the past several years, so the artist responds with a revision of the issue: "The variety of the configurations that Israel [modern Israel, as either opposed to or identical with biblical Israel] can take are unlimited, save by the number and size of the pages of Numbers itself."[4]

This is a comment on the mystical attachment to the land for those for whom it is anathema to yield one inch, even for the sake of peace. The work corresponds directly to the *Entropic Drawing*, which is its less obviously politicized counterpart. Although first created in 1988, the work bears a particular resonance in the aftermath of a succession of peace accords and the assassination of Prime Minister Yitzhak Rabin.

Moreover, the intrinsic hiddenness of mystical meaning springs from this work, whose three-ness recalls the three "mother letters" (*aleph, mem, shin*) of the *Book of Formation*, as it connotes in part the links and continuity among the three fathers of Israel, Abraham, Isaac, and Jacob, and the all-important first moment of transmission of the covenant of continuity. That moment, set forth in Gen 22, is the binding and sanctification (as opposed to sacrifice) of Isaac. The three boulders may be seen as altar-like. The prime minister, slain on the altar of blindly fervent attachment to the Land, was named Isaac [*Yitzhak*]. The other son of Abraham, who in Muslim tradition was the son offered to God, was Ishmael, ancestor of Muhammad and therefore of Islam.

The socio-political responsibility exercised by such commentary circles back to the responsibility for *tikkun olam* in the Jewish mystical tradition—mystics must enlighten the community, not only themselves—and to the statement of the artist's social responsibility first articulated over a century ago by Pissarro, Jewish Impressionist par excellence. Kliner thus draws together elements of both the Jewish mystical and the Jewish art historical traditions.

MYSTICAL VOCABULARY AND THE MYSTERY OF THE HOLOCAUST

The deconstruction of the text of the Torah can be seen to symbolize the deconstruction of the entire world when we consider that the entire world is contained within the Torah according to the Jewish mystical tradition. But when we apply the notion of deconstruction not to the philosophical and linguistic terminology of the twentieth century but to its history and theology, our focus inevitably comes to rest on the Holocaust. There is no more deconstructive moment in Jewish—indeed, in human—history than the Holocaust. It is a return to chaos that the flood story of Gen 6-9 anticipates; by paradox, it is also a return to the endless ingenuity invoked by the Nazis for the purposes of destruction reflects the darkest of negative creativity imaginable. It would be a surprise if, in addressing the Holocaust, there were not artists whose instrumentation of understanding the unfathomable and articulating the ineffable did not include the varied vocabularies of mysticism. This might be particularly true for survivor-artists.

Alice Lok Cahana managed to survive Auschwitz, where her brother and mother died. Afterward, her sister disappeared into the medical bureaucracy of the liberation and she was estranged from her adored father in the complicated aftermath of the war. From Hungary to Sweden to Israel to the United States she wandered, where the art gestating within her eventually poured forth. Within her need to remember visually and to turn the ashes of her experience into a literal rainbow of commentary, in the same way that colors often explode subtly on the canvases before us, was a mystical sensibility passed along through the countless generations of her small Hungarian Jewish village. She was drawn to the mystical tradition as one means of addressing the problematic relationship between God and us, particularly problematic in the aftermath of the Holocaust. That tradition, as we have observed, begins in a particular sense with the problem of creation and the *Sefer Yetzirah's* solution by means of letters and numbers. Not only was the Holocaust the ultimate act of de-creation in its dehumanization of its victims, but the most obvious and specific aspect of its process of dehumanization was the reduction of humans to numbers and letters. The Wannsee conference yielded numbers of Jews in numbers of European countries, and those rounded up were stamped on their arms with numbers and letters. Names, which throughout history have connected humans to the essence of what we are, were eliminated. The inhabitants of Auschwitz were reduced to personal numbers and letters; in lieu of families and addresses were the numerological system of bunker-bed-boards within bunker-buildings and places on line for innumerable roll calls.

Numbers and letters are a constant in much of Cahana's work: those from the tattooed arms of the dead, as well as those from the calendar of counting the endless days that had lost their coherent cycle in the concentration and extermination camps. By paradox, in turning these very numbers and letters into art and memorializing the numberless victims, Cahana reverses the Hitlerian process of de-creation and dehumanization: she recreates in creating a particular art of memory. In *No Names* [fig. 14], railroad tracks plunge into a dark night overwhelmed not with stars but with letters and numbers (this railroad track is at the same time an ironic Jacob's ladder connecting heaven and earth). Names are returned to those whom the Nazis sought to make nameless: the *mysterium* of God's relationship to humanity is implied in the chaotic ordering of the letters. The *mysterium* of their organization into groups that, called "names," are intended to convey some meaning to us about the entities to that the names are attached; the role of the first human, Adam, in performing the act of according names (an act made possible by divine dispensation); the *mysterium* of letters floating upward toward God to be reorganized in heaven

fig. 14 *No Names*

fig. 15 *Four Degrees of Access*

into the names and words they formed below—all of this is implied. Moreover, as the artist incorporates not only groups of numbers and letters into her work, but (as in the series, *Sacred Texts*) whole pages of texts—the prayers and biblical and talmudic pages of her pre-Holocaust childhood— she draws our attention to the specific role of letters within the Jewish tradition. They comprise the Torah, ultimate bridge between divinity and humanity. The Torah, the specific book of moral creation that centers Jewish history and geography, is the centerpiece of reclaiming the irreclaimable.

Numbers and letters, in comprising the Torah, comprise the response to the specific question of the divine-human relationship created by the Holocaust: how can such loss have been permitted to occur? Further, we must answer the question of how such loss (and such questions) can be endured; namely, by remembering the dead with a visual voice whose act of witnessing now speaks, by describing the indescribable. The letters ascend as intelligibly wordless words beyond the surface of the canvas. They are restored into names in that realm addressed by prayer. They soar beyond our everyday reality of kitchen tables, rose bushes, and railroad tracks.

The later Jewish mystical tradition speaks of the role of humans in repairing the universe damaged by the evil that we humans have allowed into it, as we have already noted. Lurianic Kabbalah speaks of gathering together the sparks of light scattered at the moment when humans disobeyed God. Cahana's art is filled with images of such sparks. She takes the fallen letters (intended to obliterate humans by being denied a place as part of names of individuals) from the tattooed arms of the dead and lifts them up. Her work restores the lettered names and the memorialized humans to whom they were attached. She gathers in the letter-number-sparks of six million broken souls and repairs their being.

SAMUEL BAK AND THE MYSTICAL LANDSCAPE OF LETTERS, NUMBERS, EXPERIENCE

Samuel Bak's *Landscapes of the Jewish Experience* record a range of issues and ideas, but their most abiding theme is the Holocaust as both trauma and triumph. Born in Vilnius in 1933, he was six years old when World War II began and not much older when it arrived into the Lithuania of his childhood, carrying away with it the innocence left buried in the ashes and ruins of his city. That innocence was exchanged for the tenuous life of the shrunken ghetto, a work camp, and refuge in a monastery, which in turn was exchanged for life in a displaced persons camp at war's end, followed by immigration to the new state of Israel in 1948, by which time the artist was an old man of fifteen years.

Bak's own features appear often on the faces and figures in his work, although most often his landscapes are devoid of humans. They are still filled with symbols of the human and the specifically Jewish presence. His visual vocabulary is both personalized and universal; the distance between these two angles of understanding is bridged by Judaism and, from within Judaism, by the mystical tradition in particular. Repeatedly the number "four" appears, often in the form of four doorways. We are reminded of the four-lettered name of God, *YHWH*, of the kabbalistic obsession with that name as the closest contact possible for humans with God itself and with that number as a rung close to the name on the ladder of contact that leads, by fourness, by letters, and by those four particular letters, toward God. We are reminded of the fourfold approach to understanding the Torah that is the word of God and the guide to understanding the covenant with God and thus to leading a living life within the context of a covenantal relationship with God.

The *Four Degrees of Access* [fig. 15] lead us through the everyday flotsam and jetsam of life's laundry into four doorways. A Hebrew letter, standing for a word, subtly marks each. Each word refers to an approach to interpreting the Torah delineated by the thirteenth century rabbis. *Pey* [P] represents *p'shat*, which seeks a literal meaning; *resh* [R] stands for *remez*, which looks for an allegorical meaning; *dalet* [D] signifies *d'rash*, which is the method of interpreting by means of midrash, filling in lacunae and excavating the text by means of legends; and *samech* [S] refers to *sod*, the hidden mystical meanings sought beneath the surface of the deepest depths of the texts.

For a people of texts, the continuous cycle of their interpretation and reinterpretation is a synonym for life. For a people whose covenant is with an invisible, intangible God, texts in which that God has spelled out the covenant are the key to the doorways of life. The four doors lie open, each at its own level: there are many paths to the garden within. The garden is the paradise left behind by our aboriginal ancestors after they disobeyed God's commandment and ate from the tree of knowledge. But without their disobedience, they would still be there, innocent as children—and we wouldn't be.

Thus, the destruction of paradise is the construction of human history with its magnificent chamber music and its unfathomable ovens. "Paradise" as a word, as text, is derived (by way of Latin and in turn by way of Greek) from Persian. Borrowed into Hebrew and transformed, it became *pardes*, meaning "garden" or "orchard." But the consonants of Hebrew's unvocalic personality yield the four letters (P, R, D, S) that are the compendium of the fourfold path of approaching the Torah. The garden within is the garden of Torah, which is the bridge between God and us. It is the creation and creator of our spiritual landscape, the mirror in which God and we see ourselves and each other.

The letters are the keys, and in Bak's landscapes keys can be as hidden as *sod* and as obvious as *p'shat*. In *Wall* [fig. 16], for example, we see a giant key embedded in the mountainous stone wall before which the stage-set houses on wheels rest—homes that are not homes, prepared to move with no more than false means of locomotion, like the Jewish people in its eternal wandering from landscape to landscape. The light that washes at a diagonal across the surfaces, engendering striped shadows, creates the stripes of a *tallit* or prayer shawl, constant companion of places and times of devotion through centuries of exilic wandering. The key's teeth form the letter *shin* [SH], standing for the word *shaddai,* God's power-name symbolizing God's protective aspect. It is on the *mezuzah* [doorpost] in Jewish homes and is the container with its scroll that marks the doorposts of our houses and our gates. It was on the doorposts and the gates of most Jewish houses left empty and insubstantial, like flat stage sets, stripped of their inhabitants who were transported to Auschwitz and other destinations.

The key opens no door, the doors lead nowhere, the empty rooms and empty skies offer no answers. Candles mark the weekly commemoration of the covenant embodied in the Sabbath (*Zakhor et Yom HaShabbat...*"Remember the Sabbath Day"), but also the annual remembrance [*yizkor*] of loved ones gone, both known and anonymous. Smoke rises out of the candles, out of the toy trains that lead to a familiar crematorial chimney, and out of smokestacks on stone ships filled with stage-set homes and the flat backs of covenantal tablets, in a *Voyage* [fig. 17] going nowhere, except perhaps out into an empty sea as devoid of answers as the sky and as devoid of connection as the barren mountains. The paradoxes of human existence become intensified as the paradoxes of Jewish experience have become focused as a series of layered symbols, with revealed and hidden meanings.

GERALD WARTOFSKY'S *GOLEMS*

Hidden meanings are the essence of Jewish mysticism's history in every conceptual, verbal, and visual sense, just as the meaning of the Holocaust

fig. 16 *Wall*

fig. 17 *Voyage*

fig. 18 *Karin and the Carousel Horse*

fig. 19 *The Golem*

can rarely be understood to offer answers other than in a hidden, senseless manner. Not only those who survived the crucible and were enflamed by the process raise the questions, but those who have been burned by reflected fire. Artists like Gerald Wartofsky exemplify this: his wife, Karin, a dancer, is often the focus of his exquisite paintings. Her worlds interweave his, and her world is embedded in a childhood lost to the Holocaust.

It is the world of *Karin and the Carousel Horse* [fig. 18]; that is, the world of the childhood carousel horse: the alter ego of the dancer (the horse is all movement) and of the painter (the horse is rooted to the ground, so that movement cannot carry it away) are fused as one, like the mystic who transcends our reality into mergence with the *sacer* without ever lifting his feet from the soil of the *profanus*. The carousel horse is decorated with the flotsam and jetsam of a dancing life, spinning around a giant carousel wheel of Fortune, telling tales of that far off land of Karin's childhood called Vienna-before-the-Nazis.

This is the world of Gerald's beloved Karin, who clutched her broken doll Peter when she was sent into hiding as a child. It is the world of the Golem, that giant doll, shapeless earth glob that through the mystical powers of Rabbi Judah Loew, became the protector of Prague's sixteenth century Jewish population but was then lost to lifelessness in the attic of Prague's Old-New Synagogue when, four centuries later, his protective force was most needed.[5] For Wartofsky, the story of the Golem is mediated by Meyerink's novelized version of his legend, in which the giant-doll figure and the figure of the novel's protagonist become intertwined (as do the dolls and Karin in her memories, on his canvasses). *The Golem* [fig. 19] is a mist-wrapped self-portrait with its eyes closed, waiting to be awakened.

The artist is God-like in that, like God, he creates; Judah Loew-like, in that like Judah Loew, he creates golems; golem-like, in that he awaits with eyes closed to be animated, to feel the in-spirit-ation to create, to open his eyes and see the invisible. Wartofsky mediates as Judah Loew does, between God and his golems; he is a co-creator, with the kabbalistic rabbi, of the golem. Rabbi Loew animates his golem with the ineffable name of God imprinted on his forehead or on paper placed in his mouth; the artist animates his painting with the Hebrew word *emet* [truth] floating, it would seem, to or from the golem/self-portrait's mouth. God's name and "Truth" are synonyms for each other. The story of the golem is the search for truth and the revelation of its elusiveness: it offers the gypsy wheel of fortune that also frequents Wartofsky's paintings, symbol of chance, of the fugitive and of the destroyed worlds of gypsies, Jews, and others. It includes the destruction of the Jews of the Prague of Rabbi Loew as it included the destruction of the Jews of the Vienna of Karin.

The world of Karin's childhood is the world of all childhood when we idealize it after its traumas have been forgotten. It is the world of the *Prague Clock* [fig. 20]: another nursery world, dominated by the dappled carousel horse and its dancer-rider, by the bright red carriage and sparkling patterns of that faraway realm, and driven by a wheel of fortune that has become the clock that lends to the painting its name—a clock that is also the kind of wheel that pulls the throne-chariot of God, moving in all directions simultaneously without moving at all, envisioned by Ezekiel by the waters of Babylon. Wartofsky's clock/wheel has ten spokes, like the ten *hechalot* of the throne mysticism that grew out of mystical commentaries on that Ezekelian image. A magical clock, it would seem, that Prague clock, for its numbers are Hebrew letters (like the letters so necessary to the process of creation) and it runs counter-clockwise. Time itself is turned on its head! This is the only public clock in the world of Europe that runs this way, in the city of Judah Loew and the Golem, with its once plentiful Jewish population.

fig. 20 *The Prague Clock*

The great numbers of Jews who populate Prague now do so in its famous cemetery that includes the grave of Rabbi Loew. The Prague clock is death because it represents a world destroyed, the belonging of the city's inhabitants' gathered, together with those of Jews throughout central Europe, into Prague, to create a museum of a dead people. But the Prague clock is life: it still ticks, and the people were decimated but not destroyed. They have slowly regenerated, even in Prague itself. The clock is unique; backward running is the ultimate symbol of timeless time, of past and present and future fused together rather than distinguished from each other. It hovers rather than hangs on the wall of the nursery of past and future.

BRURIA FINKEL AND THE DIVINE CHARIOT

Seven centuries before the clock/wheel refused to succumb to the Nazis and stop marking time backwards, Abraham Abulafia, approximate contemporary of Moses de Leon, sought the esoteric height of Jewish mystical speculation and the social connection of offering access to such speculation to any Jew wishing to learn his system. The author of perhaps more than two dozen works, a poet and a dreamer, a madman and a genius, a self-proclaimed prophetic and messianic figure reviled by the mainstream rabbinic leadership as a heretic, Abulafia more than any of his mystical contemporaries caressed the idea of language with the fingers of his mind, meditating on every sound and letter as a celestial event with nerve-like ramifications, dwelling on the God-ness of speech whose beginning point is the act of God saying, "let there be."

Among Abulafia's works are commentaries on Maimonides, on the *Book of Formation*, and on the Vision in Ezek 1 referred to as the *merkavah*, the Throne-Chariot of God. This vision, the basis for the awe-filled early phase of Jewish mysticism called *merkavah* and which becomes a point of focus for Abulafia's systems of Kabbalah, is the point of emanation that continues outward from Gerald Wartofsky's Wheel of Fortune/Prague Clock toward a series of two- and three-dimensional works of visual meditation by Bruria Finkel.

Bruria's engagement with Abulafia began twenty years ago when she slowly co-translated a prophetic work of his called *Sefer Ha-Ot* [*Book of the (Alphabetic) Letter*]. This work, offering both mental and physiological techniques (such as breathing, chanting, and visualization) for seeking through the permutation of letters that emanate from the name, reverberates with tonalities that point in the musical directions of Lurianic Kabbalah and *hasidut*. From it emanates Bruria's turn toward Abulafia and her turn towards the parts of his commentary on Maimonides that present concentric circles of text and isolated letters in Mandela-like focus.

This encounter led directly to her bronze sculptures and paintings on paper, called *The Divine Chariot*. The text in Ezekiel speaks of wheels of eyes whirling in all directions: they defy the norms of time, space, and direction. Bruria's four bronze wheels reach across time into the Bronze Age innovation of a spoked wheel and, by way of the number "ten" (each of her wheels has ten spokes), into the kabbalistic emphasis on "ten."

Four wheels, of course, suggest both the four directions of Creation and the four-lettered name of the Creator, *YHWH*, and the four worlds (Emanation, Creation, Formation, Making) of pre-*Zohar* kabbalistic thinking that emanate towards our world from God. Each of the four wheels offers a different emphasis: one offers *The One*; one *The Influx*, the divine act of Creation; one the four-directioned *The Power*, associated with the names of the four Archangels; and one the efflorescence that becomes *The Many*. These are all emanations from the central idea, like the four rivers of paradise (referred to in Genesis) that emanate from the source and are the beginning of the fertilization of the created world.

Abulafia-like, the imaged wheels are nuanced with letters: ten each, organized according to their numerological values, the focused meditation on that yields mystical rapture. Across one wheel the names of the four archangels are inscribed, hovering around the centerlessly Centered One. Each wheel may be viewed from any of the four directions; the front of each presents the theme encompassed by its circle and the back, through the motif of human hands (we are returned to a theme taken up in the work of Marilyn Banner), suggests the human role in the world as creator and manipulator.

The triangular forms articulated by the spokes in concert with the outer rims are emphasized by subtleties of patina and subsumed into the form of a five-pointed star. The star, in its five-ness, further underscores the relationship between God and us: it is like a hand with five fingers. One, the thumb, is attached to, yet separate from, the other four. The one is the One, the four is our four-directioned reality: both thumb and fingers are connected to the same hand, yet separate from each other.

The spokes of the wheels are ten in number, yet one is different from the other nine. It is presented in the process of growth, as a part of nature beginning to flower; the other nine are identical and unnaturally stagnant. The notion of transformation and growth, endemic to the universe, is reinforced by this imagery. Bruria's *merkavah* re-vision is superimposed onto the kabbalistic idea of representing the macrocosmic universe and its processes as a tree of *spherot*: the tree is a microcosm of nature, the universe, and the Torah as the ultimate "Tree of Life." This in turn is understood as a human figure (man, tree, *spherot*, universe, the Torah are analogues of each other) that Abulafia carried to an extreme.

Moreover, in the esoteric well associated with Abulafia from which the artist drinks, nine is a particularly propitious mystical number. It is the square of the number of "mother letters" (*aleph, mem, shin*), three (letters) times three. And if, using an Abulafian version of Hebrew letter numerology, we eliminate zero (which, of course, leaves nine basic numbers), then the Hebrew words for truth (*emet*: *aleph* = 1, *mem* = 4, *taf* = 4) and light (*or*: *aleph* = 1, *va* = 6, *resh* = 2) each add up to nine. Light is the most essential instrument of visual imaging; it is the substance of the ladder of ascent to the celestial realm; it is the first material called into existence by God. And truth, which is the ultimate goal sought through that ascent, the word imprinted on the Golem's forehead, or written on a piece of paper and placed within his mouth to animate him, is the totality of existence from beginning to end, for its three letters are the first, the middle and the last in the Hebrew alphabet.

Not surprisingly, there are nine *Divine Chariot* paintings to complement Bruria's four sculptures, for example, *Pathway to Power* [fig. 21]. They modulate, in concentric circles toward their centers in bristling primary colors (red, yellow, blue, like the three mother letters and the three kabbalistic elements), crisscrossed with diagonal and vertical patterns, or sometimes both. Visions of earth and sky, and of sky and clouds, interweave imagery of human-contrived geometries. As with her sculptures, we are locked in a dynamic opposition between the perfection of the circle, without beginning or end, and the stop-and-start angles and corners of our imperfect reality, between a sense of open endlessness and closed finitude.

We are webbed in abstractions that, concentrated at the centering point, prove to be emanations from the form of the letter *aleph*. We are again back at the beginning of a journey that allows no time or space measurement. In her painting of nine miniature variations, we are poured into a meditation on the permutations of the *aleph*: permutations and transformations of all that exists potentially and in actuality, from the endless pre-beginning of the universe already contained in the Torah of God's mind to the Messianic era of perfection to which we have not yet arrived.

fig. 21 *The Divine Chariot: Pathway to Power*

SHOSHANA GREENBERG AND THE ARI

The mystical heart of the land, which is the focus of Kliner's commentary and the setting-up point for Bruria's Abulafian Throne-Chariot and Banner's Ladders, is Jerusalem. The city's hills breathe a sacred fragrance that in all three Abrahamic traditions derives from a direct ladder to the celestial realm. But for Jewish mysticism in the last four centuries, the mystical soul of the land and its brain are hidden up in the sun-touched hills of the Galilee within the territory allotted, according to the Bible, to the tribe of Naphtali, in the town of Safed. There, at what was a stop along the ancient caravan route between Damascus and Akko (Acre), Rabbi Isaac Luria (1534-72) took spiritual refuge and root with his followers. In the few years before his early death, he expanded the teachings of Kabbalah in newly-enriched directions. From his time to our own, mystics and artists alike have found in Safed the inspiration to set forth complex ladders of connection between heaven and earth.

There Shoshana Greenberg found the resource to center her own work as a visual artist. Over a six month period she accomplished a rubbing in modular units of the very stones of the courtyard before the synagogue associated with Rabbi Luria, the Ari. This plays between the first letters of his name and the word *ari* [lion], a long-standing symbol of the tribe of Judah, associated with the House of David and with the hope of a Messianic redeemer descended from that House. It is also associated with the Jewish people as descendants from the tribe of Judah. Safed grew to encompass the place where the Ari and his circle would come out weekly to greet the Sabbath and where a synagogue eventually grew (*The Courtyard of the Ari* [fig. 22]). The artist has overlaid the rubbings with watercolor applied with natural sea sponges and layers of text, the texts themselves reflecting Lurianic Kabbalah and its suggested means of concentrated focus on the relationship between God and Israel.

The texts are two. The first, in Hebrew, English, and in transliteration, is *L'cha Dodi* ["Come, my beloved, let us welcome the Bride, the Sabbath"], composed by Rabbi Solomon HaLevy Alkabetz, a contemporary of the Ari, and now universally sung as a poem of greeting the Sabbath. The notion of the Sabbath as a bride goes back to the time of Akiva, who is credited with suggesting that the love poetry of the Song of Songs is an allegory of the love-relationship between God and Israel. This interpretation, that understands God as the groom and Israel as the bride, reverberates obliquely onto the notion of the Sabbath kept by Israel ("for even as Israel found two particular new directions in far-separated Tsfat and Prague. In Tsfat, **Isaac Luriya** - better known by his acronym **The Ari** (which means "lion") - evolved an esoteric system which includes the idea that the Primordial Goodness was smashed in the moment when Adam and Eve disobeyed God's word, and scattered like tiny sparks throughout Creation; that those sparks are embedded in every human soul (sometimes hidden by the un-good that we can be and do) as the God-ness that is within us all, by definition (for the spirit of the Lord, breathed into us, *is* the basis of the soul which

to recognize our past lives, to know us in way that we can't even know ourselves.

Judah Loew, in Prague, at appromately the same time, was on the one ha evolving more and more esoteric systems Kabbalah. On the other hand, he is said have used his extraordinary esoteric know edge to emulate God Itself, in creating anthropoid out of formless (which is wh the root of the word "*golem*" means) ear **The Golem of Prague** became a gigan protector of the Jewish community, and piece of Bohemian folklore shared by Je and non-Jews alike, into c own time.

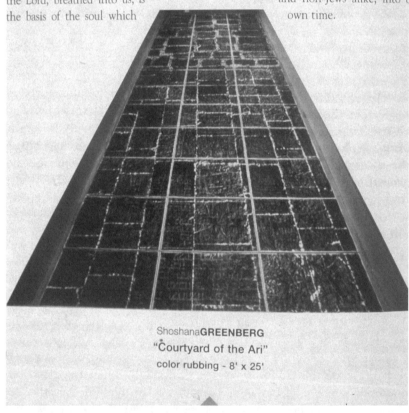

Shoshana**GREENBERG**
"Courtyard of the Ari"
color rubbing - 8' x 25'

fig. 22 *The Courtyard of the Ari*

has kept the Sabbath, so the Sabbath has kept [and defined] Israel") as a bride whom we welcome eagerly.

Akiva's contemporaries would attire themselves festively to greet "the Bride, the Queen," as Rabbi Hanina would chant; in the Safed of the Ari, men and boys, robed in white, would go out at sunset through the hills and valleys, singing passages from the Psalms and Song of Songs. The notion that the Sabbath and the God to which it connects us should be embraced not only as text but as song would become, with *hasidut*, a centerpiece of *kavannah*, the heart-filled intention of seeking God with music and dance and not only with study.

The second text used by Greenberg comes from the Jewish marriage service with its seven blessings. She arranges it on the "stones" of her work in seven concentric circles, just as a bride encircles the groom seven times in the service and as he encircles her with the seven blessings. In the same way the Sabbath consecrates the seventh day as a bride, and the universe, with its seven visible *planetes*, reached physical perfection by the seventh day. But every moment and every act calls us to continue the process of perfecting the moral universe, calls us to what the Ari entitled *tikkun olam*. The use of circles also reminds us of the Lurianic doctrine of *gilgul*, the cycling of the soul through a progression of lives in which *t'shuvah*, [return and redemption] is the ultimate goal.

So the bustling Safed of the artist's six months of stone rubbing (and one difficult evening, on a rickety ladder, of lintel rubbing), crisscrossed by residents and tourists, scholars and shopkeepers, religiously intense and secularly indifferent, is hidden in the layers of *The Courtyard of the Ari*. *L'cha Dodi*, in a traditional script, moves one way; its transliterated chorus and key words move the other way; the wedding text, in a more modern script, moves in its circles. Each is layered on the next. The work connects the profane to the sacred, the *sacer* to the *profanus*, the celestial to the mundane, by means of a multi-dimensional ladder of time and space and evolving traditions. The process of creating art recapitulates the process of history (as of the archaeology of Safed itself), which recapitulates the processes of Creation and thinking about Creation endemic to Jewish mystical contemplation.

The artist worked in modules—fragments, able to be interrupted and begun again later—as she explains: "a reflection of my life, its complexity and interruptions...developed from an exploration, during a particularly fragmentary time of my life, of the question 'How fragmented can a work get and still be a unified whole?'"[6] The viewer's necessary act of perambulation brings pieces and parts into and out of focus, "just as the future becomes clearer as we approach it and becomes the present, then recedes and becomes dim."[7] Together the fragments become monumental.

The juxtaposition of this marvelously fragile, even ephemeral, work on paper with a solid ceramic piece, a *Tzfat Wall Piece*, adds to the layers of her intention. The opposition of materials, displayed in opposed directions (horizontal and vertical), reinforces the Jewish mystical notion that time, space, and reason cease to present their ordinary senses to our sensibilities when, in seeking connection with that Ultimate Other, we enter into the process of ascent that is descent and descent that is ascent. For Greenberg, the starting point is at what, for her, became the navel of the universe: the cracked walls and cobbled stones of the dawn/dusk hill town of Safed.

DAVID FRIEDMAN AND THE CENTER OF MYSTICISM

David Friedman lives in the sacred city of Safed, at the center of the Jewish mystical brain and soul, where time can seem simultaneously like dawn and dusk. A range of aspects of Jewish mystical history inspires Friedman's work, from the *Book of Formation* to Isaac Luria to *hasidut*. He works primarily in watercolor, tempera, and pen-and-ink, using brilliant hues to articulate and to comment on principles set forth in the textual and oral forms that have spanned the Jewish centuries. As Kabbalah in all its aspects is a particularly complex form of midrash, digging beneath the surface of the text of the Torah, so Friedman's work offers a particularly complex visual midrash on midrash.

The artist seeks, for example, to represent the way in which the 22 letters of the Hebrew alphabet are understood in the *Sefer Yetzirah* to fall into three categories, relating to spirit, time, and space, as well as to air, water, and fire. Late Kabbalah continues, as we have seen, to explore three particular letters—the "mother letters," *aleph, mem* and *shin*—that are understood to correspond both to these three elements and to the three basic directional forces that define the created universe: horizontal, vertical, and diagonal [fig. 23].

To this layered mystical soul of seeking, Friedman has added the brain of geometry and color theory. *Shin* [fire] is connected to the color red and is also associated by the artist with the number three and with the form of the triangle. *Mem* [water] is associated with blue, with the number four, and with the square. The *aleph* [air] he associates with yellow, the number one, and the circle.

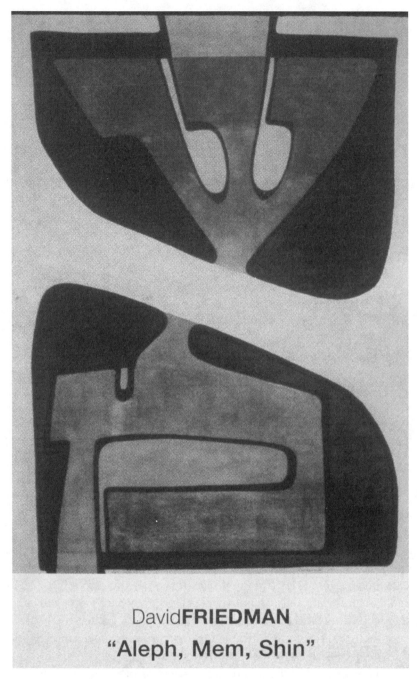

David**FRIEDMAN**
"Aleph, Mem, Shin"

fig. 23 *Aleph, Mem, Shin*

Aleph intermediates between *shin* and *mem*—air mediating between fire and water—or, in the Hegelian vocabulary that Friedman incorporates into his thinking about these principles, *aleph* is the synthesis that stands between the thesis of *mem* and the antithesis of *shin*. In terms of the kabbalistic thinking of the *Zohar*, the three letters reflect three states of consciousness expressed among the *spherot*: *mem* is *hochmah* [pure thought], *shin* is *binah* [verbal thought], and *aleph* is *da'at* [the holy spirit instilled in us by God]. As with the permutations of ideas that grew, over the centuries, from *Sefer Yetzirah* to *Zohar* to Abulafian and Lurianic teaching to *hasidut*, these concepts yield an almost endless range of others that the artist encompasses in an entire series of contemplative works that explore the paths between realms.

In some works those paths flow out of the center in circular or hexagonal formations that multiply the coloristic elements, shifting gradually among the three foundational hues in 12 zodiacal quadrants (the microcosm is the macrocosm). In others, the seven "double" Hebrew letters according to kabbalistic tradition—*bet, gimel, dalet, kaph, pay, resh* and *taph*—are the swirling circular center from which arrow-forms thrust out toward the periphery.

The artist's shimmering, maze-like paintings hover between the abstract and the representational. A seven-branched candelabrum is both a Tree-Menorah image, as described near the end of the book of Exodus, and a study in the sevenness that, because it is endemic to Shabbat as the seventh day, defines Judaism in its relationship to the world and to the God who made it. A "diagram" of the *spherot* offers to the viewer the opportunity to visualize some of the abstraction set forth in the Jewish mystical tradition. One work presents the ascent of the *spherot*, from *malchut* to *keter*, in which each *spherah* is connected to the others by vertical, horizontal, and diagonal lines; from each, concentric circles of modulated color emanate until they spill off the canvas.

The artist is engaged in different processes simultaneously in this. He suggests the intermediation between realms by contrasting rectilinear with curvilinear geometries and reinforces this with the carefully selected spectrum for which the juxtaposition of colors produces a prescribed effect that is both still and vibrating. Luminous creations explore the birth of light itself, and the notion of kabbalistic emanation is superimposed onto the photosynthetic process of growth in nature.

He acts as an intermediary or teacher in offering the means of understanding by way of visualizing ("I found that if you can give someone a picture, it helps them to integrate some of these abstract concepts," he commented a few years ago).[8] His visualization of the kabbalistic re-vision of the invisible process whereby the intangible God created and relates to the tangible universe presents the viewer with the wherewithal to see.

But this works most effectively when the viewer spends the necessary time to focus on, to engage with kavannah in, the work. This is difficult not to do, for our eye is drawn to the center of many of his paintings before oscillating outward and then returning in towards the center. Such paintings, in inviting meditation on them and in them, not merely observation of them, recapitulate the artist's own process of arriving at such work (the contemporary Jewish meditation techniques associated, for example, with Rabbi Aryeh Kaplan), as well as his process of making such work, and create for the viewer a specific means of contemporary meditation.

In this sense, Friedman draws from the traditional vocabulary of Jewish mysticism a modernist language of seeking connection with that other realm. He re-implants contemporary, secularized psychedelic pre-occupation with otherness—multiplied by Hegel, modern biology, and the *I Ching*—in a Jewish context. One of his most complex works, *Unified Field Map* [fig. 24], functions like an electrical engineer's diagram of the universe. Its circuitry connects the points of a star of David to the routes of the *Spherot*, with Hebrew terms labeling the switches by referring to the parts of the body and the parts of the soul. The gigantic letters that form the pattern's superstructure, colored with the elemental hues, spell out the Name of God, *YHWH,* the root of which name means "is-ness." The being and becoming of all being is sketched out from the holy spirit, at the upper reaches of the image, to the sacred sanctuary that rests at its foundation.

DIANE SAMUELS AND INVISIBLE TEXTS FOR THE INEFFABLE ONE

Words and letters as intermediaries between the invisible, intangible, ineffable God of pure "is-ness" and us play yet differently in works like that of Diane Samuels. Her *"Letter Liturgy (for Leon, 1993-99)"* [fig. 25] reflects on an old Hasidic story regarding what God accepts as piety: not book-learned knowledge of the prayer book or the Torah, but the purity of the heart's intention, symbolized by the illiterate Jewish peasant who cannot read the prayers but keeps reciting the Hebrew alphabet, allowing God to combine the letters into words. The Hasidic tale refers to the simple but

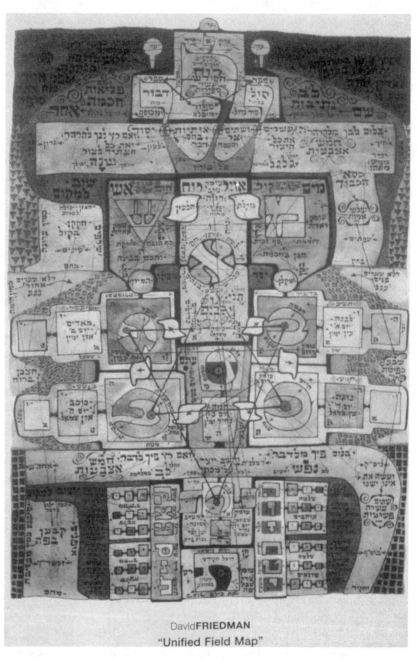

David**FRIEDMAN**
"Unified Field Map"

fig. 24 *Unified Field Map*

fig. 25 *Letter Liturgy (for Leon)*

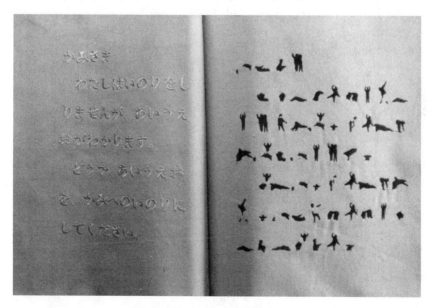

fig. 26 *The Book of Alphabet Prayers*

pious man who prays: "Dear God, I do not know how to pray. But I can recite the alphabet. Please accept my letters and form them into prayers."[9]

One is reminded of the work of both Kliner and Cahana, each of whom differently deconstructs or reconstructs the universe of letters: one from the Torah, the other from Holocaust victims' tattoos. Samuels plays emphatically on the very abstract arbitrariness of letters as symbols that in combination represent words and ideas. Are the "letters" in her "book" letters? If not, is this a book? Can non-letters form the words that comprise prayers? Do prayers require well-wrought words or, for a textual people like Jews, well-shaped letters? With what instruments—words? melodies? gestures? images?—does one most effectively address God? Is God listening and looking—is God interested any more?

What form of "art" uses only letters, white ones against white [fig. 26}? Is this "painting," "sculpture," or something else entirely? If this is in one sense neither text nor image, then it cannot be seen the way we ordinarily use that term to refer to texts and images: it is and is not part of our reality; it is and is not part of that other reality. It offers the ultimate pattern of mediation between the creator and the created, between artist and work of art, between God and humanity.

As Mordecai M. Kaplan, founder of Reconstructionist Judaism, might say, whether or not God is listening becomes secondary to the fulfillment of our human need to address God. The expanding interest in spirituality overall, including the more intense form of spirituality that we call mysticism, evident in the last part of the twentieth century and the beginning of the twenty-first makes clear how deep the need is to approach the revelation of the hidden and to make visible the unseen. For contemporary Jews, the instrumentation of fulfillment and approach clearly and emphatically includes the visual arts. Whether the address of the Other is based in the specifics of Jewish mysticism or more broadly and simply born out of a spiritual thirst, we continue to explore what we are as a people of words, ideas, and images, a people of endless range and variety. Each artist follows a unique path in envisioning the unfathomable *mysterium* that, according to centuries of esoteric exploration, lies beyond the endless recesses of the universe.

ACKNOWLEDGMENTS

All photographic reproductions in this article are provided by the author, who has full permission to use them here.

NOTES

[1] This is a long discussion beyond the purposes of this article. See, among others, Gerschom Scholem, *Modern Trends in Jewish Mysticism* (New York: Schocken, 1961), 156-204, for the most cogent of his (and others') arguments.

[2] See Morris M. Faierstein, "From Kabbalist to Zaddik: R. Isaac Luria as Precursor of the Baal Shem Tov," in *Studies in Jewish Civilization 13: Spiritual Dimensions of Judaism* (Omaha: Creighton University Press), 95-104.

[3] In a letter to the author in 1997.

[4] In a conversation with the author.

[5] The story of the Golem of Prague is a cross between Frankenstein and the Sorcerer's Apprentice—long before either of these was written. The legend claims that when it became clear that the golem could be as dangerous as he was useful, since only Rabbi Loew really knew how to control him, the Rabbi removed the name of God (or the word "Truth") from his mouth (or wiped it from his forehead), thus returning the golem to an inanimate state. The most common version asserts that he did this late at night in the attic of the Alt-Neu Schul [or Old-New Synagogue], where the clay body is said to remain hidden.

[6] In a conversation with the author in 1997.

[7] *Ibid.*

[8] In a conversation with the author in 1997.

[9] An alternate version has the simple and pious man explaining to the great mystic Isaac Luria that this is how he prays, when Luria inquires as to how and why his prayers are so effective. A third version has the Hasidic rebbe reassure the simple and pious man that, if he keeps reciting the letters of the alphabet with strong and pure intention—*kavannah*—God will know how to formulate them into prayers.

Elements of Spirituality in the Architecture of American Synagogues, 1763-2000

Thomas A. Kuhlman

In her keynote speech for this Klutznick-Harris Symposium, Dr. Hava Tirosh-Samuelson of Arizona State University stated: "spirituality implies the opposite of the corporeal."[1] How, then, can we find spirituality in architecture, which by nature is physical, material, and very much of this finite world? My paper rests on the assumption that a relationship exists between spirituality and architecture when a building succeeds in providing a designed and built environment in which an individual or a congregation of individuals are inspired to perform, in a serious, intense, and significant way, three elements of their religious faith: worship, study, and humane social interaction.

At different times and places, and among different peoples, buildings that may be impressive for secular and aesthetic reasons have failed in this purpose. As Tirosh-Samuelson says, for much of the twentieth century, an affluent and secure culture offered its younger generation splendid suburban facilities that did not inculcate a vibrant spirituality, but instead turned the young to secular rather than to religious paths and actions for the fulfillment of their spiritual hunger.[2] I nevertheless maintain that in both the acts of designing and building synagogues, as well as in the acts performed by various members of congregations in these physical spaces, inspiration can be found, and thus spirituality—as the root of the words "inspiration" and "spirituality" is, of course, the same.

Jon D. Levenson beautifully expresses the relationship between Jewish spirituality and architecture when he discusses the concept of cosmos and ritual in regard to the Jerusalem Temple, where these were expressed as perfectly as the human mind can grasp them. The synagogue of recent centuries, to those who await the rebuilding of the Jerusalem Temple, may only imperfectly express the divine will for the cosmos and ritual, but it must have to some degree the same function.[3] In recognition of this special nature of the synagogue, my purpose in this paper is twofold: first, to integrate the synagogue into the larger narrative of American architecture with a chronological survey emphasizing the presence of Jewish spirituality in a variety of times and places of structural representations, and second, to identify those elements of design that have as their achievement unique but characteristic expressions of true Jewish spirituality.

Chronologically, the tradition in America began in Newport, Rhode Island, with Touro Synagogue [fig. 1], today the oldest existing Jewish place of worship in the United States. Only synagogues in Curacao and Surinam go back farther in time in the Western Hemisphere. Dr. Isaac de Abraham Touro, who had come from the Rabbinical Academy in Amsterdam, formed the congregation in 1759. The Sephardic Jews he led had been attracted by the statement of Rhode Island's founder, Roger Williams, many decades before: "All men may walk as their conscience persuades them, everyone in the name of his God." This synagogue and its burial ground inspired Henry Wadsworth Longfellow to write the poem "The Jewish Cemetery at Newport" in 1852—at a time when the building was closed and seemed unlikely to open again.[4]

The Touro synagogue represents Georgian architecture in a city rich with many examples of the style, some by one of America's earliest architects, British-born Peter Harrison, who is also responsible for Touro's design. The exterior includes arched windows, a small entrance porch with two Ionic columns and a triangular pediment, and a belt course separating the two principal stories. Inside, Harrison's details are more elaborate, characteristic of the sophisticated English baroque; the ark, a cabinet carved after a pattern by the great English architect William Kent, exhibits swags, volutes, and a dentiled pediment on the frame surrounding the painted Ten Commandments. Grey and cream colors for the walls and woodwork increase the elegance and delicacy of the scheme, and brass chandeliers express the restrained formality of Colonial period architecture. The superbly carved cornice displays modilions and dentils, and twelve Corinthian columns supporting the gallery for women symbolize the twelve tribes of Israel.[5]

After the American Revolution, American architectural preferences were for Roman and Greek Revival buildings. In Charleston, South Carolina, the Beth Elohim Synagogue (a Sephardic congregation founded in 1748) is an 1840 structure designed by Charles F. Reichart and Charles B. Tappan in the Greek Revival style, with a portico with six Doric columns, an entablature with the customary metopes and triglyphs, and a triangular pediment with modilions along the cornice. Huge numbers of Protestant

fig. 1 Touro Synagogue, Newport

and Catholic churches were being built in the Greek Revival or Roman Revival style across the nation; this building shows how an American synagogue could display the latest architectural fashion of its time.

After the vogue for buildings in the Roman and Greek Revival styles came a fascination with the exotic. The Plum Street Temple in Cincinnati has been identified as "Moorish-Mudejar-Gothic-Jewish-Victorian" in style.[6] This is the Isaac M. Wise Temple, built in the years 1865 and 1866. Leading the B'nai Yeshuran congregation from 1853 to 1900, Wise was considered the founder of Reform Judaism in the United States; he established Hebrew Union College in 1875. This is where the first rabbis were ordained in the United States. The building, designed by James Keyes Wilson, is of brick and highly decorated stone, with two minarets rising fifty feet above the roof. It stands today across from a Greek Revival Roman Catholic cathedral from the 1840s and catercorner to a Romanesque City Hall designed by one of America's most celebrated architects, Henry Hobson Richardson, late in the same century, making a striking ensemble of varied styles and purposes.

Richardson's ideas were not confined to the design of city halls or his famous railroad stations, warehouses, and libraries. His ideas about massiveness and solidity, rough textures, and dramatic contrasts of light and shadow influenced Louis Sullivan, who, with his partner Dankmar Adler, brought these features to the design of a building that stands today on Chicago's South Side as the Pilgrim Baptist Church. Sullivan and Adler built this in 1890 and 1891 as the Keheleth Anshe M'ariv Synagogue. Architectural historian Roger C. Kennedy has cited Adler as "a great engineer and a part of Chicago's German-Jewish elite."[7] Adler's father-in-law had founded the congregation, and his father headed it. Kennedy considers this building, built of brick, Joliet stone, and pressed sheet metal, "extremely powerful," and after praising its "marvelous acoustics" and an interior "once shining with gold and rich, dark wood," concluded:

When the congregation is all present and the singing resounds under that great barrel vault, it celebrates the continuity of a religious space, which continues to serve a purpose so close to the original that only some shifts of accent and liturgy mark the passage of time. It remains dedicated to serving the Mystery, and the ghosts of Adler, his father, and father-in-law, must be pleased.[8]

By the beginning of the twentieth century, American architects were turning to the École des Beaux Arts in Paris for their training and their ideas. This influence is seen in a synagogue in Richmond, Virginia, where Temple Beth Ahabah was designed in 1904 in a Beaux Arts version of Greek Revival, with a dome and a Doric portico with four columns. The interior attempts a grandeur not imagined in the antebellum version of the Greek Revival, with a stained-glass window by Lewis Comfort Tiffany of "Mt. Sinai erupting at the very moment when God's presence became manifest to Moses."[9]

Cleveland, Ohio, saw a major step forward in American synagogue design in 1923 and 1924 with the building of a structure for Congregation Tiffereth Israel. The seven-sided modified Byzantine plan featured a dome over a sanctuary 90 feet in diameter, only 17 feet less than the dome of the Hagia Sophia in Istanbul, and 88 feet high. The architect was Charles R. Greco of Boston. Eric Johannesen has described the effect:

A warmth is imparted to the sanctuary by the dark wood of the ark and the balconies occupying four sides of the room. The overall impression if one of somber heavy richness, illuminated partly by the clerestory windows, but depending largely on artificial lighting. The exterior of the Temple is much more simplified than many eclectic Byzantine buildings. In fact, the severe geometry of the central mass and the twin entrance towers resemble the stripped-down historical forms best exemplified in the early twenties by Bertram Goodhue's Nebraska State Capitol, begun the year before.[10]

In this way, literal historicism is tempered by a modernist concern for clarity and strength of architectural line. These qualities in the architecture serve to represent and convey a spiritual, even prophetic, vision and religious commitment.

America had become the richest nation in the world after World War I, and New York was of course our richest city. There, at the corner of Fifth Avenue and 65th Street, a Reform congregation in 1929 erected the most magnificent of all American synagogues, Temple Emanu-El. It exemplifies the basilican tradition, with references to ancient Rome and with the use of Byzantine and Romanesque forms. The size is overwhelming: 150 feet along Fifth Avenue; 253 feet along 65th Street, a sanctuary 30 feet in depth and 40 in width, and an auditorium seating 2500—more than St. Patrick's Cathedral located a mile down the Avenue—and measuring 150 by 70 feet. The architects, Robert D. Kohn, Charles Butler, and Clarence S. Stein, specified Siena travertine marble for the walls of the vestibule, and red, green, and yellow columns for the support of the side galleries. The lavishness, says Kennedy, recalls Isa 54:11: "O afflicted one [Jerusalem] I lay your pavements in carnelians, and your foundations in sapphires; I will make your battlements of rubies, your gates of carbuncles, and all your walls of precious stones."[11]

The European-born architect Erich Mendelsohn gave Cleveland his own modernist design for another synagogue. Johannesen, quoted above in reference to the Tiffereth Israel Temple, praises "Mendelsohn's Park Synagogue, one of his last projects...generally regarded as a major work of twentieth century architecture...the largest and most ambitious of four synagogues designed by him and built in the United States between 1943 and 1953." Johannesen quotes Mendelsohn's own view of the project: It is "a community center, sheltering the three activities of a contemporary congregation: the house of worship—the House of God; the school for the education of the children—the House of the Torah; the auditorium for the assembly and the recreation of the adult members—the House of the People."[12]

The 100-feet-in-diameter dome was the third largest in the United States when built. Johannesen goes on to report:

Mendelsohn believed that in Judaism, God is not remote or mysterious but rather He is near and the heavens and earth are united in the Spirit of God. This is why the synagogue is virtually all dome....The drum of the dome is entirely glazed with large plate glass windows. Although many members wanted...stained glass, Mendelsohn rejected the idea, insisting that the view of nature through the clear glass would bring the congregation closer to the Spirit of God.[13]

Here in the Park Synagogue, Mendelsohn endowed his creation with a balance of traditional religious expression and form and twentieth century sensibility. His words and design both speak of how the synagogue is indeed the House of Jewish spirituality.

In Elkins Park, Pennsylvania, a suburb of Philadelphia, Frank Lloyd Wright, in 1954 at the apex of the second stage of his brilliant but stormy career, designed the synagogue for the Beth Sholom congregation quite without any traditional historic references or stylistic borrowings. Here was the master acting free of precedent as usual, but in sympathetic collaboration with the commissioner, Rabbi Mortimer J. Cohen, and his congregation. As the name "House of Peace" had been chosen as far back as 1920 to commemorate the end of the First World War, so the tent-like shape of the building reflected the Tabernacle that God had instructed Moses to build for the wandering Jews. The roof was supported by three aluminum uprights rising 117 feet into the air. Maria Constantino offers additional description of this near-miracle of modernism:

The forty-foot high concrete monolith which represents the stone tablets given to Moses forms the backdrop to the Ark containing the 10 Torah scrolls, one for each of the commandments.... The Ark had to be made of wood because metal was...[a symbol of war] and it must always be approached by steps—never fewer than three and as many as 12, as in the ancient Temple in Jerusalem. Over the Ark Wright had argued for a representation of the Burning Bush as a feature of the lighting. Cohen, however, was against the concept and sent Wright his design for the triangular aluminum and glass sculpture, "Wings," the colors of which symbolizes divine emanations.[14]

Constantino also refers to the hexagonal plan of the synagogue taking the form of "the cupped hands of God in which the congregation rests" and notes that "the ramps of the broad, deep stairs with shallow risers...suggest the ascent of Mount Sinai, and the light which filters through the walls symbolizes the divine gift of the law."[15] In other words, towards the end of his life, the nation's greatest architect participated with vigor and empathy in the creation of another milestone in the history of American synagogue design. And again, a particular Jewish congregation of mid-twentieth century America used the finest contemporary architectural ideas to foster and to express its own spiritual aspirations and religious traditions.

Continuing the movement to offer new forms for twentieth century religious life in America, Minoru Yamasaki designed Congregation Israel Synagogue in Highland Park (Glencoe), Illinois, in 1964, with walls and a roof of white concrete that remind many of delicate rose petals. Also in the 1960s, Walter Gropius in Baltimore and Philip Johnson and Louis Kahn in the New York suburbs of Port Chester and Chappaqua designed synagogues in a dramatically modernist style. Thus, the greatest names in the architecture of the late twentieth century are part of the story of our synagogues.

These buildings, from very old to the quite recent, represent the linear development of American architectural style. We may now consider the elements that, in addition to the symbolic effects referred to above, promote or facilitate spirituality. Although this spirituality may result from the traditional forms, symbols, and artifacts already mentioned, spirituality might also result from something else. Charles Jencks quotes the great twentieth century architect-utopian philosopher Le Corbusier (Eduard-Charles Jeanneret) commenting on his own world-famous chapel, Notre Dame du Haut, at Ronchamps, France. Le Corbusier asserted that the source of his design was not so much a concern for theology and dogma, but rather "an answer to a psychophysiology of the feelings." As Jencks explains, "Joy and meditation were the primary feelings [Le Corbusier] had in mind,"[16] Certainly Wright and Mendelsohn showed in their synagogue designs that they had similar concerns and goals.

Spirituality may also have its source in will, the will which worshipers, students, and philanthropists deliberately bring to a building as the motive for their actions within it. Thus we may consider that the first American synagogue, in Newport, turned its congregants' thoughts to spirituality through a pronouncement of its warden Moses Seixas in a letter to George Washington in 1790:

> Deprived as we heretofore have been of the invaluable rights of
> free citizens, we now (with a deep sense of gratitude to the Almighty
> Dispenser of all events) behold a Government erected by the

majesty of the people, a Government which gives to bigotry no sanction, to persecution no assistance.[17]

Is this spirituality? Pragmatism, it surely is, but idealism too; that this first synagogue in the United States had as its warden a man with such thoughts as these invested the structure with a meaning both eternal in its validity and specific in its period. The twentieth century novelist Herman Wouk seems to have experienced this spirituality within the building: on a visit in 1972 he wrote in the visitor's book a passage from Ps 30: "I will extol Thee, O Lord; for Thou hast delivered me, and has not made my foes rejoice over me."[18]

Idealism and spirituality are clearly related. But what about material richness in spirituality, as in the case of Temple Emanu-El in New York? If "spirituality implies the opposite of the corporeal," as Tirosh-Samuelson has said, how do we reconcile these opposites? For all its worldly grandeur, New York's Temple Emanu-El does indeed exhibit the spirituality of will, in light of the statement made by its President, Louis Marshall, on the occasion of the laying of its cornerstone on May 4, 1928:

> The concept of the architects is that of symbolizing monotheism and the deathless story of Israel. This in itself will be significant, but in the end will be of little use if it does not evoke and emphasize the spiritual values of those teachings of our prophets, our poets and our sages which have made Judaism through all the centuries a great civilizing force. Within this synagogue must dwell the Shechinah. Here Mercy and Truth must meet together, and Righteousness and Peace must kiss each other. Here Justice and Charity and the love of one's fellowman must be the line and plummet by which right living is to be attained. Here must be acquired that fear and knowledge of God which are the perfection of wisdom.[19]

I conclude by discussing some synagogues in Omaha, Nebraska, the city in which these symposia are held. Synagogue design continues here, and thus we are brought up to the twenty-first century.

Although today the structure houses the Greek Orthodox parish of St. John, the former Temple Israel building on Park Avenue, designed in 1908 by the local architect John Latenser, presents the familiar Beaux Arts dome-and-portico form. The congregation moved westward in 1954, into a building bearing the inscription, "This is the gate of the Lord. The Righteous shall enter it" [figs. 2 and 3]. A menorah stands in relief on a high slab on a western wall. Historic artifacts enhance the spirituality of

fig. 2 Temple Israel, Omaha

fig. 3 Temple Israel (New), Omaha

fig. 4 Old Beth El, Omaha

fig. 5 New Beth El 2000, Omaha

the interior. The chapel ark has two scrolls: an Ashkenazic Torah, rescued in 1938 from Germany by a family who later became members of the congregation, and a Sephardic scroll smuggled out of Egypt in 1963.

Omaha's Beth El Synagogue was housed in a fine structure in Dundee, in the central part of the city, designed by the locally prominent architect John McDonald [fig. 4]. The Conservative congregation moved with much of the city's Jewish population to the west in the 1990s, to a building designed by Boston architects Notter, Finegold, and Alexander in association with the Omaha firm of Wilscam Birge. The sprawling complex includes a sanctuary whose exterior roofline [fig. 5] is reminiscent of the wooden synagogues of Europe, and the exterior colors of the building and the shape of the windows evoke images of Jerusalem and the Holy Land. Inside, the west court has five arches [figs. 6-10] representing the five books of the Torah.

On Sunday, September 10, 2000, Rabbi Howard Kutner of the orthodox Beth Israel congregation, in their central Omaha synagogue designed in the 1950s by the Kansas City firm of Kivett and Myers [figs. 11 and 12], presided as local architect Martin Shukert presented to a large audience his ideas for a new synagogue, also to be built in the booming west of the city [fig. 13].20 Rabbi Kutner first quoted the Torah: "Build for me a sanctuary, says God, that I may dwell in their midst." Then Shukert, who had recently made a study tour of many East Coast synagogues, listed the characteristics of his design for the new Beth Israel. The structure should, following tradition, be built on the highest piece of land in the neighborhood. It would be sited close to the street and convenient for those who choose to walk to services. There would be separate entrances and aisles for men and women, and a five-row deep, twenty-five foot modesty wall would be included within the auditorium. Most important, the physical and spiritual heart of the complex would be the sanctuary, and special attention would be paid to its acoustics and those of the auditorium. Of course, a kosher kitchen and storage area would be part of the design, as well as flexible spaces for study, meetings, and recreation. Contemporary practical and legally required matters, such as fire codes and handicap accessibility, would receive attention: the bimah would be barrier-free. "Beth Israel Village" would be a small set of town homes for those who wish to live immediately adjacent to the synagogue.

Shukert stressed his intent to "quote"—as architects of our time so often do—from previous structures, using representations of architectural forms or details from earlier orthodox synagogues in order to give a sense

fig. 6 New Beth El

fig. 7 New Beth El Sanctuary-Chapel

fig. 8 New Beth El--Chapel

fig. 9 New Beth El

fig. 10 Beth El 2000

fig. 11 Beth Israel, Omaha

fig. 12 Beth Israel Chapel

fig. 13 Proposed West Omaha Beth Israel

of continuity in the new synagogue. And is not continuity an element of spirituality? Shukert's "quotations" will remind worshippers not just of their heritage, but also, and more importantly, of the eternal truths shared by all generations of Jews.

Having found it immensely pleasing to learn of the great tradition of synagogue building in America through the words and pictures provided by architectural critics and historians, I conclude my comments on spirituality in the Jewish tradition by quoting from the Tridentine Latin Mass of my childhood, words taken from Ps 26:8: *Domine dilexi decorem domus tuae, et locum habitationis gloriae tuae*: "I have loved, O Lord, the beauty of thy house, and the place where thy glory dwelleth."

ACKNOWLEDGMENT

Photographic illustrations for this essay are courtesy of the author.

NOTES

[1] Hava Tirosh-Samuelson, "Jewish Spirituality: Past Models and Present Quest," in *Studies in Jewish Civilization 13: Spiritual Dimensions of Judaism* (Omaha: Creighton University Press), 4.

[2] *Ibid.*, 2-3.

[3] Jon D. Levenson, "The Jerusalem Temple in Devotional and Visionary Experience," in *Jewish Spirituality: From the Bible Through the Middle Ages.* (ed. Arthur Green; New York: Crossroad, 1988), 32-61.

[4] Rabbi Dr. Theodore Lewis, "History of Touro Synagogue," *Bulletin of the Newport Historical Society* 48 (part 3; 159; Summer 1975): 281-320. Roger Williams is quoted on page 282; the reference to Longfellow is on page 299.

[5] Lewis, "History of Touro Synagogue," 284.

[6] Walter C. Langsam, *Cincinnati in Color* (New York: Hastings House 1978), 76.

[7] Roger C. Kennedy, *American Churches* (New York: Stewart, Tabori, and Chang, 1982), 35.

[8] Kennedy, *American Churches,* 35.

[9] John G. Zehmer, *Old Richmond Today* (Richmond: Council of Historic Richmond Foundation, 1988), 97.

[10] Eric Johannesen, *Cleveland Architecture: 1876-1976* (Cleveland: Western Reserve Historical Society, 1979), 159-60.

[11] Kennedy, 259.

[12] Johannesen, *Cleveland Architecture,* 204.

[13] Johannesen, 207.

[14] Maria Constantino, *The Life and Works of Frank Lloyd Wright* (London: Courage, 1998), 134-35.

[15] Constantino, *Frank Lloyd Wright*, 135.

[16] Charles Jencks, *Modern Movements in Architecture* (London: Penguin, 1985), 155.

[17] Lewis, "History of Touro Synagogue," 292.

[18] Lewis, 303.

[19] Lewis Marshall, dedication speech printed in display, with photograph of group at laying of cornerstone (May 4, 1928), in museum of Temple Emanu-El, New York, October, 2000.

[20] Martin H. Shukert, "Designing for God: Personal Reflections on Designing a Synagogue," in *Studies in Jewish Civilization 13: Spiritual Dimensions of Judaism* (Omaha: Creighton University Press), 179-84.

Designing for God: Personal Reflections on Designing a Synagogue

Martin H. Shukert

The chance to design a synagogue is a special opportunity for a Jewish architect. It is particularly important to a practitioner like me: my primary work is town planning and urban design, and building projects tend to be few and far between. I am an interpreter of relationships, one who delights in finding connections among things, ranging from parts of a city to sections of Torah commentaries and Hebrew texts. As such, I am strongly drawn to Thomas Kuhlman's formulation at this Klutznick-Harris Symposium that a relationship between spirituality and architecture exists "when a building succeeds in providing a designed and built environment in which an individual or a congregation of individuals are inspired to perform in a serious, intense, and significant way, three elements of their religious faith: worship, study, and humane social interaction." The statement is profound because it transcends the qualities that we often associate with "awe-inspiring" architecture and is in many ways a fundamentally Jewish way of looking at the building of synagogues. Indeed, *bet ha-k'nesset*, one of the Hebrew equivalents for the word "synagogue," means literally a house of gathering.

It has always been difficult to define Jewish architecture, partially because of the unique and often unsettled nature of Diaspora Judaism. Interestingly, Jewish architects have emerged at the forefront of the American and even world architectural scene in the late twentieth century. But synagogue architecture has always had something of a protean quality. The Torah describes the fittings and features of the *mishkan*, or the Tabernacle in the desert, and we can derive a floor plan from these descriptions. Yet no one, Frank Llloyd Wright at Beth Shalom notwithstanding, really knows what this portable structure looked like. Similarly, the Hebrew Bible tells us the size of Solomon's Temple and the expense and ornateness of its furnishings, but we have no real idea about its architectural style.

179

Authoritative writings on halacha [Jewish law] and traditions also provide some guidance to the designer. Such a guideline is the statement, more often representing the ideal than the real, that a synagogue should be taller than any other building in a town, except for those structures built solely for beauty.[1] Such prescriptions were often modified by expedience. In Italy, for example, many ornate synagogues looked like rather ordinary urban buildings from the street to avoid attracting undue attention. Similarly, such famous European synagogues as Amsterdam's Sephardic synagogue and London's Bevis Marks synagogue, are located off inner courtyards separated from city streets. While partially a nod to the hierarchy of courtyards of the *mishkan* and the Temple, this site device also served to avoid attracting the attention of those who wished the buildings and their congregations ill.

Synagogue architects, in augmenting traditional standards and guidelines in search of spirituality, have sought inspiration from two sources: the prevailing architectural motifs of their working environments and associations with major themes of Jewish literature, philosophy, and history. Buildings like Beth Elohim, the Wise Temple, and Temple Emanuel, all of which are discussed by Kuhlman, and New York's grandly restored Central Synagogue reflect the first trend. Modernists, on the other hand, tended to pursue the second direction. Thus, Mendelssohn's Park Synagogue interpreted the unity of heaven and earth, Wright addressed his conception of the form of the Tabernacle, and Percival Goodman's Shearith Israel in Southfield, Michigan, expressed the upreach of the congregation to the heavens.

However, many contemporary architects, while incorporating historical and scriptural antecedents and themes, seem to me to follow Kuhlman's formula that a synagogue is spiritual if it succeeds in encouraging the performance of things spiritual. The building is the supporting player, not the star of the show. Maurice Finegold's excellent Beth El Synagogue in Omaha (1991) is a fine example of this approach. The building's design incorporates allusions to both the hierarchy of the courts and the architecture of Jerusalem and the Polish synagogue. Yet, it is first and foremost a building designed for social interaction, creating a sanctuary that encourages and inspires prayer, but does not overwhelm it. When I had the opportunity to design an addition to the building, adding a social hall, an educational wing, a new interior courtyard, and an outside Peace Garden, I felt that the guiding principle was simply to listen to and remain consistent with the rhythms and integrity of the original building.

About three years ago, Beth Israel Synagogue, Omaha's Orthodox congregation, asked me to develop a master plan and conceptual design for a new building, a project that is now proceeding toward a fall, 2002 groundbreaking. The congregation's current home was designed by Kivett and Myers in the early 1950s, dating from a period of both a more expressionistic architecture and a time when many Orthodox congregations followed the "Chicago school" by allowing mixed seating and amplified sound on Shabbat and holidays. Previously, I had designed three buildings of importance to Omaha's Jewish community: the Gordman Center for Jewish Learning at the Jewish Community Center, housing Omaha's day school; a chapel at Beth El Cemetery; and the previously mentioned addition to Beth El Synagogue. Each was a special experience. Yet, the design of a completely new synagogue is a unique opportunity, purportedly a chance for spiritual self-expression. I say "purportedly" because my own self-expression can detract from what I believe is the real purpose of the building, to serve as a catalyst for the spiritual expression and work of the congregation. In approaching the project with Beth Israel, we considered three types of spirituality: the spirituality of place, the spirituality of the word, and the spirituality of continuity.

In trying to achieve the design of a spiritual place—a vessel for prayer, study, and interaction—we considered two quotations from the Hebrew Bible. The first is from the book of Kings and describes Elijah's vision of God after fleeing to a cave to escape the murderous persecution of prophets by Jezebel:

> The Lord passed by. There was a great and mighty wind, splitting mountains and shattering rocks by the power of the Lord; but the Lord was not in the wind. After the wind—an earthquake; but the Lord was not in the earthquake. After the earthquake—fire; but the Lord was not in the fire. And after the fire—a still, small voice. When Elijah heard it, he wrapped his mantle about his face and went out and stood at the entrance of the cave (1 Kgs 19:11-13).[2]

Adapted to the problem at hand, Jewish spirituality is not in the structural tour d'force or the soaring form, although in some traditions architecture does have the power to elevate the spirit. But Jewish spirituality is truly found in a place that encourages people to hear the "still, small voice," both from within and without.

The second quotation, one that I have always loved and that expresses so much of what I believe is wonderful about the fundamental outlook of Judaism, comes at the end of Moses' valedictory summary of the commandments of the Torah in Deuteronomy. Speaking of God's commandments to the people of Israel, Moses says:

> Surely this Instruction which I enjoin upon you this day is not too baffling for you, nor is it beyond reach. It is not in the heavens, that you should say, "Who among us can go up to the heavens and get it for us and impart it to us, that we may observe it?" Neither is it beyond the sea, that you should say, "Who among us can cross to the other side of the sea and get it for us and impart it to us, that we may observe it?" No, it is very close to you, in your mouth and in your heart, to observe it (Deut 30:11-14).

In synagogue design, this can be expressed by a building that is wonderful, yet down to earth and accessible; a building that welcomes, encourages, and does not intimidate. It also means accessibility in the literal sense: there is an element of spirituality in a bimah that is fully accessible to all users, whether disabled or able-bodied. This permits all congregants to participate seamlessly in the service without special arrangement or loss of dignity. Mendelsohn was clearly guided by these principles in the design of the great enclosing dome in his Cleveland synagogue.

The spirituality of the word also infuses synagogue design and character. For example, the walls of the famous wood synagogues of Poland were usually covered with illuminated texts. Because I love the Hebrew alphabet and the poetry of Hebrew texts, I believe that these words have a fundamental role to play in the space of the synagogue. Such words should speak to the users of the building, in a sense forming a prism against which they reflect their actions in the space. For example, the Hebrew expression "Know before whom you stand" is placed above arks in many sanctuaries. Text will also play a significant role in the Beth Israel sanctuary. On opposite walls, we will display two fundamental expressions of the Covenant at Sinai: "If you will obey Me faithfully and keep My covenant, you shall be My treasured possession among all the peoples" (Exod 19:5) and "You shall be to Me a kingdom of priests and a holy nation" (Exod 19:6). These words help provide both a measure and promise for prayer, which is expressed by a Hebrew word [l'hitpallel] implying self-judgment.

Finally, the spirituality of continuity and history is important to the Beth Israel design. Architects in general, building on the thinking of designers such as Robert Venturi and Robert Stern, frequently quote the past in contemporary buildings. Some may criticize this trend as a lack of confidence in the capacity to create new forms. Yet, architecture that builds on people's experiences and memories is now being incorporated into buildings from shopping malls to museums. Moreover, history is so fundamental for Judaism that it takes on emotional and even spiritual dimensions. Jews sometimes collapse history into an experiential singularity. Consider, for example, the commandment for parents to tell their children the story of the Exodus as if they were personally there to experience it. History and continuity are key to the Beth Israel design. This congregation was built on the foundation of two earlier congregations. Two predecessors, Beth Hamidrash Hagadol and B'nai Israel, each with grand downtown buildings, merged to create Beth Israel; the new congregation then built its new building in what was once the western part of the city. Our new building design acknowledges this history by incorporating elements of its predecessors in a unified whole that we hope will recall the spirit and energy of these earlier institutions. In this way, the new building can also merge the efforts of previous generations into a renewed Orthodox Jewish enterprise in Omaha.

Thus, spirituality in synagogue design—"designing for God"—is very different, I think, from conceiving of soaring spaces and dramatic lighting. It is about three types of spirituality: a spirituality of place, which conceives of the building as a catalyst for prayer, study, and interaction; a spirituality of the word, which uses our beautiful and special texts to advance and enrich these activities; and a spirituality of continuity, which unites the generations of this congregation across the years into a unified and renewed Orthodox enterprise. My prayer is that the finished building is capable of being transformed, when inhabited by its congregation, from a physical container into a spiritually enriching House of Israel.

NOTES

[1] Rabbi Yisrael Meir Kagan (The Chafetz Chaim), *Mishnah Berurah* (Jerusalem: Pisgah Foundation, 1993).
[2] All translations are from the *JPS Hebrew-English Tanakh* (Philadelphia: The Jewish Publication Society, 1999).

Visual Art as a Pathway to Prayer and Meditation

Jenni L. Schlossman

Works of art, ordinarily used to engage one's visual imagination, can also help people approach prayers in a new manner. Imagery integrated with text engages those who ordinarily would not be drawn into prayer, or cannot understand or read Hebrew. The artists, who often combine English with Hebrew, literally help people "see" prayer in a new and different way. Betsy Platkin Teutsch's *shivitis* in the Reconstructionist *Kol Haneshamah* prayer books fulfill the promise of how works of art can combine visual beauty with spiritual text. Teutsch said, "My *shivitis* create a different entry point into prayer for people who do not find the texts meaningful."[1] This essay considers imagery in contemporary prayer books that enhances prayers and helps to focus the worshippers' thoughts on prayer in a manner similar to Teutsch's *shivitis,* as well as works of art by two other artists combining art with prayer.

Considering the second Commandment's ban on graven images, artists, among others, have interpreted the prohibition in ways that allow them to create visual art, so long as the works are not to be worshipped as idols. If art is used to decorate or beautify an object, visual imagery is allowed, as in Exod 15:2, "This is my God and I will beautify (glorify) him." This passage, known as *hiddur mitzvah,* is used to support making beautiful ritual objects.[2] For example, during the time when the Jews wandered in the desert, the instructions given to Moses by God (Exod 25:27) directed the artist Bezazel to create two sculptured figures to decorate the ark that held the Ten Commandments: Create "two cherubim of gold: of beaten work shalt thou make them, at the two ends of the ark cover" (Exod 25:18).[3] There is a distinction between the early use of visual art for *hiddur mitzvah,* as in an individually produced prayer book with illuminations and beautiful calligraphy, and the use of visual images to create *kavannah* [intention or consciousness], or the proper state of mind for prayer, as in Teutsch's *shivitis.* Tzvee Zahavy has written, "Samuel said, 'I count birds [to help me induce the proper state of mind].'" Zahavy also relates Rabbi Ben bar Hiyya's words: "I count rows of bricks [in a wall to aid me in achieving the proper state of mind]."[4] Birds and bricks can be represented to beautify a text; however, these images seen in nature can also be used to help one cultivate a meditative state; that is, they may be used as a "means to enhance one's concentration, to modify a person's state of consciousness, perhaps to induce a special state of consciousness, close to what we might call a simple form of trance."[5] Therefore, not only can bricks and birds be pretty decorations, but they can also be visual aids that help to focus one's mind in order to be able to meditate on prayer. This article discusses the use of visual art to enter into a meditative state—not just counting birds or bricks (or sheep, for that matter), but works of art made by professional artists who want to contribute to their viewers' concentration for prayer.

HISTORICAL USES OF VISUAL IMAGERY IN A JEWISH CONTEXT

Synagogues as early as the 3rd century CE were decorated with paintings, as seen, for example, on the walls of the Dura-Europos synagogue (c. 245 CE) in present-day Syria. It has been suggested that if it was permissible to decorate a house of worship, it is likely that Hebrew manuscripts intended for personal use were also illuminated as early as the third century CE.[6] The leader of the Jewish communities in late thirteenth century Germany, Rabbi Meir ben Baruch of Rothenburg, wrote that illustrations in prayer books would distract a worshipper, but he did not ban the use of imagery because of the second Commandment.[7] Throughout Europe, in the fourteenth through eighteenth centuries, there were a number of illuminated prayer books and other manuscripts. A variety of rules governed what imagery was allowed to be included.[8]

Sometimes decorative texts use micrographic script. Using miniature letters, the words of texts themselves create contour line drawings of assorted shapes, architectural forms, animals, plants, and figures. The earliest extant Jewish micrographic script appears in the late ninth century Moshe Ben Asher Codex. Many times, but not always, the shapes relate to the subject matter.[9] In this way, micrography actually does integrate text and visual art. The makers of these images were scribes rather than visual artists. Scribes were able to show off their proficiency rather than enable viewers to expand their comprehension of the texts while praying or meditating.

CONTEMPORARY PRAYER BOOKS

Much of this paper focuses on imagery found in contemporary daily, Shabbat, and High Holiday prayer books. Because of the narrow scope of this analysis, the rich tradition of visual art illustrating the Hebrew Bible, the Passover Haggadah, and the Book of Esther, for example, is not considered. There seem to be far fewer examples of art in contemporary prayer books. However, the current spiritual climate found in the United States appears to be accepting of visual art in conjunction with prayer.

In the nineteenth and twentieth centuries, the individualistic touch of the artist's hand that had been found in personalized illuminated manuscripts was replaced by mass-produced printed prayer books. Many twentieth century prayer books are professionally designed and beautiful to look at, but are completed with few if any illustrations.[10] For example, the *Complete Artscroll Siddur*, 1984, employs different styles of typography, layout, and ornamental graphics throughout the volume, all of which make it pleasing to look at.[11] Besides the small leaf and scroll design to mark the names of the prayers, each paragraph begins with bold type, and some text is included in gray boxes to show prayers not included for everyday recitation. There are, however, no illustrations.

Another example is the *Conservative Siddur Sim Shalom, A Prayerbook for Shabbat, Festivals, and Weekdays*, 1985, which incorporates a graphic design of two small flowers with a curving line between them.[12] The layout of the Conservative prayer book is precisely crafted, as is the *Artscroll* prayer book. However, there is nothing included that could be called an illustration or a work of art that stands on its own. The power and history of traditional texts engage the worshipper.

Some Hasidic prayer books have traditional *shivitis* printed in them. In the *Siddur Korban Asher* [The Sacrifice of Asher Prayer Book], 1986, there is a *shiviti*, as well as drawings, including pictures of food on pages with blessings before meals and depictions of how to place *tefillin*. The drawings are illustrations, describing actions and helping to identify prayers, rather than works of art themselves.[13] The *shiviti*, with its standard texts, follows the established look of nineteenth century *shivitis*. It is probably included in the prayer book for the same reason a *shiviti* plaque hangs on the wall near the ark of a synagogue; namely to help focus worshippers' concentration on God and improve their state of mind for prayers.

The Reconstructionist movement also updated its prayer books in the 1980s. The first to be published in 1989 was an experimental edition, *Kol Haneshamah, Shabbat Eve,* which reproduced Teutsch's first *shiviti* as well as her numerous illustrations.[14] In the 1990s, the Reconstructionist Press published the complete *Kol Haneshamah* prayer book series: *Shabbat and Holidays*, 1994; *Daily Prayer Book*, 1996; and *Prayer Book for the Days of Awe* (the High Holidays), 1999, all of which include text illustrations and *shivitis* by Teutsch.[15]

During the 1990s, at least two Jewish Renewal groups prepared their own prayer books, both of which include visual material: the *Meta-Siddur*, version 5.0, "A Jewish Soul-Development Workbook," originally published in the early 1990s by Rabbi David Wolfe-Blank for Eitz Or Congregation in Seattle; and *An Invitation to Prayer*, 2000, for Temple Adath Or, Fort Lauderdale, Florida.[16]

Rabbi Wolfe-Blank developed his *Meta-Siddur* from handouts for a conversion class held in the early 1990s. It is a spiral-bound, black-and-white collection of photocopies, to be updated periodically. Inspiration stemmed from the Aquarian Minyan prayer books that he had helped develop in the 1980s, which also included illustrations.[17] On the cover of his *Meta-Siddur*, he wrote:

This book is not meant to be...davvened as a prayerbook....It is intended as an aid and adjunct to the traditional *Siddur* [prayer book]; to spark the reader's ability to be creative with prayer; and to deepen the appreciation of the possibilities inherent in the *Siddur*....Retranslating and re-interpreting the *Siddur* in our own time continues the ancient process of integrating inherited tradition with modern experiences and needs.[18]

He included a number of meditations with pictures, and combined text and imagery to "inspire" the worshipper.[19] For example, on a page with morning prayers, there is a figure with hands raised in the priestly blessing, and within his body is the phrase *ufros aleynu sukkat shelomecha* [Spread over us the shelter of your peace], from the *Hashkivenu* [Divine Help] prayer [fig. 1]. This is only one of many examples of figurative art in the *Meta-Siddur*.

An Invitation to Prayer includes colorplates of works by professional Florida artists and by the rabbi of the congregation, Shoni Labowitz. Rabbi Labowitz and a congregant wrote, compiled, and edited the prayer book. The book is ten inches square, to "symbolize the Ten Gates of the Kabbalistic Tree of Life and the Ten Utterances of God [later translated into the Ten Commandments]."[20] The page layout is uncluttered, with the feminine Hebrew on the left page in gold lettering and the masculine Hebrew on the right with blue lettering, followed by two pages of transliterations and one page of English translation. In two colorplate sections, works of art are reproduced to accompany prayers or for meditative purposes. The pictures are not integrated with the prayers, but stand alone as avenues that can lead the worshipper down a visual route of devotion.

The painting *Shema Prayer* by Cheyenne Chernov [fig. 2] uses color and the placement of words to evoke the spirituality and meditative quality of the prayer, "Listen, Israel: The Eternal is our God, The Eternal One alone!"[21] A golden glow outlines each word and frames Chernov's square painting. The blue lines inside the golden frame are neither perfectly straight nor square, underscoring the countless subtleties of even simple things such as lines as well as the nuances of what could be a simple, six word prayer. The artist gives each word its own line, allowing the worshipper to meditate on it within the context of the whole prayer. Separated by the most space, the first word, *shema* [listen], and the last words *adonai* [God] and *echad* [one] emphasize the importance of each of these words apart from the overall prayer. It is as though the worshipper is to meditate upon each word separately for a number of seconds before moving on to the next, quieting one's mind and slowing one's breath while contemplating the meaning and visual beauty of each word. Here, the visual art is used to help focus thought wholly on the prayer. Traditionally, during the Shema prayer, worshippers close their eyes to block out everything else so that they can concentrate completely on the words and the meaning of the prayer; in this case, however, one's eyes must be open to fully concentrate on the nuances created by the visual image. Eva-Lynn Diesenhaus, another contemporary artist, also uses the Shema prayer in an artist's book discussed later in this essay [fig. 11].

RECONSTRUCTIONIST *KOL HANESHAMAH* PRAYER BOOKS
The Reconstructionist *Kol Haneshamah* series, first published in 1989, before the *Meta-Siddur* and *An Invitation to Prayer,* uses Betsy Platkin Teutsch's black-and-white drawings and *shivitis* throughout the text. She was commissioned to enhance the prayer books with calligraphic artwork and to create five *shivitis* as alternative meditations for the Amidah prayer. In the introduction to the Shabbat prayer book, the editor wrote:
Most of the artwork in this Siddur is calligraphic because representational art has not been a frequently used Jewish form. While including artwork in a Siddur is uncommon, it reflects a deep commitment to all aspects of Jewish civilization. That commitment has been the hallmark of the Reconstructionist movement.[22]

Teutsch said that she could not find a precedent for "illustrating" a prayer book in the manner in which she chose and that her *shivitis* are not really "illustrations" or "illuminations" because she is "integrating imagery with the prayers."[23] Her works of art enhance the meaning and experience of the prayers and Psalms. For example, in the borders surrounding the grace after meals, her drawings sequentially depict a seed sprouting and growing larger on each of the following pages, as well as a branch blossoming and bearing fruit.

The *Kol Haneshamah* editorial committee included the *shiviti* drawings as "tools for inner exploration...to enrich the prayer experience."[24] There are also guided meditations in English that walk worshippers through steps that help them pray and meditate with the *shivitis*. These meditations must be done with one's eyes open in order for the words of the prayers to be enriched by the visual design. Teutsch's first *shiviti*, published in the experimental edition of the Friday evening *Kol Haneshamah*, was a fascinating addition to the Reconstructionist prayer book.

HISTORY OF *SHIVITIS*

Since the eighteenth century, a *shiviti* has traditionally been hung in a synagogue, sometimes on the eastern wall like a *mizrach*. *Mizrach* [east] is an acrostic that translates "from this side comes the spirit of life."[25] A *mizrach* is typically hung on the eastern wall in a European or American Jewish home to identify the direction of Jerusalem and to remember the Holy Temple. Therefore, when facing a *mizrach*, people know they are facing in the correct direction to pray. It is also a symbol of God's protection of the family's home.[26] Since the 1970s, *shivitis* can also be found in American homes, not just in synagogues, since some feel "that one should *always* be conscious of God's presence."[27]

Shivitis are a form of folk art, not a prescribed ritual object, so there are few rules to follow to create them. The only thing that a *shiviti* plaque must have are the words from Ps 16:8, *shiviti adonai lenegdi tamid*, which may be translated as, "I place God before me always" or "I have set the Lord always before me";[28] one of Teutsch's translations is, "I will be ever aware of God's presence."[29] She says, "Because of its devotional nature, a *shiviti* generally has God's four-letter Name centrally displayed."[30] Said as part of daily prayer, Ps 16:8 came to be seen as showing one's devotion to God. This prayer is different from most because it is in the first person, "shiviti" [I place or I have set], rather than the usual "we."[31]

Teutsch explained that *shiviti* is similar to *shivion*, meaning equality in

Hebrew. A more nuanced meaning of *shivion* is that we are on a balance, like a seesaw, on which one person balances against another. Therefore, the *shiviti* verse also connotes that we are in balance with God in front of us on the other side of the seesaw.[32]

Shoshana Cooper, composer of a musical chant for the *shiviti* verse, wrote, "*Lenegdi* means 'as up against me.' It was used first in Genesis in relationship to Adam and Eve. There are other Hebrew words that could be used to say 'before me.' This one has a distinct call for both a sense of separate and yet connected."[33] Therefore, there is a sense that God is both within and outside of worshippers as they chant God's name during the recitation of Ps 16:8. It is this closeness to God that makes the *shiviti* verse so appealing and its succinctness that makes it attractive in visual form.

Traditional *shiviti* plaques are intricately decorated with biblical verses and Psalms, buildings symbolizing Jerusalem, animals, amulets, or magical symbols and verses. They are larger than a typical contemporary prayer book (approximately 6" x 9") because they were made for wall decorations with free-hand calligraphy and other visual elements. They are typically rectangular and black and white, with a text border surrounding Ps 16:8. Most often, centered below the *shiviti* phrase, is the seven-branched menorah from the Temple in Jerusalem; the "Menorah Psalm," Ps 67, within or surrounding the candelabra, gives thanks for a good harvest. It is known as the Menorah Psalm because its seven verses form the seven-branched symbol.[34] "The 'menorah'...is the most enduring symbol of Judaism, tracing its origins back to the 'mishkan,' the portable sanctuary in the wilderness."[35] "Psalm 67, according to legend, was engraved in the form of a menorah on David's shield, has been frequently reproduced in the form of a menorah in amulets, *shivitim*, and Sephardi prayer books."[36]

"Most *shiviti* plaques derive from Eastern Europe in the nineteenth century....Some plaques...come from North Africa, mainly Morocco."[37] Three nineteenth century *shiviti* plaques will be discussed before presenting Teutsch's contemporary interpretations. Nineteenth century *shivitis* were created as freestanding wall plaques; Teutsch's original concept was to create a black-and-white *shiviti* to be included in a prayer book. The idea for her *shivitis* to be separate color prints came after the original conception.

The first example is a traditional black-and-white *shiviti* from North Africa, from the mid-nineteenth century [fig. 3]. The Tetragrammaton is emphasized within its black-and-white, rectangular format. YHWH is the largest, darkest word, placed centrally above all else except the verse creating the border. Within the tops of the black letters spelling God's name, the artist inserted in small white letters *adonai*, the name of God to be pronounced when reading the large YHWH. A menorah, created from the text of Ps 67, is centered below; the rest of the design consists of written verses. Because it is all black and white calligraphy, it looks most like Teutsch's published *shivitis*. However, within the plaque are traditional verses, prayers, and imagery, unlike Teutsch's. Flanking the word YHWH are two Jewish symbols, stars of David. The top line of the border of this *shiviti* (and a number of other standard *shivitis*) begins, "Know before whom you are standing." The top edge continues, "The King of Kings, the Holy One, blessed be he."[38] Psalm 121 forms the other three edges. The second largest and darkest writing, centrally placed on the bottom within an eye shape, alternates the four letters of the Tetragrammaton with the four Hebrew letters of *adonai*, a combination also found in other *shivitis*. The smallest calligraphic writing forms symmetrical circular and semi-circular designs around the bolder printing, adding an artistic element to an image filled with words. Much of the plaque is filled with intricate calligraphy containing "names of angels and letters of the alphabet whose arrangement has mystical or magical value."[39]

Intricate and ornate drawings filled with symbols and emblems of mysticism are also found in a colorful nineteenth century *shiviti* by Solomon ben David Attias [fig. 4]. It contains words and imagery intertwined in a stimulating visual context. The size, 23 ¾" x 17 ¼", is significantly larger than the 8 ¼" x 5 ¼" *Kol Haneshamah* prayer book. As in many *shivitis*, the Tetragrammaton is centrally placed on the top of the page, although in this example it is not the largest and most emphasized word. The largest names are those of four angels: Michael, Raphael, Gabriel, and Uriel; however, the Tetragrammaton is centrally located above the menorah and higher than all the rest of the names. This YHWH is a word in the *shiviti* verse, and while the work of art is a *shiviti* plaque, Ps 16:8 does not seem to be the most emphasized element. Above YHWH is written, "was, is, and always will be," an interpretation of the name of God. On the upper left and right, under the arches, are the hands of the priestly blessing. Under the names of both Michael and Gabriel is a pitcher of oil, surrounded by biblical names. The larger circles contain some of the forty-two mystical names of God.[40] Surrounding the centrally located menorah that contains the words of Ps 67 are delicately rendered flowers, some growing from a vase below the menorah. Surrounding the central image are over a hundred circles with mystical, kabbalistic writing in a serpentine design. Simplified flowers in an intricate, abstract arrangement frame the entire work. The entire layout is completed by a muted two-color scheme of red and green, along with black. While the overall design is busy and complex, the *shiviti* as a whole helps to focus one's mind on God's presence.

A much less complex nineteenth century *shiviti* is from the United States, a paper cut with gold ink by Phillip Cohen, 1861, 25 ¼" x 19 3/8" [fig. 5]. He encloses Ps 16:8 within two white circles, enlarging and emphasizing God's name and the word *tamid* [forever]. Underneath, in a pointed archway, the words, "This is the gate of God," appear in black writing against a white background, as also found in the circles above. White light in the archway and circles appears to be inviting the viewer into a holy time and space for prayer. These words are placed within a design using a gate and columns to refer to the architecture of the Temple in Jerusalem, with keys to the gate of God hanging within the columns. Above the columns, in an unusual addition to a *shiviti*, Cohen included his own symbols, two flags of the United States. In the lower half of the plaque an intricate menorah, formed without the words of Ps 67, is surrounded with floral designs. The menorah's base is supported by the text of Ps 50:1, "From the sun rising in the East until it sets in the West." To the left of the menorah Cohen wrote, "Tree of knowledge," and to the right, "Tree of life," as though the menorah were also a symbol of the tree in the Garden of Eden and a metaphor for the Torah. Three contemporary artists included in this essay also include the tree of life in their works, Teutsch [fig. 8], Eva-Lynn Diesenhaus [fig. 12], and Peggy Davis [fig. 13].[41]

BETSY PLATKIN TEUTSCH'S *SHIVITIS* IN THE RECONSTRUCTIONIST *KOL HANESHAMAH* PRAYER BOOK SERIES

As documented above, the *shiviti* form is not new. What is new is its use in a Reconstructionist prayer book that is meant for mass production, as opposed to *shiviti* plaques that were created as single works. Teutsch created *shivitis* that diverge from the standard texts and their rectangular shapes. Using texts from *Kol Haneshamah*, she created *shivitis* for specific occasions, including Shabbat, Rosh Hashanah, and Yom Kippur, and for those in mourning. After 1989, when she published her most traditional-looking *shiviti*, *Shabbat Eve* [fig. 6], in the Friday night experimental edition of the Shabbat prayer book, Teutsch continued to revise and refine the *shiviti* format, basing her personal renditions and unique designs on the thematic texts involved [figs 7, 8, 9, 10].[42] She added English translations for most of the Hebrew, thereby opening the use of the *shivitis* to those who cannot understand Hebrew. Teutsch also simplified. Her *shivitis* needed to be readable in small scale because they were to be published in a prayer book with pages measuring 8 ¼" x 5 ¼", which meant her images would be approximately 6" x 4 ½".

The idea of including *shivitis* in Reconstructionist prayer books arose in a subcommittee of the prayer book commission. This group of rabbis was considering how to integrate art into the prayer books and came up with the idea of including a full-page work of art that would be based on a *shiviti*, as well as other illustrations that would augment the text. The commission selected Teutsch. Although she was not trained as a scribe, she had illustrated Michael Strassfeld's *Jewish Holidays: A Guide and Commentary*.[43] At first, Teutsch treated the *shivitis* as any artistic assignment. Nine years later, when she sat down to think about making her *shivitis* for the High Holiday prayer book, she put on a *kippah* [skull cap] and entered into a state of prayer. By the time the High Holiday prayer book was compiled, Teutsch's artistic input was seen as so important that she became a member of the prayer book commission.

Teutsch's first *shiviti, Shabbat Eve* [fig. 6], was created in 1989 as an alternative means of praying the Amidah during the Friday night Shabbat service. While the format was conventional, the content was not. The Tetragrammaton is the largest word and placed centrally within the *shiviti* verse. A black rectangular shape, emphasizing these letters above all else, surrounds the white letters YHWH. The white shapes of the letters against the black create the only sense of depth found in this *shiviti*, and it is an infinite space, not defined by lines of perspective. Small, calligraphic writing fills the page. There is the usual horizontal border of words along the top and bottom, yet the sides are simplified, consisting only of vertical lines. There is a centralized menorah, mimicking the form of standard *shivitis*, but the verses are not from Ps 67, but instead are drawn from the Friday night Shabbat service. Also, the left side of the menorah is the English translation of the Hebrew. Within the rest of the *shiviti* there are symbols: the sun, moon, eyes, and hands. However, the hands do not stand for the priestly blessing, but rather for doves.

The words from Ps 150, which incorporate the name of the prayer book and create three arches above the menorah, may be translated, "Let every living thing Yah's praises sing!" The Hebrew in the central arch is emphasized by its dark, ornate calligraphic script; decorative flourishes, or crowns, are found on certain letters of the alphabet in Hebrew scribal writing in the Ashkenazic tradition.[44] Teutsch was excited about the name of the new series of prayer books, *Kol Haneshamah*, usually translated "your whole soul or spirit";[45] but "*kol haneshamah*" could also mean, "all the soul." As the editor-in-chief, Rabbi Teutsch explained, "Let it be the soul's voice that offers praise."[46] Teutsch's five *shivitis* visualize her praise for God in a manner befitting an artist.

The theme of Teutsch's first *shiviti*, breathing, is reflected in a number of verses she picked that focus on breathing and/or have the "ah" sound at the end of the word (to emphasize breathing out while saying "ah"). This slows down the worshipper's pace, making it more meditative. Also, as written in the guided meditation that corresponds to this *shiviti*, "As you follow your breath, reflect on the divine energy it contains."[47] Teutsch subtly influences the reader of the verse on the right side of the menorah to focus on the "ah" sound by making the letter *hey* at the end of words slightly bigger. It starts, *elohay neshamah* [My God, the soul]. Rabbi Teutsch's commentary reads, "When this prayer is chanted slowly, you breathe these words. Thus this prayer suggests an opportunity, through breathing, to explore the connection between *neshamah* as breath and as soul."[48] Rabbi Teutsch affirms the connection between the name of the prayer book and the theme of *Shabbat Eve*.

The underlined verses to the left of the menorah are from Isa 42:5-6, which speaks of God's giving breath to people on earth; the bottom line, which helps to form the arch under the menorah, is from Gen 2:7, where God created humans and breathed into their nostrils the breath of life. The three words below the arch say that *neshamah* [your soul] equals *hashamayim* [the heavens]. The verses to the right and left of the menorah, and those that support it, the eye shapes, and surprisingly, even the *shiviti* verse are not translated into English. As a result, many of the references to "breath" and "breathing" are not available to the non-Hebrew reader.

Since this *shiviti* may be used as an alternative Amidah meditation, there are also a few references to the Amidah. The sentence above the menorah, for example, "Open my lips, God, and let my mouth declare your praise," is the line preceding the beginning of the Amidah and sets the mood for the whole prayer. This line is centrally located and larger than most of the text. The line parallel to it, under the *shiviti* verse, is the third prayer of the Amidah, "May my words of prayer and my heart's meditation be seen favorably, *Yah*/Beloved One, my rock and my redeemer." These Amidah verses are translated into English on the *shiviti*.

Near the end of *Kol Haneshamah: Shabbat Vehagim* are alternative Amidah meditations in English, based on Teutsch's *shiviti*. The editor explains:

> The *shiviti* is a spiritual tool. It provides a visual focus for efforts to sense the divine presence. Facing that presence through the *shiviti* design, feeling surrounded by the divine embracing the divine within ourselves leads to awareness of the fullness of God—and to the godliness which fills us. The *shiviti* meditation can yield new insight—a sense of harmony and balance. It can give us a sense of our place in the order of things. It can provide fresh perspective, clarity, and energy....The first time user can begin by exploring the *shiviti*—responding to its overall shape, reading its words, contemplating their meanings.[49]

Essentially, people can use the *shiviti* to help focus their thoughts and to "feel the presence of God."[50]

While the first *shiviti* was designed to be in the Shabbat prayer book as a small, black-and-white design, it ended up as a large, lithographic print as well. Serendipitously, when Teutsch and Rabbi Mordechai Liebling were examining the negative image (on a photostat, a process rarely used anymore), they saw the white writing against a dark background. Rabbi Liebling, on the spur of the moment, recognized the beauty of the negative image and decided to print a series of color lithographs of *Shabbat Eve* to sell or give away with the prayer book orders the Reconstructionist Federation received. Thereafter, all the remaining *shivitis* were planned both as small, black-and-white images and as larger color prints to sell separately as wall hangings—as traditional *shiviti* plaques had been conceived.

In 1993, when the second edition of the Shabbat prayer book was being compiled, Teutsch and the art committee examined her first *shiviti* page. Teutsch was not completely satisfied with the standard rectangular shape, the four corners, and the centralized menorah. Someone noticed that the gates above God's name were closed, and everyone agreed that they should be opened. Teutsch opened the gates for the second edition. Also, the committee had received some comments that the writing was too small to read. Teutsch responded by simplifying and clarifying the rest of her *shivitis*.

TEUTSCH'S SECOND SHABBAT *SHIVITI*

Teutsch's *Creation: Shabbat Vehagim*, 1994 [fig. 7], an oval-shaped flower, abandons the traditional rectangular format. The overall design is easier to read than *Shabbat Eve*, and there is substantially more white space to rest one's eyes. Teutsch also presents the *shiviti* verse in English as "I will be ever aware of God's presence," while she did not translate it in her first *shiviti*. The large color lithograph has gold embossed letters of the Tetragrammaton and purple petals.

The Tetragrammaton is both horizontal and vertical, with the vertical name included as part of the *shiviti* verse. The second YHWH is one of the seven different Hebrew names of God, with English translations, found within the inner set of arched petals. The gender-neutral appellations for "God" follow examples found within Reconstructionist prayer books. The curves of the outer petals are formed from sections of the fourth and fifth blessings of the Amidah. Connecting the inner and outer petals are arched, opened gates surrounding the names of the Jewish ancestors in the first Amidah blessing.

The artist herself wrote the commentary in the prayer book for *Creation: Shabbat Vehagim*:

> The images of the *shiviti* can provide a spiritual entry point and aid in concentration. This *shiviti* is built around the liturgical themes of creation, revelation, and redemption. The vertical oval is associated with women's procreative power, which echoes divine creation. The overall shape of the *shiviti* is inspired by Eastern meditation Mandalas, which often include a circular image of the rose or lotus. The opening flower is meant to suggest the gradual revelation of the perfection and mystery of creation. To the opening petals seven gateways are added. There is one for each of the patriarchs and matriarchs to remind us that each person finds his or her own path to God. No two journeys are alike.

At the heart of the *shiviti* is the Tetragrammaton, which is the most holy name of God. It is surrounded by petals/archways with other names of the Divine. A second Tetragrammaton crowns the *shiviti*, with Jerusalem, a symbol of redemption, rising from the top.[51]

Teutsch reveals the influence of Eastern Mandalas instead of traditional Jewish *shivitis* in her choice of format. The central placement of YHWH provides an entry point into the *shiviti* and a point of comparison with the other names of God in each of the petals. Rather than using letters to outline many diverse forms, as in the first *shiviti*—the sun, moon, eyes, doves—along with one set of gates, here she uses just a few forms, including architecture, gates, and semi-circles. The second theme is "creation, revelation, and redemption" rather than "soul" and "breath," as in the first *shiviti*. Nonetheless, the significance of breath and breathing as meditative techniques to bring us closer to God is still an important part of her second *shiviti* because of its emphasis on the vertical placement and isolation of the Tetragrammaton.

One of the most distinctive changes is Teutsch's presentation of the YHWH as vertical rather than horizontal. God's name is presented vertically on another contemporary *shiviti* designed by Rabbi Wayne Dosick. He writes:

> There is a way that we can feel and know God within us, that we can feel and know God filling up our whole beings.
>
> One of the earliest biblical names for God is made up of four Hebrew letters: "yud, hey, vav, hey." It is taken from the root word that means "to be," affirming that God was, is, and always will be....
>
> By seeing these letters as symbols—what all letters really are— fully standing for and representing God, we can bring God within.[52]

He then discusses how one can look at and meditate along with the vertical placement of YHWH. In abstract art, for example, in Barnett Newman's painting *Covenant*, 1949, a vertical line can symbolize, among other things, the human figure. Writing YHWH vertically also creates the feeling of a human form, with the *yud* as a head, the *hey* as the shoulders and arms, the *vav* as the torso, and the final *hey* as legs. The Reconstructionist meditation for this *shiviti* suggests that when we concentrate on the vertical YHWH, we may "reach for the holiness it embodies."[53] Each letter is not just a part of "a" body, but a part of "your" body; that is, the body of the person meditating. In this manner, by visualizing the letters and breathing slowly, we can "feel the godliness rise and fall within you, with each breath. Focus on your sense of oneness, of unity, with the divine."[54] During another meditation, we are to breathe in while focusing on the letter *yud*, to breathe out while saying *hey*, breathe in for the *vav*, and out for the final *hey*, which allows us to "feel godliness flowing in and out of you, and flowing all around you. Feel the links to all other breathing vessels of God."[55] In other words, as Rabbi Dosick writes, "Feel God's continuous flowing—in you, through you....God flows within you. God flows through you."[56]

Rabbi Dosick uses Teutsch's *Creation: Shabbat Vehagim* [fig. 7] in his book, *Dancing with God*, as a visual counterpart to his description of a *shiviti* as being:

> The most authentic Jewish symbol for guiding thought and

enhancing meditation....It is a beautiful artist's rendering of the four-letter name of God. By staring at the *shiviti*, thoughts can be directed right toward God, for God is "placed right before me." This *shiviti* by the contemporary artist Betsy Platkin Teutsch is especially compelling.[57]

He designed his own *shiviti* card, containing only the Hebrew and English words of Ps 16:8 without any additional visual art, to be given out to participants at his lectures. His English translation, on the back of the card, follows the format of the Hebrew, showing the name of God vertically.

TEUTSCH'S *FOUNTAIN/TREE: LIMOT HOL*

Teutsch's third *shiviti* is not only for a weekday *minyan* [prayer meeting], but also for use in a house of *shivah* [mourning]. *Fountain/Tree: Limot Hol*, 1995 [fig. 8], is intended for those who are in mourning, and also those who are ill or in need of solace. The themes revolve around death, comfort, and mourning. Teutsch was looking within Jewish tradition for symbols, and she learned that water was a powerful image of healing. Therefore, the tree can also be seen as the fountain of God, and God as the fountain of life. The color lithograph is blue, with the Tetragrammaton written in flat gold. The blue airbrush spray is equivalent to both water and a blossoming tree. Teutsch's design, including the shape, imagery, and verses, has moved even farther away from the standard nineteenth century *shiviti* format. The overall design also has become even more simplified and, therefore, more clear on the small page of the prayer book.

The *shiviti* verse creates the top of a sacred arch, to enhance the border design. In her translation of Ps 16:8, she substituted a different English phrase for the name of God, to reflect the theme of the *shiviti:* "I will be ever aware of the SOURCE OF LIFE'S presence." The YHWH within Ps 16:8 is the largest word in the *shiviti*, written horizontally with letters outlined in black, unlike any other word. God's name, written vertically as part of the *Hashkivenu* prayer for divine help, is in a large size, solid black, and forms the trunk of the tree and lower limbs. Here, Teutsch represents God as the heart of a sheltering tree, in order to emphasize the comforting presence of God.

The tree theme is repeated by the verse from Prov 3:18, written as the ground supporting the tree and the base of the *shiviti*: "For it is a tree of life." The branch on the left side that reads, "How precious is your love," continues unbroken to form the top arch on the right to represent a bird in the tree, where we can "find the shelter of your wing."[58] The wavy lines below the tree, from Ps 23:2-3, represent water: "God leads me by the calmest waters, and restores my soul." This Psalm and other verses, including those from the second Amidah blessing, represent the theme of water's healing properties, and God as healer and nurturer. On the right side of the image, God is referred to as one who "heals the sick." To the left of the tree, under the canopy, is another part of the second Amidah blessing, which refers to God with water imagery as "the Fount of Life, who gives and renews life." *Fountain/Tree* is striking in its overall simplicity, and it is much easier to comprehend in the small-scale version published in *Kol Haneshamah* than Teutsch's two earlier Shabbat *shivitis.*

TEUTSCH'S *ROSH HASHANAH* AND *YOM KIPPUR*
It is unusual to find *shivitis* centered upon a single holiday, as are Teutsch's fourth and fifth from *Kol Haneshamah: Prayer book for the Days of Awe,* 1999: *Spiral* [fig. 9], her 1999 *shiviti* for Rosh Hashanah, and *Gates* [fig. 10], created in the same year for Yom Kippur. The *shiviti* verse is not translated in either of the High Holiday images, perhaps because Ps 16:8 does not have anything to do specifically with a holiday. However, it is quite appropriate to include this verse in the High Holidays prayer book, since God is foremost in worshippers' minds at this point of the year.

The concepts for the High Holiday *shivitis* are complete breaks with the traditional *shiviti* format. Teutsch explains her Rosh Hashanah design in the prayer book commentary:

> On *Rosh Hashanah* we celebrate renewal, but we hope to live our lives without endlessly repeating ourselves. Instead, through the process of *teshuvah/*turning, we attempt to change a bit each year. We pray that when we return to the beginning in the cycle of the year, we will stand at a higher point, our lives an ascending spiral over our years. This *shiviti* plays on that theme of spiraling, and also hints at the double helix, another spiraling mystery of life.[59]

She wants to emphasize that people's lives are not going around in circles, but rather spiraling; that is, changing and not stagnating, and that there can literally be upward movement in our spiritual growth. The spiral goes up, and the text reads down. Teutsch believes that meditation on the ascending spiral will put worshippers in the mood for self-evaluation and contemplation. The design of the Rosh Hashanah *shiviti* is even clearer than the three preceding ones. Fewer verses create one large image emphasizing repetition, not only of the design but also of the chosen texts.

Teutsch found that it was difficult to take verses out of context, isolate them, and still find them inspiring to meditate upon, so she had to carefully arrange them to serve her purpose. The *shiviti* verse is in the center, with the Tetragrammaton as the spiral's axis; so God is the center of the axis of life. The spiral curves around YHWH, in front of the *yud* and *vav*, and behind both of the *heys*. Therefore, the spiral surrounds and embraces God.

A verse from Lam 5:21 is repeated in large Hebrew letters: "Return us Eternal One, let us return! Renew our days, as you have done of old!" going from the upper left and spiraling down to the lower right.[60] The verse is repeated in English as the outer edge of the spiral, starting from the lower left and going up to the top, where it reads, *l'aila u'l'aila* [higher and higher] from the Kaddish. These two Hebrew words read down again. The English phrase, "Today the world is born," begins on the bottom of the spiral, where it is also found in large, outlined Hebrew calligraphy. This phrase is repeated four times, as the Hebrew words surround each letter of the Tetragrammaton and connect the verses on each side. The central verse, from the Amidah, emphasizes God as the one who "guides constellations, and seasons, and years." This, of course, reiterates the cycle of the seasons, the same year after year. This *shiviti* is reproduced twice in the prayer book, and each full-page image is opposite a page in which the changing of seasons is a theme.

The color lithograph depicts a yellow airbrushed spiral floating within a blue background, which acts as a vision of the sky. The Tetragrammaton is not flat black but airbrushed and translucent, with the edges blurred and the tips left white, which enables God's name to be more amorphous than in the black and white version.

The Yom Kippur *shiviti, Gates,* is Teutsch's favorite design and the most striking one in color, with a gold background and raised black and red lettering. The coloring and the use of a single theme, an open gate, make it stand out from her other *shivitis*. Except for the last line, which is the *shiviti* verse, Teutsch had to come up with verses from the Yom Kippur liturgy that were inspiring when taken out of context, a problem she also had to solve in her Rosh Hashanah *shiviti*. In the High Holiday prayer book, the Yom Kippur *shiviti* stands alone, with a blank page across from it, on the page preceding the *amidah*.

For Teutsch, the obvious choice was to use gates as the theme. She had previously used the image of gates to illustrate Rabbi Michael Strassfeld's chapter about Yom Kippur in his *Jewish Holidays* book.[61] These are the gates from the Ne'ilah service, during which the gates of Heaven swing shut. Yet, as it says in the commentary about the Ne'ilah service, "the gates move slowly in this last hour [of Yom Kippur]. We have one more chance to squeeze from ourselves the last bit of impurity still in our hearts, to voice the last unspoken hope and give it power in the new year. The gates are closing, but they are not yet shut."[62] Therefore, Teutsch's gates are still open to worshippers' voices, and the central verse from Ne'ilah is written in red to emphasize this. It is important to note that this verse is written in the feminine. Teutsch changed the Hebrew to show that the davening voice is female, stressing that women have a role in prayer and decision making in Reconstructionist Judaism.

Lettering forms the decoration between the scrollwork on the gates. The verses emphasize life, the goodness of life, and the mysteries of life. The wish that God "remember us for life" is on the upper left, while on the bottom left there appears in Hebrew, "King who delights in life." The gates also reveal a compassionate God (middle right) who listens to our prayers. God's presence is shown in the lower center, where the *shiviti* verse is written. The Tetragrammaton is still the largest word in the *shiviti*, but not so large as to overpower everything else. The letters of God's name are literally holding the gates open, so as to allow the last few prayers to enter heaven before the gates close.

OTHER ARTISTS WHO COMBINE WORKS OF ART WITH PRAYERS

Teutsch is not alone in her creation of imagery that enhances prayer with beautiful calligraphy. Her interpretation is in the tradition of works by Ben Shahn, one of the premier American artists of the twentieth century. He integrated Hebrew calligraphy in a number of paintings and prints. However, he never intended to publish his work in a prayer book, as did Teutsch.

To Shahn, Hebrew letters were full of mystery. The artist referred to the Kabbalist Rabbi Abraham Abulafia's feelings about letters when he wrote: "In the contemplation of their shapes the devout might ascend through ever purer, more abstract levels of experience to achieve at last the ultimate, ineffable abstraction of union with his God."[63] In the 1930s, Shahn explained:

> I began to use letters...for their own sake, for their beauty and their own meaning....There is the glory of the Hebrew that I had sensed so deeply as I had first learned to make the letters. Now I

did not hesitate to register my own feelings; the prohibitions of art must melt before one's own authority, one's sure knowledge of what he feels and what is right for him. I made many paintings using the Hebrew letters...realizing with Rabbi Abulafia their mystery and their magic.[64]

As an example, Shahn's 1954 work, *The Alphabet of Creation*, depicts the divine origin of letters written about in the *Sefer Ha-Zohar* [The Book of Splendor].[65]

Shahn's Judaism informed his art. Many of his best-known works from the 1930s use secular themes, but by the 1950s and 1960s, he was attracted to biblical themes and Jewish history. In one example, he uses a text from a prayer book, from the *musaf* service for Yom Kippur. [66] The image represents a person covering his face with his hands. The lettering and the image use a similar style of scratchy lines, magnifying the sadness of the figure.

Shahn influenced the work of many contemporary Jewish artists. Two artists who unite Hebrew prayers with visual imagery are Eva-Lynn Diesenhaus and Peggy Davis. English translations are frequently integrated into their works, in a manner similar to Teutsch's *shivitis*. Similar to Shahn, prayers inspire Diesenhaus and Davis, but their works are not published in prayer books. Each of these contemporary artists approaches prayer differently.

Diesenhaus, a Judaic artist and calligrapher, prefers to make art that is personal. She credits Judaism with a vital role in her life and work. Inspired by Torah, prayers, songs, images, and history, the work expresses her feelings about Judaism. She writes in her artist's statement: "There is an inner need for me to relate our joys and sorrows and the hope for peace. With words and color, my art reflects my soul....It is my hope to bring moments of spirituality to others."[67]

Diesenhaus chose to use the Shema prayer, as did Chernov, while creating a completely different feeling from the latter's painting [fig. 2]. The *Sh'ma* book by Diesenhaus [fig. 11] opens up into a three-inch-square Star of David. She used this prayer because it is important to her, and thus she placed it within a symbol of the Jewish people. The design also engages the attention of its viewer. The gold on the edges of the pages, the tassel, and the tie reveal the preciousness of the book and its contents, and the color reflects light to make the work shine like a star in the night sky. The physicality of holding this book, reading it, and turning the pages relates to the feeling of holding a prayer book and the holiness of a book containing

God's name. There is also something mystical in the ability of this book to transform into a symbolic shape. When the book is in the star shape, the reader must turn it around and around to comprehend its full meaning. The beauty of this book enhances our meditation upon the Shema prayer.

In a 1996 papercut, , *A Tree of Life* [fig. 12], Diesenhaus uses the same "Tree of Life" symbol and verses (Prov 3:17-18) as do Teutsch in her *Fountain/Tree: Limot Hol* [fig. 8] and Davis in her *Tree of Life* screenprint [fig. 13]. Diesenhaus and Davis incorporate a black image on a solid background, as does Teutsch in her version published in *Kol Haneshamah*. The design of Diesenhaus' tree lends itself to a graphic presentation, in which it plays a supportive role, literally and figuratively, to prayer. The "Tree of Life" verses, the only phrases that Diesenhaus chooses to translate into English, are especially significant, as they are said when the ark is opened and the Torah placed inside. The phrase, *etz hayim hi* [tree of life], is understood to mean that the Torah is a tree of life because "the book of Genesis tells us that the tree of life is in the Garden of Eden. The Torah is our tree of life; it is our way back to the garden."[68] Also, "the Torah is our lifeline to Judaism and to our heritage, to where we have been and to where we are going. The torah derives its essence from the divine realm and shares its fruits with us on earth."[69]

The branches of the tree, interspersed with four Hebrew verses along with the one English phrase, blossom into two Torah scrolls.[70] Above on the right, the Torah has the Hebrew letter *bet* in it, representing the first letter of the first word of the Torah: *bereshit* [in the beginning]. The scroll is shown rolled to the beginning, with the thicker part on the left side shown as a black rectangle. The Torah on the upper left surrounds the Hebrew letter *lamed*, representing the last letter of the Torah, from the word Yisrael. The thicker side of the scroll is to the right of the *lamed*, representing the full Torah rolled open to its last section. The tree of life supports the Torah above it and below nurtures a garden, with the words "love" and "peace" within the flowers. It is a provocative image, deceptively simple, while at the same time providing a viewer access to a variety of interactions between verse and imagery.

Davis also combines Hebrew and English verses within beautiful, thought-provoking works of art that appeal to a broad audience. Her artist's statement says that she "draws inspiration from traditional texts, old Hebrew manuscripts and Jewish folk art for her work, which celebrates Jewish ritual and ceremonial life in home and synagogue."[71] Like Teutsch and Diesenhaus, Davis usually uses Hebrew and its English translation to make the work accessible.

In her 1989 screenprint, *Tree of Life* [fig. 13], Davis literally creates a tree, with the verses printed in English in all capital letters on either side of the trunk. Its starkness and linear style, reminiscent of Vienna Workshop prints from the end of the nineteenth century, create a striking image that catches and holds a viewer's attention. The letters are placed within horizontal lines, creating a similar feeling to Teutsch's depiction of a gate whose cast-iron elements are letters in *Gates*. Therefore, Davis' tree/Torah could appear to be within gates. If the gates are seen as doors, they can be construed as the doors of a holy ark containing the Torah. In Davis' *Tree of Life,* the tree and the verses take on an abstract life of their own, adding to the visual complexity of an otherwise simple image.

Davis' *Jerusalem Hills*, 1995 [fig. 14], is a "microcalligraphy print containing verses from Psalms which mention Jerusalem or mountains. The words create the landscape looking towards the Dead Sea from Jerusalem."[72] As in Teutsch's *Creation: Shabbat Vehagim* [fig. 7], this image includes references to Jerusalem, but not to the city's buildings or to the Holy Temple. Rather, Davis represents the hills around the city, created by her lettering and pastel coloring. We are, therefore, not looking east to Jerusalem, but southeast, away from the city. Yet, Davis positions viewers as if they were in Jerusalem, and in that manner sets the mood for contemplating Jerusalem as well as its surroundings.

In the Hebrew and English version, Davis translates each of the Psalms. She starts with Ps 114:1-4 and 7-8 for the upper hills, using imagery of hills and mountains from verse four, "The mountains skipped like rams, and the hills like lambs." The first two verses of Ps 121, creating the hills in the center, read: "I lift my eyes to the hills; whence will my help come? My help comes from God who made heaven and earth." The lowest hills, formed by Ps 137:1-6, include the familiar reference in verse five to Jerusalem: "If I ever forget you, O Jerusalem, withered be my right hand."

The viewer's eyes meander from left to right reading the English, and right to left reading the Hebrew, as we are taken from the blue sky above to the red and green hills below. The rolling hills set a slow pace—horizontal lines are considered to be slow; lines get faster as the angle increases—and there are only a few lines acting as lines of perspective (on the central left section and the lower/central right) to draw the viewer back into the hills. The lines that make up the hills are placed farther apart in the foreground and come closer together in the background, creating a sense of depth. Davis' design allows us to read either from top to bottom, as though this were a flat page of text, or bottom to top, foreground to background, as if it were a three-dimensional picture of hills that grow smaller as they move into the distance.

One difference between this print and Teutsch's *shivitis* or Diesenhaus' work is the way Davis writes the name of God: she uses "G-d" in English, and *hey* [*hashem*] in Hebrew. She believes this spelling increases the audience for her prints. She also feels that abbreviating the name of God allows her the option of destroying prints that do not turn out to her satisfaction. Otherwise, the rejected prints may have to be stored in a genizah, a depository for worn-out sacred books or manuscripts containing the Tetragrammaton.[73] Also, once the prints are sold and she has no control over what happens to them, this spelling of God's name resolves a problem for her.

CONCLUSION

Chernov, Teutsch, Diesenhaus, and Davis have been inspired by Psalms, verses from the prophets, and prayers from prayer books to make beautiful works of art that enhance the spirituality of the texts to create a pathway to prayer and meditation. Teutsch's *shivitis* and illustrations in the Reconstructionist prayer books have broken new ground, reviving and transforming a traditional Jewish format. The works of art by Teutsch, Diesenhaus, and Davis, which combine Hebrew and English verses, not only broaden the appeal of the texts, but expand their meanings in ways unimaginable without the visual context. The pictures are not a substitute for the texts—used together they develop a new and visually exciting way of approaching familiar Jewish territory. Through their works of art, these artists enable individuals to journey through Jewish prayers and texts at their own pace, absorbing nuances of visual and textual meaning through personal contemplation over time. The texts have retained their power over the centuries; these artists have adapted and transformed the texts for a twenty-first century audience, each in a unique manner.

LIST OF FIGURES

fig. 1 *Ufros Aleynu Figure*

fig. 2 *Shema Prayer*

fig. 3 *Shiviti* Plaque

fig. 4 *Shiviti*

fig. 5 *Shiviti*

fig. 6 *Shabbat Eve*

fig. 7 *Creation: Shabbat Vegahim*

fig. 8 *Fountain/Tree: Limot Hol*

fig. 9 *Spiral*

fig. 10 *Gates*

fig. 11 *Sh'ma Book*

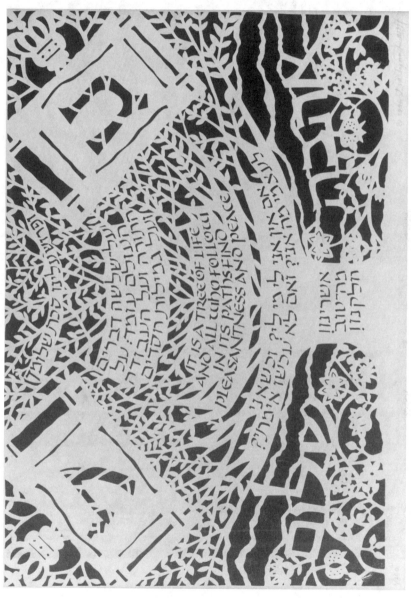

fig. 12 *A Tree of Life*

fig. 13 *Tree of Life*

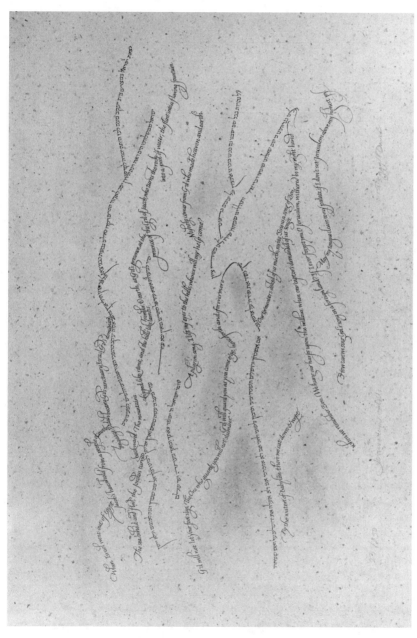

fig. 14 *Jerusalem Hills*

NOTES

[1] Betsy Platkin Teutsch, author interview, telephone, June 20, 2000. For the term *shiviti*, see below.

[2] Susan Kriegel Leshnoff, "The Influence of Jewish Mysticism on Jewish Contemporary Artists: An Investigation of the Relationship Between a Religious Tradition and Creative Expression" (Ph.D. diss., Columbia University Teachers College, 1988), 26-27; Leshnoff refers to BT 111:b, 27.

[3] Leshnoff, "Jewish Mysticism," 27.

[4] Tzvee Zahavy, "*Kavannah* (Concentration) for Prayer in the Mishnah and Talmud," *New Perspectives on Ancient Judaism* (Lanham: University Press of America, 1987), 35-48. Cited August 3, 2000. Online: <http://newark.rutgers.edu/~zahavy/kavvanah.html>.

[5] *Ibid.*, from *y. Ber.* 2, *m. Ber.* 4.

[6] Cecil Roth, "Illuminated Manuscripts, Hebrew," *Encyclopaedia Judaica, CD-ROM Edition*, 1997, n.p.

[7] *Ibid.*, and Leshnoff, "Jewish Mysticism," 46.

[8] Roth, "Illuminated Manuscripts," n.p.

[9] Stanley Ferber, "Micrography: A Jewish Art Form," *Journal of Jewish Art* 3-4 (1977): 12. Also, Leila Avrin, "Note on Micrography: A Jewish Art Form," *Journal of Jewish Art* 6 (1979): 112-117.

[10] Two exceptions that come immediately to mind are Hasidic and children's prayer books.

[11] Rabbi Nosson Scherman, ed., *The Complete Artscroll Siddur, Weekday, Sabbath, and Festival* (Brooklyn: Mesorah Publications, Ltd., 1984).

[12] Rabbi Jules Harlow, ed., *Conservative Siddur Sim Shalom, A Prayerbook for Shabbat, Festivals, and Weekdays* (New York: The Rabbinical Assembly, The United Synagogue of America, 1985).

[13] Rabbi Howard Kutner, author interview, Omaha, NE, March 14, 2001. The Hasidic Siddur is by Rabbi Asher Anshol Krausz, *Siddur Korban Asher* [The Sacrifice of Asher Prayer Book] (Williamsburg, Brooklyn: Moriah Offset Co., 1986), 26.

[14] Rabbi David A. Teutsch, ed., *Kol Haneshamah, Shabbat Eve* (Wyncote, PA: The Reconstructionist Press: 1989).

[15] Rabbi David A. Teutsch, ed., *Kol Haneshamah: Shabbat Vehagim* (2nd ed.: Wyncote, PA: The Reconstructionist Press: 1995); Rabbi David A. Teutsch, ed., *Kol Haneshamah: Daily Prayer Book* (Wyncote, PA: The Reconstructionist Press: 1996); and Rabbi David A. Teutsch, ed., *Kol Haneshamah: Prayer Book for the Days of Awe* (Wyncote, PA: The Reconstructionist Press: 1999).

[16] Rabbi David Wolfe-Blank, *Meta-Siddur, A Jewish Soul-Development Workbook* (rev. ed., version 5.0; Seattle: Eitz Or Congregation, 1998); and Rabbi Shoni Labowitz and Dr. Judith Gulko, *An Invitation to Prayer* (Fort Lauderdale, Florida: Temple Adath Or, 2000).

[17] Miriam Stampfer, author interview, telephone, June 7, 2001. See *The Aquarian Minyan Siddur for Friday Evening Service* (Berkeley: The Aquarian Minyan, n.d.); *The Aquarian Minyan Shabbat Morning Service* (Berkeley: The Aquarian Minyan, 1994); and *The Aquarian Minyan Makhzor for the High Holy Days* (Berkeley: The Aquarian Minyan, 1995).

[18] Wolfe-Blank, *Meta-Siddur*, cover.

[19] *Ibid.*, 7.

[20] Labowitz and Gulko, *Invitation to Prayer*, 10.

[21] Translation from D. Teutsch, *Kol Haneshamah: Shabbat Vehagim*, 64.

[22] *Ibid.*, xxiv.

[23] B. P. Teutsch, author interview, June 20, 2000.

[24] D. Teutsch, *Kol Haneshamah: Shabbat Vehagim*, xxiv.

[25] Ellen Frankel and Betsy Platkin Teutsch, "East," in *The Encyclopedia of Jewish Symbols* (Northvale: Jason Aronson, 1992), 44.

[26] *Ibid.*, 45.

[27] Richard Siegel et al., eds., *The Jewish Catalogue* (Philadelphia: The Jewish Publication Society of America, 1973), 17.

[28] Bezalel Narkiss, "*Shivviti*," *Encyclopedia Judaica CD-ROM Edition*, 1997, n.p.

[29] D. Teutsch, *Kol Haneshamah: Shabbat Vehagim*, 293, from B. P. Teutsch's shiviti: *Creation: Shabbat Vehagim*, 1994.

[30] Siegel, et al., 17.

[31] Rabbi Wayne Dosick, author interview, telephone, July 13, 2000.

[32] B. P. Teutsch, author interview, June 20, 2000.

[33] Shoshana Cooper, e-mail to author, July 20, 2000.

[34] Efraim Gottlieb, "Menorah (ritual object), subsection 'In Kabbalah,'" n.p., *Encyclopedia Judaica CD-ROM Edition*, 1997.

[35] Frankel and B. P. Teutsch, "Menorah," *Jewish Symbols*, 105.

[36] *Ibid.*, 106.

[37] Narkiss, "*Shivviti*," n.p.

[38] Linda Altshuler, *In the Spirit of Tradition: The B'nai B'rith Klutznick Museum* (Washington: B'nai B'rith International, 1988), 73. The catalogue entry for this *shiviti* plaque states that this quote is a "variation on Babylonian Talmud, *Berakhot* 28b."

[39] *Ibid.*

[40] Jacobo Furman, *Treasures of Jewish Art: From the Jacobo and Asea Furman Collection of Judaica* (Southport: Hugh Lauter Levin, 1997), 88, 89.

[41] Grace Cohen Grossman, *The Skirball Museum Collections and Inaugural Exhibition* (Los Angeles: Skirball Cultural Center, 1996), 88. In the lower left and right, Cohen signed his name and included the date in English and Hebrew.

[42] B. P. Teutsch, author interview, June 20, 2000. The information about the *shivitis* in *Kol Haneshamah* is from this interview. Also see the Jewish Reconstructionist Federation website that shows all five *shivitis* in color: <http://jrf.org/pub/cat-posters.html>.

[43] Michael Strassfeld, *The Jewish Holidays: A Guide and Commentary* (New York: Harper & Row, 1985).

[44] Leila Avrin, "Calligraphy, Modern Hebrew," *Encyclopaedia Judaica, CD-ROM Edition*, 1997. See the chart in the media section of this entry.

[45] B. P. Teutsch, author interview, June 20, 2000.

[46] D. Teutsch, *Kol Haneshamah: Shabbat Vehagim*, xxvi.

[47] *Ibid.*, 165.

[48] *Ibid.*

[49] *Ibid.*, 728.

[50] *Ibid.*

[51] *Ibid.*, 292.

[52] Rabbi Wayne Dosick, *Dancing with God: Everyday Steps to Jewish Spiritual Renewal* (San Francisco: Harper San Francisco, 1997), 25.

[53] D. Teutsch, *Kol Haneshamah: Shabbat Vehagim*, 729.

[54] *Ibid.*

[55] *Ibid.*

[56] Dosick, *Dancing with God*, 27.

[57] *Ibid.*, 50.

[58] From Ps 36:8-11; see D. Teutsch, *Kol Haneshamah: Prayer Book for the Days of Awe*, 143.

[59] *Ibid.*, 104. Commentary by B. P. Teutsch.

[60] *Ibid.*, 415.

[61] Strassfeld, *The Jewish Holidays*, 110.

[62] D. Teutsch, *Kol Haneshamah: Prayer Book for the Days of Awe*, 1144. Commentary by Rabbi David Teutsch and Micah Becke-Klein.

[63] Ben Shahn, *Love and Joy about Letters* (New York: Grossman, 1963), 5.

[64] *Ibid.*, 17.

[65] *Ibid.*, 18. Moses de Leon, a 13th century Spanish scholar, wrote most of the *Zohar*. See Gershom Scholem, "Moses Ben Shem Tov de Leon," *Encyclopedia Judaica CD-ROM Edition*, 1997, n.p..

[66] Shahn, *Love and Joy about Letters*, 22, 76.

[67] Eva-Lynn Ratoff (née Diesenhaus), "Artist's Statement." Cited 20 July 2000. Online: <http://www.jccoc.org/cv/cv9810/calligrapher.html>.

[68] Dan Ehrenkrantz, commentary in *Kol Haneshamah: Prayer Book for the Days of Awe*, by Teutsch, 545.

[69] Rabbi Matthew Kaufman, "*Tu B'Shvat* 5760 Tree of Life sermon, January 21, 2000." Cited 23 May 2001. Online <http://www.congregationbnaitikvah.org/rabbi/000121.TuBshvat.TreeOfLife.htm>.

[70] Diesenhaus's *A Tree of Life* papercut has the following verses: The upper verse is from *Hashkivenu*, "Spread over us the shelter of your peace," (see Teutsch, *Kol Haneshamah: Shabbat Vehagim*, 80); the second is from the Torah service; the lowest branches are formed by Hillel's quote: "If I am not for myself, who will be for me?" (*Pirke Avot* 1:14); the tree trunk is from a prayer cited in the Talmud (*b.*

Yoma 87b).

71 Peggy H. Davis, "Artist's Statement." Cited 20 July, 2000. Online: <http://www.crocker.com/~ganeydn/~artist.html>.

72 Peggy H. Davis, "Jerusalem Hills." Cited 20 July 2000. Online: <http://www.crocker.com/~ganeydn/~jerhills.html>.

73 Peggy H. Davis, e-mail to author, May 25, 2001.

Some "Earthy" Dimensions
of the Spiritual in Jewish Liturgy

Charles D. Isbell

To speak of "spiritual things" is something like discussing one's spouse or sweetheart, for both involve such personal matters that we often hesitate to broach either subject. Some among us stoutly maintain that they have advanced beyond the spiritual to a higher level of the intellect, which they sometimes refer to with pride as enlightened or intellectual or modern. Others descend to the maudlin, regaling listeners with tales of deeper levels of mystical meaning seen only by a select and superior few; much as endless talk about one's perfect wife is wont to do, they leave us convinced of the truth of the old proverb, that "a satisfied man don't brag."

But those who belong to a civilization with a history of several millennia of spiritual perception need not forget that there is a comfort zone within the boundaries of which it is possible to accept the spiritual dimensions of life and faith without embarrassment. Even then, it is difficult to articulate what we mean by spiritual or to define our own personal experiences of spirituality. Another proverb avers that "nobody's sweetheart is ugly," which we might take also to mean that individual definitions of spirituality vary widely as well. So these opening words may be taken as my advance apology for the intensely personal nature of what I write below. I am describing things that I know, incidents that happened to me, and perceptions of reality that have been filtered through my own private thought and language screen.

As I have stated, the very word "spiritual" evokes many diverse mental images. In common American parlance, spiritual serves as the bipolar opposite of words like material or physical, while in Jewish life specifically, spiritual more often than not serves as the counterpoint to religious. But there are several phrases in the Jewish liturgy indicative of the fact that such a dichotomy would have been deemed inappropriate in the thought world of our forebears. Of course, the cultural worlds, and thus the linguistic referential fields, of those from whom we have inherited our modern *siddurim* [or prayer books] were radically different from modern categories of understanding or expression. The rabbis knew nothing of our modern world of cause and effect, even as we know increasingly less about their simple agrarian one. Many of them, we should recall, were people whom our society would call common— laborers, farmers, craftsmen, shepherds—who worked with the soil, with animals, and above all with their hands. When they thought about God, when they contemplated "miracles," even when they composed prayers for worship, they did not divest themselves of their "earthy" (not earthly!) occupations and modes of expression. Rather, they frequently expressed their faith and their hopes for this world and the next in common (what I am calling "earthy") language, often eschewing more elegant forms of expression that one might expect from scholars.

My first Hebrew teacher was my grandfather, עליו השלום [of blessed memory]. Although he was but a simple farmer, all of the expressions that I discuss below were quite obvious and plain to him. In fact, it was while living with him as a small child that I first began to understand many of the concepts that I offer in this paper. Today, the young bar and bat mitzvah candidates whom I tutor often find these same expressions quite unintelligible precisely because the world in which they live and the referential fields of their modern language are so different from his. That is why the words and expressions chosen for examination, while all are well known from virtually every rescension of the *siddur* [prayer book], must be discussed in light of the cultural and linguistic world from which they stemmed.

Let me state at the outset my belief that our search for "spiritual" dimensions within Judaism must be securely tied to our own classical texts. And with respect to the pursuit of spirituality generally, I would suggest a simple formula. If spirituality is made the goal of our endeavor, we may well find ourselves adrift in a sea of bewildering dimensions, cut off from rigorous methodology or textual moorings. Taking aim at such an amorphous and intensely personal goal makes each individual a law unto him or herself, for who can deny the reality of what another says he or she has experienced in a private moment with the divine! But I believe there is a more authentic way to approach the subject of spirituality. If our commitment can be to a lifestyle of study, the study of all of our texts and all of our historical experiences, there is a greater likelihood that deep and authentic spirituality can become a by-product of our engagement with the full range and diversity of Judaism.

The methodology I follow is simple. I have chosen five examples of language that must be translated not only linguistically but also culturally in order for us to appreciate their meaning. And I have recalled in some instances a very personal and "spiritual" moment when I believe some of these phrases came into focus for me.

THE WISDOM OF THE ROOSTER

The first expression is found in the morning blessings, specifically the phrase אֲשֶׁר נָתַן לַשֶּׂכְוִי בִינָה לְהַבְחִין בֵּין יוֹם וּבֵין לַיְלָה [{YHWH} who gave to the rooster insight to distinguish between day and night].[1] Few if any of my young students, and surely only a small percentage of modern adult urban Jews, readily understand the reference employed here, even when they can translate all the words. And this is admitted by the paraphrases offered in two modern *siddurim*. For example, Reform Judaism's *Gates of Prayer*, speaks of God "who has implanted mind and instinct within every living being."[2] Now of course Jews believe that God did in fact do this, but the point is that this particular blessing is inviting us to celebrate something far more specific. The Conservative *Siddur Sim Shalom* comes a bit closer to the meaning of the phrase, speaking of God, "who enables his creatures to distinguish between night and day."[3] Both of these paraphrases succeed in sidestepping the literal meaning, while both actually come rather close in their attempts to approximate the referential value of the ancient phrase to a modern context. Yet both versions struggle because their modern audiences are presumed not to be able to identify with the referential field of the original.

While it may be granted that the lexicons define שֶׂכְוִי as either "a rooster" or as a generic term for "insight" or even "heart," only rooster makes any syntactical sense in the phrase as it stands. We are surely not expected to thank God for giving "understanding to the insight," for such a phrase is nonsensical. Besides, what amount of insight does it take to distinguish between night and day? Even the dumbest bird should be able to do that. On the other hand, for God to give a rooster the unique ability to which the rabbis were referring was apparently meaningful to the framers of this blessing, and is still easily understood by anyone who has lived on a farm where chickens and roosters are present.

I must insert here an observation that will be self-evident to those who know a bit about chickens. The chicken is basically quite a stupid bird. My own anecdotal evidence of this fact began with the observation of older uncles flicking lit cigarette butts into the yard just to watch the chickens peck and swallow and then dance frantically around. And this they would do repeatedly, apparently incapable of learning that swallowing fire is never a smart thing to do, no matter how practiced one becomes at it.

Again, we might ask what is so special about the fact that even an animal this dumb can distinguish between day and night. But that is not what the ברכה [blessing] in question celebrates. The farmer knows well that a rooster does not crow when it becomes light, but invariably just a moment or two before the sun appears each morning. As a young man, I discovered that it is quite a wonderful experience to stand in the pre-dawn moments and watch for the sun as it pops suddenly into view. One moment all is gray and gloomy, and the next moment the world is bathed in light once again by what appears to be the rebirth of the sun. And it is during these final moments of gray that the rooster crows, not at the moment after the sun's appearance. The ability of such a dumb animal to know even slightly ahead of time that a new day is about to dawn was perceived by the rabbis to be a true miracle, deserving of its own special "blessing."

I am not able to explain how a rooster knows when to crow. But I know, because I have observed it firsthand, that roosters do in fact crow just before the light of the morning sun tells the rest of the world that a new day has arrived. Asserting that such understanding derives from God alone, our liturgy calls this a miracle. And to this otherwise unremarkable fact they assigned a place among the "everyday miracles" [בכל יום נסים] for which we give thanks in our Shabbat morning worship. Is there a more appropriate word in our day?

מעריב ערבים

The second example is actually a series of expressions found among the וברכות קריאת שמע [prayers in connection with the Shema], specifically in the section known as מעריב ערבים. We know today, of course, that the round earth, as it spins on its axis around the sun, routinely presents one side of itself to the sun ("day"), leaving its other side away from the sun ("night"). But our ancestors perceived this simple routine far differently. In their minds, God brought on each evening because God controls what we now call nature, including the cycles of light and darkness as well as the longer seasons of the year. For them, God personally created each evening and personally brought the sun out from its hiding place each morning. In addition, to their way of thinking, God continued to vary both the season of the year and the weather conditions during each season from moment to moment (משנה עתים ומחליף את הזמנים) [the one who alters periods of time and changes the seasons]), just as he continually arranged the stars properly in the sky (מסדר את הכוכבים במשמרותיהם ברקיע [the one who arranges the stars in their heavenly constellations]). The specific expression that lends its name to the entire blessing, ערבים מעריב, is best understood to mean that God "causes evenings to become evenings." And this event, which happens every day, was to them more than a repeated illustration of natural law. Not a single evening could become evening apart from the continuing involvement of God with the world. Were we rewriting this part of the *siddur*, I doubt that any modern expression could more accurately express what happens every twenty-four hours. Indeed, however accurately we might describe the onset of an evening in scientific terms, we would certainly run the risk of losing the wonder, the sense of awe, that lurks in their simple expression.

THE SHELTER OF HIS WINGS

A third example is attested in two similar phrases expressive of a single concept. One form of the phrase in particular, "in the shadow of your wings" [בצל כנפיר], comes both from עטיפת טלית [the prayer said when putting on a tallis or prayer shawl] and from the השכיבנו [the second blessing after the Shema].[4] The origin of the phrase is, of course, biblical, where "the shadow of your/his [God's] wing" is described as a place of refuge for the faithful,[5] a secure place in which to hide from enemies,[6] or a place in which one may confidently sing a song of joy even in the hour of loneliness and pursuit by those who are seeking one's very life.[7] Here we might well ask how many modern Jews perceive God as winged, even metaphorically, and also ask how many urban dwellers have experienced via personal observation the miracle of a mother bird sheltering her chicks under her own wing.

When I was seven years old, I witnessed, in the company of my grandfather, a sight that I still remember vividly forty-nine years later.

Learning that the barn of our neighbor had caught fire, my grandfather and I ran to his adjoining small farm, only to learn that we were too late to help rescue anything of value. Standing at the edge of a still smoldering hen house, my grandfather inadvertently kicked what appeared to be merely a lump of smoldering ash. To our astonishment, from under that smoldering lump ran two tiny chicks, alive and well because their mother had sheltered them at the cost of her own life. And she had saved them by having tucked them securely under her wings as the fire swept over them. It is hard to imagine the impact of such a scene on a seven year old child and even more difficult to describe it to anyone who was not there to see it in person.

A perhaps equally remarkable sequel also remains fresh in my memory. My grandfather, a typical farmer whose physical strength and toughness were legendary, bent down and scooped up both chicks into his hands, looking at them with something that can only be described as awe. Then, while my gaze alternated between the charred body of the mother hen and the helpless chicks, I heard my grandfather whisper the words יסתירם בסתר כנפיו [may he hide them in the shelter of his wings]. Not sure what the words meant, I asked him what he had said. In his Cajun dialect of French, he answered merely, "J'ai jamais vu aucune chose aussi merveilleuse" [I've never seen such a marvelous sight]. Much later, when my knowledge of Hebrew had improved and I was able to connect his words with the startling experience we had shared that August afternoon, I realized how appropriate had been his insight into the meaning of this earthy expression from our worship. The idea of God spreading his (or her!) "wings" of protection over his children no longer seemed outlandish at all in light of the evidence showing how far a humble bird will go to protect her young. I further believe that only common, "earthy" scholars, men who might even have seen situations similar to my own experience, could have conceived such an image for the protection of God that they were certain they enjoyed.

נקבים נקבים חלולים חלולים
[Numerous Openings and Many Cavities]
Phrase number four is found in the ברכות השחר [the morning service], specifically in the graphic words נקבים חלולים חלולים נקבים [numerous openings and many cavities]. Now, if one is seeking

"earthy" terms, these two words are an appropriate place to explore. The only biblical appearance of נקב is in Ezek 28:13. Following a list of precious stones, there is this description: מלאכת תפיך ונקביך, a phrase whose meaning JPS describes as "uncertain."[8] "Neqev" is a noun formed from the verbal root נקב, meaning "to pierce" or "to bore," perhaps with the aid of a jeweler's tool.

But in post-biblical Hebrew, the plural form נקבים acquires a whole new field of reference that included the familiar phrase under discussion. נקבים and חלולים are two of the words chosen by the rabbis to depict the internal channels of the human body, and this field of reference was adopted into early dialects of modern Hebrew: [a] נקבים was used to describe the "bowels," or more broadly the process of waste elimination including both the easing of the bowels[9] and the process of urination.[10] [b] חלולים carries the more general meaning of a "hole" or a "cavity,"[11] but an organism described as חלול is one that contains a bowel system.

In Talmudic discussions, נקבים most frequently refer simply to holes or cavities, and these may be holes in anything from a flute[12] to a human skull.[13] A particularly pertinent text contains the following vivid and earthy description:

שני נקבים יש בו באדם אחד מוציא שתן ואחר מוציא שכבת זרע.[14]

But we must note also the use of Mybqn in the context of describing what can only be understood as a rather delicate social condition; namely, the breaking of wind during the Tefillah [that is, prayer]. Such an eventuality is not to be considered sinful, but rather should be overlooked—on the rationale that since the good Lord created us in a specific way, נקבים נקבים חלולים חלולים [i.e., with numerous openings and many cavities], he should certainly understand that we are not always able to restrain ourselves from doing certain ungraceful things even during moments of great solemnity and holiness.[15]

Returning to the wording of our ברכה [blessing], the Talmudic passage shows that it is referencing the internal channels of the physical system by the following explanation:

It is clear and well-known in the presence of your glorious throne, that if one of them should be open [when it should be closed], or if one of them should be blocked [when it should be open], it would be impossible to rise up and stand in your presence.

This explanation became very personal to me in June of 1999, when I was diagnosed with a kidney stone. After undergoing a surgical procedure to remove the stone, I had the privilege of explaining to my doctor that not only had his skillful hands restored my physical system to proper working order, but I also had gained a deeper insight into the *siddur* as a result of the experience. And, of course, my experienced urologist had little trouble in believing my testimony that I had indeed found it impossible to "rise up and stand" in the presence of God when one of my internal channels that is designed to remain open had become "blocked." Once again, a rugged and earthy expression speaks volumes.

YOKE

Finally, I want to examine the referential field implied by the word "yoke" in the well-known phrase עול ממשלת השמים [the yoke of the kingdom of the heavens]. In biblical literature, the word עול [yoke] is used in two distinct ways. Literally, it refers to the yoke used on cattle or oxen.[16] Figuratively, it is used to refer to transgression[17] or to involuntary servitude.[18] Thus, in certain early poems and in prophetic literature we find references to the breaking of such a yoke with divine assistance.[19]

Of signal importance is the use of עול in Jer 27. There, the prophet perceives the inevitability of the conquest by Nebuchadnezzar of Babylon and reports that God himself has commanded him [Jeremiah] to make "bonds and yokes"[20] to place upon his own neck. The symbolism involved is clarified immediately in the prophetic oracle that follows. Any nation that refuses to submit willingly to Nebuchadnezzar, by placing its neck voluntarily under his "yoke,"[21] will be punished and destroyed by God, and only those who submit to the plan of God to use Nebuchadnezzar will be spared (27:11). Accordingly, in the following verse, Jeremiah gives this advice to the Judahite King Zedekiah: "Place your neck into the yoke of the King of Babylon. Serve him and his people, so that you may live."

Here we see for the first time the idea of a difficult "yoke" that may be accepted or rejected, with drastic consequences attendant upon either choice. It is this picture that the Tannaim [rabbis of the earlier Talmudic period] draw upon in their discussions. In rabbinic thought, recitation of the Shema is connected with the act of accepting the "yoke of the kingdom of the heavens"[22] and is perceived as the acceptance of God as one's king. In terms of language only, there is an apparent Mishnaic distinction drawn between "the acceptance of the yoke of the kingdom of the heavens" and "acceptance of the yoke of the commandments."

In fact, however, as a well-known Mishnaic passage makes clear, through the recitation of the Shema the pious Jew both voluntarily takes upon himself the "yoke" of the kingdom of the heavens and accepts for himself the obligation of the commandments of halakha.[23] The importance of such an acceptance is illustrated by the fact that Rabban Gamaliel himself was known to have recited the Shema even on the first night of his wedding, reminding his students that he would not avoid "the yoke of the kingdom of the heavens even for a moment."[24]

Two things seem clear. First, we note the voluntary nature of the choice between whether to accept the "yoke" or not; second, we find the assumption that acceptance of the "yoke" leads to a halakhically correct life. This background prepares us to investigate a famous passage in the New Testament, which portrays Jesus speaking about his own idea of halacha or his perception of a Jewishly appropriate life of obedience to God. Matthew 11:29 attests a figure of speech chosen by Jesus that would have been quite familiar to his audience: "Take my yoke upon you and study with me." What else could Jesus have meant than a call for students to learn and follow his unique interpretation of halakha? Overlooked by most commentators on this passage is that Jesus cites Jer 6:16 here, assuring his audience that through observance of his halakhic interpretations, "you will find rest for your souls."

Now, the passage in Jeremiah specifically refers to the necessity of searching out the classical ways of faith for the purpose of learning where "the good way" [דרך הטוב] may be found, and to "walk in it" [לכו בה]. I take both Jesus' choice of the word "yoke" and his citation of Jeremiah to imply that he perceived his own halakhic teachings to represent the "good" and acceptable way in which Jews should exercise their Judaism in order to obtain a life of peace and rest. Further, I feel it is not pressing beyond the evidence to note that Jesus was doing what many a good first century rabbinic teacher would have done, namely commending his own halakhic interpretations in preference to those of other Jewish authorities.[25]

I also believe it clear that the Mishnaic interpretation of "yoke" is pertinent to all of these New Testament passages. For the Tannaim, it would not be the halakha of Jesus as reflected in the way followed by his disciples, but their own understanding of halakha that the recital of the Shema and its blessings implied.[26] What I find noteworthy in the context of this paper is the common use of the ordinary word "yoke" to express such a lofty concept. Once again we see that spiritual truths need not be cloaked in mystical terminology that is difficult to decipher, but may be expressed in elegant fashion by simple and well-known "earthy" terms.

CONCLUSION

Surely there is no denying the spiritual depths of those who bequeathed to us our forms of prayer and blessings and worship. What is significant is that they did not always resort to a specialized or mystical language, but often used what must have been for them quite ordinary, everyday modes of speech and expression. Accordingly, their "spirituality" must be understood correctly. They studied and worshipped, both of which were for them acts of piety and devotion, as they lived—plainly and humbly. The context in which they described God and his miracles was real life, and it is remarkable that many of the metaphors they chose to describe the religious life of piety and worship derived from the most ordinary of words. In short, their "earthy" words often expressed deeply "spiritual" ideas.

I also believe that a survey of the ideas our ancestors found "spiritual" or "miraculous" can inform efforts to define "spirituality" in our modern world. Our rabbis routinely began with the text of the Bible and then carefully drew into the world of their day the concepts that they had mined exegetically. We could do worse!

Perhaps we could begin again to look for a life of piety in sources other than the spectacular or the strange and far away, the ineffable or the "mystical." In short, perhaps a search for the goodness, or the "God-ness," in the plain and simple aspects of twenty-first century life may prove more fruitful than flights into the ethereal and the fanciful. We too may be able to discern God in the eyes of an infant, in the delighted yelp of a puppy at the return of its master, at the drops of rain that wash away some of the pollution with which we have soiled our home, at the devotion of a child for aged parents, at the caress of a beloved one.

Their language involved common animals, the field, the pasture, the barn. And since our linguistic expressions should reflect our culture and our times, we will need to call upon modern terminology, including cyber terms that our forebears could not possibly have anticipated. But it can only be to our detriment if we neglect to look for God in the common places where our forebears found him so often.

NOTES

[1] This phrase answers the question posed in Job 38:36b: מי נתן לשכוי בינה [Who gave insight to the rooster?].

[2] *Gates of Prayer: The New Union Prayerbook*, ed. Chaim Stern (New York: CCAR, 1975), 268.

[3] *Siddur Sim Shalom*, ed. Jules Harlow (New York: The Rabbinical Assembly, 1985), 11.

[4] A close referential parallel is attested in אל מלא רחמים [O God full of compassion] by the phrase יסתירהו בסתר כנפיו [may he hide him in the shelter of his wings].

[5] חוס/חסה in Ps 36:8; 57:2; 61:5; 91:4; Ruth 2:12.

[6] סתר in Ps 17:8.

[7] Cf. ארנן in Ps 63:8.

[8] *Tanakh: A New Translation of the Holy Scriptures According to the Traditional Hebrew Text* (Philadelphia, Jerusalem: Jewish Publication Society, 1985).

[9] נקבים גדולים.

[10] נקבים קטנים.

[11] Or even a "pore."

[12] *Hul.* 45:1; 57:2; 126:2 and elsewhere

[13] E.g., *Sanh.* 39:1, where שני נקבים are said to be the two holes in the head for the eyes and ears.

[14] *Bek.* 44:2: "There are two channels in a man. One discharges urine and one discharges semen."

[15] *Ber.* 24:2.

[16] E.g., in Num 19:2 or 1 Sam 6:7.

[17] As Lam 1:14 makes clear.

[18] As the example of Rehoboam in 1 Kgs 12 illustrates repeatedly.

[19] See, for example, Gen 27:40; Jer 2:20, 5:5, 30:8; Ezek 34:27; Isa 9:3.

[20] מוסרות ומוטות (Jer 27:2).

[21] יתן את צוארו בעל מלך בבל.

[22] *Ber.* 13b: בשעה שמעביר ידיו על פניו מקבל עליו עול מלכות שמים.

[23] *Ber.* 2:2. We should also compare the expression עול תורה [the yoke of the Torah] in *Avot* 3:6, which is juxtaposed to עול מלכות [the yoke of the kingdom] and עול דרך ארץ [the yoke of appropriate behavior]. Of course, acceptance of "the yoke of the commandments" is one of three things (along with circumcision and *miqvah* [the ritual bath]) expected of a convert to Judaism.

[24] For this, see *m. Ber.* 2:2,4.

[25] Further indications of this concept may be found in the search of Saul for "any of this" way (Acts 9:2), as well as in the description of Apollos as a man who "had been instructed in the way of the Lord" (Acts 18:25) and Felix as one who possessed "a more exact knowledge about the way" (Acts 24:22). It may even be possible to

connect here the statement of Jesus in John 14:6: "I am the way." Surely the statement in Hebrews 10:20, speaking of "a new and living way," is also appropriate in this context.

[26] No one should be surprised that the Tannaim do not refer to Jesus specifically. They seldom cited their own Scripture either, an omission that the later Amoraim were at pains to correct.

Birth, Midlife, Menopause: Rites of Passage as Expressions of Spirituality in Contemporary American Judaism

Rela Mintz Geffen

As a result of a confluence of factors internal to Jewish life and community, and of contextual trends in American society more generally, rites of passage have become an important vehicle for exploring and evoking spirituality in contemporary American Judaism. There are several internal factors promoting new and expanded rites of passage.[1]

The first is the increased level of Jewish education on the part of American Jewish adults and their consequent familiarity with existing life cycle rituals. Not only are many more Jewish children attending supplementary religious schools, but there has also been a dramatic increase in day school attendance from kindergarten through grade twelve. The first adult beneficiaries of this increase are now forming their own families. Many of them have also been to Jewish summer camp, participated in youth movements, and gone on extended educational trips to Israel. The burgeoning of Jewish studies on college campuses has also enlarged the number of adult Jews who have studied Jewish law on a higher level. Finally, the last decades of the twentieth century saw an explosion of adult learning across all of the religious movements. Many of these courses took as their subject matter the Jewish calendar and life cycle rituals.[2]

The second factor promoting embellishment of rites of passage is the lessening of clericalism and the enfranchisement of the laity as exemplified by the havurah movement. From its inception in the 1960s, leaders of the havurah movement have insisted that every member of the community is responsible for leading rituals or, at the very least, being an active participant in worship. The roles of the rabbi and cantor were de-emphasized; innovation in liturgy was encouraged.[3]

A third factor is the Reform community's greater acceptance of and education toward the practice of home ritual, including openness to such practices as observance of dietary laws and immersion in the mikvah (or ritual bath). During its classical phase, Reform Judaism eschewed ritual practice as vestigial; however, beginning in the 1960s a range of customs was gradually reintroduced into public and private liturgy. For example, bar and bat mitzvah, *aliyot* to the Torah for lay people, carrying the Torah around the synagogue for congregants to touch and even to kiss, and the use of Hebrew in the liturgy are now commonplace in Reform congregations, along with lively communal singing and chanting of liturgy, such as Debbie Friedman's settings of the traditional healing prayer and the Havdalah blessings that mark the close of the Sabbath.[4] With the newest version of the Pittsburgh Platform, Reform Jews have officially embraced the concept of mitzvot between people and God in a way that could not have been predicted even twenty-five years ago.[5]

The fourth factor leading to innovations in rites of passage is the growing openness to conversion to Judaism during the last quarter century. The outreach movement and sophisticated, compelling introduction to Judaism classes for adults, which the Jewish partner would attend with the potential convert, brought with it experimentation in the ritual arena.

The drive of the feminist movement to include women in traditional rituals and to create new ones, where none previously existed, to mark moments of significance in women's lives was the fifth factor promoting innovation. The traditional liturgy has been expanded to include the mother's name in circumcision and naming ceremonies, and to create covenantal ceremonies to welcome baby girls to the world. Sometimes the focus is on bringing women in, while in other instances, such as the creation of childbirth or menopause rituals, the aim is to enable women to give expression to the power of their experience that tradition had failed to recognize.[6]

A sixth internal factor spurring ritual innovation has been the emergence of new family structures. Life-long singlehood, single parent households, remarried couples with children who are "yours, mine and ours," gay and lesbian couples—all of these configurations have led to the development or modification of rituals so that more Jews and their partners could mark critical moments in their lives in a religious context.

Finally, a greater search for spirituality among liberal as well as traditional Jews in the closing decade of the last century has provided a framework within which experimentation is welcomed. Taken together, these seven trends have led to innovative rituals for rites of passage for which no rites existed in the tradition. They have also led to the reconceptualization and reinterpretation of existing rites of passage.

Contextual or external factors have also enhanced or led to innovative expressions of spirituality. The first of these is the fluidity of American society and the growth of a generalized search for meaning through personalized religion. Wade Clark Roof, an important scholar of American Protestantism, has dubbed Americans "switchers."[7] He speculates that, distinct from people in the rest of the world, Americans view religion as changeable. This willingness to experience religion in a fluid way has profoundly influenced American Jews.

The second external factor mirrors an internal one: the legitimation of new kinds of families in American society. The ability to celebrate the differences in alternative life styles is made possible by their growing acceptance in the society at large. Thus, if gay marriages are at issue in general elections, or if surrogate mothering makes it possible for gay men to father children through artificial insemination, or if the law of the land permits adoption by lesbian couples, then it is easier for Jewish gays and lesbians to follow suit.

The third and final external factor leading to the creation of new rites of passage is the multi-cultural and individualistic ethos that has led non-Jews to explore Kabbalah and other aspects of Judaism as a path for their own spiritual growth. If it is good enough for Madonna and Michael Jackson, then it becomes the vogue for Jews to follow non-Jews and take their own heritage more seriously.

Having briefly sketched out the seven internal and three external factors encouraging the burgeoning of life cycle rituals, I will devote the remainder of this essay to a few concrete examples of new or embellished rites of passage.

WELCOMING BABY GIRLS INTO THE JEWISH COVENANTAL FOLD

One of the first active steps taken by the Jewish feminist movement in the mid 1970s was to write ceremonies to publicly sanctify the entry of Jewish baby girls into the covenant. For generations, their baby brothers had benefited from multiple ceremonies—*ben* or *shalom zachor* on the Friday night after birth, a party with protective Torah study and special foods before they were named; the actual covenantal ceremony, *brit milah*, with all of its elaborate mystery and joy; and, for firstborn sons of non-priest related mothers, the rite of *pidyon haben*, the redemption of the son from sacred service on the thirtieth day after birth. On the other hand, daughters often had no ceremonial welcome at all, or they were named in a brief ceremony on a Torah reading day as soon after the birth as possible—often with few family members or friends present and almost never in the presence of the baby girl or the new mother.

Over the last thirty years numerous versions of *brit bat* [the covenant of a daughter] or *simhat bat* [the joy of a daughter] ceremonies have been developed for home and synagogue usage by parents and rabbis alike. It is now more frequently necessary for parents to explain why they are not having a ceremony than why they are. In other words, public welcoming of baby girls has become normative in American Judaism.[8]

Typical ceremonies encompass a formal welcome by those present as the baby is carried in, spelling the Hebrew name out with biblical verses, explaining the rationale for the names given to the child, the priestly benediction, the traditional naming prayer, an expression of thanks for the return to good health to the mother, and a series of short blessings. These include the blessing over wine and others in the format of the seven benedictions of the traditional Jewish wedding ceremony [*sheva brachot*] and the special added benedictions to the grace after festive meals [*seudah shel mitzvah*], all of which accompany the ritual. Often booklets are printed and distributed. These announce the baby's name and provide a script for the ceremony, so that all present may participate.

THE PROLIFERATION OF EXPLANATORY MANUALS

The development of printed scripts for birth ceremonies for baby girls has had ramifications for other life cycle rituals. These manuals serve as vehicles for innovation and as educational tools to enable assimilated Jews and the growing number of non-Jews who attend Jewish life cycle rituals to understand and follow what is going on. Booklets in honor of baby girls led to similar ones for *brit milah* [circumcision] ceremonies. These, in turn, have led to wedding manuals, which announce the names and relationships of the participants and also explain the nuances of all aspects of the traditional Jewish wedding ceremony, along with any special prayers or props unique to a particular wedding. Thus, a wedding booklet might include the fact that the bride's mother made the *huppah* [marriage canopy] or that the bride is carrying a Bible given to her by her grandparents. In the case of interfaith marriages, booklets are now written to explain the symbols brought in from the different faiths. Gay and lesbian wedding booklets note the use of and alterations to traditional passages.

The latest addition to the booklet phenomenon has appeared at bar and bat mitzvah ceremonies. Here the service at the particular synagogue is detailed, along with the names of the individual family members and friends participating in the service and sometimes the names of charitable organizations to which the celebrant has donated a percentage of her gifts or for whom he has done a mitzvah or service project. [9]

While I have not seen booklets for funerals, there are now folios from funeral homes produced from the internet that include a brief biography of the deceased, his or her favorite charities, a psalm, the address of *shiva* and service times, and printed driving directions to the house of mourning. One Jewish funeral director told me that this idea was copied from Catholic funeral homes, which pioneered the map idea.

The proliferation of explanatory manuals of various types is a by-product of the search for roots, the reclamation of public ritual by the laity, the availability of technology, the deliberate push of the Jewish feminist movement, and the recognition that both Jews and a growing number of non-Jews want to be active listeners and participants in these rituals.

CONCLUSION

The flow of the life cycle clearly affords an opportunity for most people to mark off time through rites of passage celebrated in community. In an era of impersonality and given the corporate nature of life in the world of work, moments based on sentiment, family ties, and friendships bring meaning to the everyday life of groups. Within contemporary American Judaism, life cycle rituals have become a major vehicle for the expression of social and political trends in communal life. Thus, the politics of Jewish feminism, the reclamation of worship by the laity, the embrace of new family constellations, and the recognition of new stages such as adolescence and midlife have all been marked by innovative or enhanced rites of passage.

NOTES

[1] For an expansion of these ideas, see Rela M. Geffen, "Introduction," in Rela M. Geffen, ed., *Celebration and Renewal: Rites of Passage in Judaism* (New York: Jewish Publication Society, 1993), 3-10.

[2] Discussions of these general findings about the nature of the American Jewish Community in the 1980s and 1990s may be found in various analyses of the National Jewish Population Survey of 1990 and a variety of community studies completed during the decade of the nineties. See, for example, Sidney Goldstein, "Profile of American Jewry: Insights from the National Jewish Population Survey," *American Jewish Year Book*, vol. 92 (New York: American Jewish Committee and JPS, 1992), 77-177. For an excellent analysis of these trends in one community,

see Sherry Israel, *Community Report on the 1995 Demographic Study* (Boston: Combined Jewish Philanthropies, 1997).

[3] For more about the havurah movement, see Bernard Reisman, *The Chavurah: A Contemporary Jewish Experience* (NY: Union of American Hebrew Congregations, 1977, and Riv-Ellen Prell, *Prayer and Community: The Havurah in American Judaism* (Detroit: Wayne State University Press, 1989).

[4] The *mi shebeirach* melody and English words written by Debbie Friedman and sung as part of the liturgy in many Reform and some Conservative synagogues each Sabbath can be found on her audiotape, "And You Shall Be A Blessing," as well as in Debbie Friedman, et al., eds., *BLESSINGS* (New York: Sound Write Productions, 1990).

[5] For the text of the original Pittsburgh Platform of 1885 and later platforms of the Reform movement from Columbus and Los Angeles, see the classic work, Michael A. Meyer, *Response to Modernity: A History of the Reform Movement* (New York: Oxford University Press, 1988). Rejection of ritual was made clear in item 4 of the 1885 Platform, which stated: "We hold that all such Mosaic and rabbinical laws as regulate diet, priestly purity, and dress, originated in ages, and under the influence of ideas, entirely foreign to our present mental and spiritual state. They fail to impress the modern Jew with a spirit of priestly holiness; their observance in our days is apt rather to obstruct than to further modern spiritual elevation." In striking contrast, the 1999 Platform states: "Through Torah study we are called to *mitzvot*, the means by which we make our lives holy. We are committed to the ongoing study of the whole array of *mitzvot* and to the fulfillment of those that address us as individuals and as a community. Some of these *mitzvot*, sacred obligations, have long been observed by Reform Jews; others, both ancient and modern, demand renewed attention as the result of the unique context of our own times. We bring Torah into the world when we seek to sanctify the times and places of our lives through regular home and congregational observance. Shabbat calls us to bring the highest moral values to our daily labor and to culminate the workweek with *kedushah* [holiness], *menuchah* [rest], and *oneg* [joy]. The High Holy Days call us to account for our deeds. The Festivals enable us to celebrate with joy our people's religious journey in the context of the changing seasons. The days of remembrance remind us of the tragedies and the triumphs that have shaped our people's historical experience both in ancient and modern times. And we mark the milestones of our personal journeys with traditional and creative rites that reveal the holiness in each stage of life."

[6] On the development of the Jewish feminist movement, see, for example, Sylvia B. Fishman "The Impact of Feminism on American Jewish Life" in *American Jewish Year Book* (NY and Philadelphia: JPS and American Jewish Committee, 1989), and Rela Geffen (Monson), "The Impact of the Jewish Women's Movement on the American Synagogue: 1972-1985," in *Daughters of the King—Women and the Synagogue* (eds. S. Grossman and R. Haut; Philadelphia: JPS, 1992), 227-37.

[7] See in particular Wade Clark Roof, *A Generation of Seekers: The Spiritual Journey of the Baby Boom Generation* (New York: Harper Collins, 1993).

[8] I have a collection of about sixty such ceremonies. Several graduate students have analyzed them by decade to see which forms persist and which innovations did not "make it." The latest book about birth ceremonies for baby girls is a self-styled self-help, how-to guide, Debra Nussbaum Cohen's *Celebrating Your New Jewish Daughter: Creating Jewish Ways to Welcome Baby Girls into the Covenant: New and Traditional Ceremonies* (Woodstock: Jewish Lights, 2001).

[9] One of the more recent self-help books on planning bar and bat mitzvah rites is Judith Davis, *Whose Bar/Bat Mitzvah Is This, Anyway? A Guide For Parents Through A Family Rite of Passage* (New York: St. Martin's, 1998).